MODERN DANCE IN GERMANY

AND

THE UNITED STATES

Choreography and Dance Studies

A series of books edited by Robert P. Cohan, C.B.E.

This book is part of a series. The publisher will accept continuation orders which may be cancelled at any time and which provide for automatic billing and shipping of each title in the series upon publication. Please write for details.

MODERN DANCE IN GERMANY

AND

THE UNITED STATES

Crosscurrents and Influences

by

Isa Partsch-Bergsohn
University of Arizona, Tucson, USA

harwood academic publishers
Australia • Austria • Belgium • China • France • Germany • India
• Malaysia • Netherlands • Russia • Singapore • Switzerland • Thailand
• United Kingdom • United States

Copyright © 1994 Harwood Academic Publishers GmbH

Harwood Academic Publishers
Poststrasse 22
7000 Chur
Switzerland

British Library Cataloguing in Publication Data

A catalogue record for this book is available from the British Library

Front cover photo: *Orpheus* (choreographer, Margaritha Wallman; courtesy of Louise Kloapper)
Back cover photo: the author, photographed by Harold Bergsohn

Library of Congress Cataloging-in-Publication Data

Partsch-Bergsohn, Isa.
    Modern dance in Germany and the United States : cross currents and
influences/Isa Partsch-Bergsohn.
      p. cm.—(Choreography and dance studies; v. 4)
    Includes index.
    ISBN 3-7186-5557-8 (hardcover)
    ISBN 3-7186-5558-6 (softcover)
    1. Modern dance—Germany—History.   2. Modern dance—United
States—History.   3. Modern dance—Germany—American influences.
4. Modern dance—Cross-cultural studies. I. Title. II. Series.
GV1782.P36   1993z
792—dc20   92-35807
                                                          CIP

CONTENTS

INTRODUCTION TO THE SERIES

Choreography and Dance Studies is a book series of special interest to dancers, dance teachers and choreographers. Focusing on dance composition, its techniques and training, the series will also cover the relationship of choreography to other components of dance performance such as music, lighting and the training of dancers.

In addition, *Choreography and Dance Studies* will seek to publish new works and provide translations of works not previously published in English, as well as to publish reprints of currently unavailable books of outstanding value to the dance community.

Robert P. Cohan

ACKNOWLEDGEMENTS

Many people, on both sides of the Atlantic, have helped me to write this book. In Germany, Anna Markard generously provided me with material from the Jooss Archive Wiesbaden. I also appreciated the competent help of the librarians of the Wigman Archive, particularly of Hannelore Erlekamm, at the Academy of the Arts in Berlin. My thanks go to Hedwig Müller in Cologne, Germany, the founder of the Mary Wigman Gesellschaft, who was supportive of my research, as well as to Frank Manuel Peter from the German Dance Archive, Cologne. In England, Bonnie Bird and Dr. Marion North generously gave me a chance to observe the work of the Laban Centre in London, and to familiarize myself with the most recent teaching of Laban's concepts by Dr. Valerie Preston-Dunlop.

In the United States, I am particularly indebted to Martha Hill for generously discussing Martha Graham's early work with me as well as sharing her impressions of Mary Wigman's first concert in 1929; to Hanya Holm for describing her early years as teacher and director at the Mary Wigman School in New York, and for commenting on differences in temperament and attitude between American and German dance students; to Louise Kloepper for giving me insights into Holm's choreographic process; and to Bella Lewitzky, who explained to me the perspectives of West Coast dancers, especially in connection with Lester Horton's work. Walter Sorell very generously helped me in my research; Gertrude Shurr gave me most vivid descriptions of her early dance experiences at Denishawn; and, finally, Dr. John M. Wilson gave me insights into the philosophy of Margaret H'Doubler.

My husband, Harold Bergsohn, has assisted me in many ways to carry through the difficult project of completing this book. He also helped with the layout and provided some of the photography. I am indebted to the office of International Travel of the University of Arizona, Tucson, for awarding me a foreign travel grant. I thank the Faculty of Fine Arts for supporting me with an incentive grant, and Michalene Cardella for her help in preparing the manuscript. Muriel Topaz, the former Director of the Juilliard School Dance Division, provided fine and much appreciated editorial help. Last, but certainly not least, I have to thank Dr. Gail Lee Bernstein of the Department of History at the University of Arizona, Tucson, whose valuable advice led me through the process of writing this book.

INTRODUCTION

Contemporary artists are very often looked upon as undisputed geniuses. This attitude is especially prevalent in dance, where the persona is inseparable from the artistic medium. Dancers such as Isadora Duncan, Mary Wigman and Martha Graham have been hailed as innovators and prophets, and a whole literature has evolved celebrating their uniqueness.

It takes a half century or more before this image of the artist as a genius yields historical perspective. Generations succeeding the pioneers become aware of general trends inherent in a particular period. The individual contributions of artists appear in a new light against the background of a cultural pattern shaped by political influences, economic change, and international events that inspired and molded their work, giving it a characteristic stamp. Art and artist do not emerge in a vacuum.

Dance scholars of the 1920s, contemporaries of the creators of Modern Dance in Europe, presented a highly idealized image of these pioneers. Their point of view mirrored a world that has since changed radically. The rise of Nazism in the 1930s, the devastation of World War II, and the restorations of the postwar period make it particularly difficult to gain a perspective on the first thirty years of the twentieth century. Since that time, three generations of dancers have grown up in Europe and America. Although there now exists a literature tracing the development of American Modern Dance, and some of this literature recognizes the influence of European Modern Dance from the 1920s on the emerging art of Modern Dance in America, a discussion of Modern Dance in Germany since the nineteen-thirties does not exist. Neither side of the Atlantic has produced a comprehensive view of the "New Dance" that examines the crosscurrents between Europe and the United States beginning around the turn of the old century and extending into the thirties, forties and fifties.

This book attempts to fill the gap, focussing on the origins of European Modern Dance in the twenties; tracing its evolution through the Nazi regime, the Second World War, and the postwar period; and demonstrating the numerous interactions and crosscurrents with American dance. I chose to start with 1902, when Isadora Duncan first entered Germany and started her rebellion against formalism and the conventional image of dance. I limit my discussion of "Modern Dance" to the years between 1920 and 1968, since that generation of the founders, Rudolf Laban, Mary Wigman, Doris Humphrey, Martha Graham and Kurt Jooss, had made their decisive contributions by 1968. After this time, student revolts all over Europe and in the United States changed the cultural climate as the arts became politicized. In America, post-modern choreographers turned away from spectacle, virtuosity and the magic of theatre, in Germany, the old structure of the municipal ballet ensemble connected to the opera, finally gave way to the contemporary form known as "Tanztheater," formulated most clearly in the works of Pina Bausch. As different as Pina Bausch and the post-modern American choreographer Yvonne Rainer might appear, both stress as their priority "to be truthful to everyday life"; the motivation for using movement has changed. This different attitude toward the art of dance might be discussed in a further book on post-modern developments.

Even today, contemporary dance scholars and professional acquaintances of the leading artists of German dance find it difficult to deal objectively with the socially and politically controversial aspects of this generation of pioneers. Indeed, this may be the reason why published material on the post 1942 period is so sparse. The principal founders, Rudolf Laban, Mary Wigman and Kurt Jooss, made very different choices which later influenced their work. Jooss chose to leave Germany in 1933, while Wigman chose to stay in Germany through the Nazi regime and the Second World War. Laban prepared mass movement choir events for the Olympic Games of 1936, but was incarcerated shortly thereafter and escaped to England, where his work changed its focus. The different consequences of their choices left each of them open to various criticism. They were either defended or simply ignored by those who knew them or studied their lives. It is my hope to contribute a fresh interpretation that neither condemns nor condones the path each took, but rather sees them in the political context of the times and shows how this context also influenced their work after 1945. Insights gained from unpublished wartime sources help to answer the puzzling question of why Modern Dance failed to regain its original vitality in postwar Germany.

American modern dancers first became aware of striking artistic similarities between their group and the Laban-based European Modern Dance through the writings of the first dance critic of the *New York Times*, John Martin. He had experienced the upheaval in Modern Dance while studying modern theatre in Europe; he took the Modern Dance movement in Europe very seriously. In 1929, when Harald Kreutzberg, the first German modern dancer of stature, spent a full year on tour in America with his Wigman-trained partner Yvonne Georgi, John Martin focussed American audiences' attention on this new European dance, discussing in detail Kreutzberg's superb masterfulness and originality.

In the following year, the great impresario Sol Hurok brought Mary Wigman to America. Wigman was at the height of her career and she represented the zenith of German Expressionism. A student of Laban, Wigman created movement directly out of her body without referring to any known vocabulary. This was very new to Americans, and they responded enthusiastically to her first solo tour program. Because of this success, Hurok arranged a second solo tour in 1931/1932, and in 1933 Wigman appeared once more, this time accompanied by a group of young dancers.

On March 23, 1933, one week after Wigman returned with her group to Germany, Hitler took over the government. The cross-Atlantic exchange in Modern Dance between Germany and America was gradually paralyzed. The next encounter between German and American Modern Dance (though actually caused by these turbulent political events in

Europe) was of a very different nature than Kreutzberg's and Wigman's tours. Four months after the seizure of power by the National Socialists, the choreographer of *The Green Table*, Kurt Jooss, was warned to leave Essen immediately, and he and his company managed secretly to cross the border to Holland. The Ballets Jooss was the first group trained in a different, dramatic ensemble style, with expressive elements of the new dance based on Laban's concepts and integrated with classically derived elements. Homeless and in exile, Jooss agreed to an American tour of his Ballets Jooss with a six week run in New York at the Forest Theater.

Jooss did not have the chance to prepare the American audience for his choreographic language. Also, the title "Ballets Jooss" was misleading in America, since it created associations with the old country's Imperial Court, that is, with pomp, stardom and etiquette. Nevertheless, the debut performance of *The Green Table* in New York in November 1933 had a particularly strong impact, presenting a new contemporary language of European Dance-Theater.

After the Nazi take-over in 1933, Modern Dance in Germany gradually declined from a position of leadership to provincial mediocrity, while American Modern Dance experienced its most vigorous growth at the Bennington School of Dance in the years from 1934 to 1938, when the esthetics and objectives of American Modern Dance were clearly articulated. In contrast to the various encounters of American audiences with Wigman, Kreutzberg, Jooss and several other German dancers, as a consequence of the cultural isolation of the thirties under the Nazi regime and the aftermath of World War II, German audiences had no exposure to the main trends in American Modern Dance as defined by Martha Graham, Doris Humphrey, Charles Weidman and Hanya Holm, nor to the lesser known independent choreographers such as Helen Tamiris.

The first postwar attempt to bring back Wigman, Harald Kreutzberg, Rosalia Chladek and Jooss as important teachers and counteract the prevailing isolation of European Modern Dance occurred at the International Summer Courses in Zürich, Switzerland, in 1948. In the fall of the same year, the Sadler's Wells Ballet appeared in Cologne and exposed the gap between international standards and Germany's municipal opera house ballet ensembles. In the early fifties, George Balanchine's neoclassicism, as performed by the New York City Ballet, completely overwhelmed German audiences, who were still culturally deprived, and, from then on, classical dance had an easy and complete victory over the few, still existing choreographers of German Modern Dance.

For most Europeans, the first direct exposure to American Modern Dance came in 1956, when Anna Sokolow taught choreography and American Modern Dance techniques at the International Summer Courses in Zürich. Studying with her made me realize that the American Modern Dance was very different from the European approaches derived from Laban and Dalcroze, and I wanted to learn more about the roots of this American idiom. When Anna Sokolow introduced Martha Graham's falls to the European students, they were shocked by their percussive attack. The following year, in 1957, Germans had their first chance to see Martha Graham in her first solo performance in Berlin. Wigman led the standing ovation that followed. The situation was now reversed: American modern dancers brought contemporary dance to postwar Germany. At this time only the older generation still remembered that there had once been a German Modern Dance. The younger generation responded with particular enthusiasm to the performances of Merce Cunningham and his dancers with John Cage as music director, and to Paul Taylor's Company; the new contemporary dance seemed to be a revelation particularly to young Germans who had grown up without theater and dance experiences during the last years of the war and in postwar times.

In 1961, the International Summer Academy in Krefeld, Germany, offered the first of several courses, taught by American teachers. Later, Cologne became the new center, promoting American Modern Dance in an annual extended summer program. Out of the summer courses, a group of young dancers, now trained in the Graham technique, created the "Tanz-Forum" in Cologne. In 1970 they presented their own choreography as well as a reconstruction of Kurt Jooss's *The Green Table*. Exposure to American Modern Dance had led these young people back to their own German traditions. This rediscovery of Germany's Modern Dance heritage paralleled the death in 1967 of Chancellor Adenauer, whose passing signaled the end of the conservative postwar era in West Germany. Dance as well as politics had reached a turning point in Germany and in America, but it seems to me too early to include in this book the discussion of possible crosscurrents between the American Contemporary Dance and the German Tanztheater of the last twenty-five years.

Since 1985, six publications have focussed on the life and work of the European Modern Dance leaders. Anna Markard, the daughter of Kurt Jooss, and her husband, Hermann Markard wrote *Jooss*,[1] published in both English and German, in connection with an exhibition on Kurt Jooss's life and work. The book contains German dance historian Hedwig Müller's brief article on "Jooss and Expressionism," with a preface by Anna Markard, followed by a thorough biography with photos and program examples that cover Jooss's career. In the following year, Müller published a detailed biography of Mary Wigman, *Mary Wigman: Life and Work of the Great Dancer*, which coincided with the artist's one-hundredth birthday. This event was celebrated in a four-day conference at the Academy of the Arts in West Berlin.[2] Simultaneously, Müller assembled an exhibition of photos, program notes and memorabilia that gave the astounded younger German generation a first glimpse of this apparently completely forgotten German dancer. The dance writer Walter Sorell added a further biographical reflection on Mary Wigman, supplementing the earlier work based on her diaries, *The Mary Wigman Book* (1975).[3] With his publication in German, *Mary Wigman: Ein Vermächtnis* (*Mary Wigman's Legacy*) (1986),[4] Sorell tried quite sensitively to explain some of the incongruities that obscured Wigman's artistic productions during the Nazi era. He also recorded some of his conversations with the older Wigman looking back at past experiences. Although Sorell did not idealize Wigman, he gave the reader an understanding of and sympathy for some of the difficulties she faced.

In 1987, one of the leading Laban scholars, Dr. Vera Maletic, thoroughly analyzed the life and work of this European dance pioneer. Her publication, *Body-Space-Expression*, focussed particularly on the development of his movement theories.[5] In 1990,

John Hodgson, collaborating with Dr. Valerie Preston-Dunlop from the Laban Centre, London, published *Rudolf Laban: An Introduction to His Work and Influence*.[6] This work acquaints the reader with Laban's personality and conveys a sense of this extremely versatile artist who influenced the development of the New Dance in Europe. The book also describes his concepts in clear and intelligible terms. The authors recognize the amazing lack of political instinct that led Laban, in 1936, to be arrested by the National Socialists. The work also sheds new light on the circumstances of Laban's flight from Nazi incarceration. Part II contains a very valuable reference file of Laban's entire works in movement, dance, and theatre, as well as a bibliography of his writings in German and English and commentaries about Laban.

These recent biographies of the three leading personalities of the European Modern Dance, Laban, Wigman and Jooss, helped me gain a comprehensive perspective on Modern Dance's development in Europe. I also benefitted from the Mary Wigman Archive at the Academy of the Arts in Berlin, where I read Wigman's diaries, her own records of her American tours, and her entries of the thirties and forties, which described her increasingly difficult political dilemma. I knew Wigman personally. I was one of the few students she taught in Leipzig in the last year of World War II. The events described in this book, therefore, are not purely dance history to me, but are part of my life. So, too, is the fate of Kurt Jooss. In 1948, when he decided to return to the Folkwang School in Essen, Germany, I pursued advanced studies in choreography, Modern Dance and dance education under his tutelage. I worked closely with him throughout the 1950s as a faculty member and as his assistant, and I was teaching at the school when financial pressures forced him to dismiss his company.

In 1976, the Robert Joffrey Ballet presented the original "Ballets Jooss" program from 1932 in honor of Kurt Jooss's seventy-fifth birthday, at the New York City Centre. At that time,I was on the dance faculty of the University of California, Santa Barbara, and a member of the University of California Intercampus Committee. One of its functions was to organize special courses involving all seven campuses. I proposed a special choreographic workshop focussing on the creation of *The Green Table*. The participants would be selected students, and it would run for three weeks. I was able to convince Professor Jooss to accept the position of instructing the workshop. During those three weeks in September 1976, we had lengthy discussions on subjects ranging from his years of studies under Laban to the present situation in dance, and I was fortunate enough to have my husband record those conversations on tape. That vivid exchange with Kurt Jooss motivated me to write this book.

I would like to give a firsthand account of the overpowering political pressures on this generation of European Modern Dance artists. The generation of dance historians in Germany or America who followed them interpreted their lives on the basis of present-day criteria. However, without experiencing a fascist regime, a war, and the aftermath, it is very difficult to understand how hard it was for artists to keep their integrity, not only during the Nazi reign, but also, ironically, in postwar Germany, in the age of the "economic miracle" during the Adenauer years.

Thanks to a grant from the German Academic Exchange office, I was given the opportunity to become a visiting scholar at the Juilliard School Dance Division in New York in 1957. There I witnessed American Modern Dance firsthand. At Juilliard in 1957, I was fortunate to be in Doris Humphrey's last choreography class. I also came in direct contact with the teaching of artists such as José Límon, Martha Graham and Louis Horst, and with Merce Cunningham's performances. Martha Hill, then head of the Juilliard School Dance Division, generously gave me access to the work of the dance division, including rehearsals, examinations and faculty meetings, so that I was able to study the organizational structure of this exemplary program and to learn about the best of American dance education from the inside.

After fifteen years as a dancer and teacher in Europe, and after observing American Modern Dance and teaching it in American universities for another twenty- five years, I see Modern Dance, in spite of its considerably different forms in America and Europe, as a single radical rebellion of young dancers against nineteenth-century formalism. The new dance arose out of a need to express bodily a new rhythm felt in all of the contemporary arts. This new motivation stood in contrast to the Renaissance foundations of classical ballet—visual balance and harmony of line. Studying Modern Dance on both sides of the Atlantic Ocean convinced me that there is a commonality in the way the body serves as the primary source of invention, producing the disharmony, asymmetry and countertensions of Modern Dance. I discovered interrelations and interactions between German and American modern dancers which, I think, are particularly meaningful in explaining the evolution of Modern Dance as a distinctive twentieth-century performing art.

Many people, on both sides of the Atlantic, have helped me write this book. In Germany, Anna Markard generously provided me with material from the Jooss Archive Wiesbaden. I also appreciated the competent help of the librarians of the Wigman Archive, particularly of Hannelore Erlekamm, at the Academy of the Arts in Berlin. My thanks go to Hedwig Müller in Cologne, Germany, the founder of the Mary Wigman Gesellschaft, who was supportive of my research, as well as to Frank Manuel Peter from the German Dance Archive, Cologne. In England, Bonnie Bird and Dr. Marion North generously gave me a chance to observe the work of the Laban Centre in London, and to familiarize myself with the most recent teaching of Laban's concepts by Dr. Valerie Preston-Dunlop.

In the United States, I am particularly indebted to Martha Hill for generously discussing Martha Graham's early work with me as well as sharing her impressions of Mary Wigman's first concert in 1929; to Hanya Holm for describing her early years as teacher and director at the Mary Wigman School in New York, and for commenting on differences in temperament and attitude between American and German dance students; to Louise Kloepper for giving me insights into Holm's choreographic process; and to Bella Lewitzky, who explained to me the perspectives of West Coast dancers, especially in connection with Lester Horton's work. Walter Sorell very generously helped me in my research; Gertrude Shurr gave me most vivid descriptions of her early dance experiences

NOTES FOR THE INTRODUCTION

1. Markard, Anna & Hermann (1985) *Jooss*. Köln: Ballett-Bühnen-Verlag

2. Müller Hedwig (1986) *Mary Wigman,* Leben and Werk der Grossen Tänzerin. Berlin: Academy of the Arts

3. Wigman, Mary (1975) *The Mary Wigman Book*, edited and translated by Walter Sorell. Middletown, Wesleyan University Press

4. Sorell, Walter (1986) *Mary Wigman: Ein Vermächtnis*. Wilhelmshaven: Florian Noetzel Verlag

5. Maletic, Vera (1987) *Body-Space-Expression: The Development of Rudolf Laban's Movement and Dance Concepts*. Berlin, New York, Mouton de Gruyter

6. Hodgson, John & Preston-Dunlop, Valerie (1990) *Rudolf Laban, An Introduction To His Work & Influence*. Plymouth: Northcote House Publishers

CHAPTER I: BREAKING THROUGH TO MODERNITY.

THE DECADE OF FERMENTATION

During the first decade of the twentieth century, a rebellion against conventional notions of society spread across Europe. Sparked by a desire for spiritual and physical renewal, the rebellion stimulated a trend toward self-reflection that was heightened by Freud's discovery of the meaning of dreams. The turn to the unconscious self, documented in the dramas of Strindberg and Chekhov, was also recognizable in Moscow's Art Theater, where Konstantin Stanislavsky focused on "inner feeling."

In the visual arts, a group of German painters, the so-called Brücke (bridge) artists were the most radical in voicing their revolt against the restrictive academic formalism that was now identified with nineteenth-century thinking. In the first decade of the twentieth century, this brotherhood of artists created together an aggressive, anti-bourgeois style. The founders of this movement were Ernst Heckel, Ludwig Kirchner, Fritz Bley, and Karl Schmitt Rotluff; they were inspired by examples of primitive art, at the same time that Picasso rediscovered African tribal art. They aimed for a renewal of life through the arts, freed from "the ballast of tradition." In 1906, the catalogue to their first exhibition in the "new session" in Dresden affirmed that "everybody belongs to us who directly and genuinely expresses what motivates him to create."[1] The work of the Brücke artists showed clearly their aim to see the human figure in relation to the cosmos, not as a realistic portrayal, but as a reflection of an inner landscape of men. The nude female figure, in harmony with nature and painted in bright colors, appeared in their paintings to symbolize the purity of nature.

Another group of artists, established under the name of "Der Blaue Reiter" (the Blue Rider), further pioneered the twentieth-century revolt by searching for a "mystic-spiritual construction" of a new perspective on life. The group consisted of two Germans, Franz Marc (1880-1916) and August Macke (1887-1914), and the Russian Wassily Kandinsky (1866-1940). Their rebellion against academic formalism led Franz Marc in particular to create animals, occasionally combined with nude figures, symbolizing the basic unity within the cosmos. It is Kandinsky who is often mentioned as the first purely abstract painter, however. He gave his abstractions the names of musical compositions, indicating the parallelism that he saw between sound and color, and he also reflected on the relations between sound, color and movement characteristics. In his famous book, *Concerning the Spiritual in Art*, Kandinsky articulated the credo of the Blaue Reiter: "Form is the outer expression of inner meaning.... The artist may use any form which his expression demands; for his inner impulse must find suitable outward expression."[2]

It is hard to say if Isadora Duncan's meteoric appearance had exerted any indirect influence on these groups of artists, or whether she was one of the "crosscurrents" that John Martin referred to when he called Duncan "a peculiarly sensitive channel for an idea whose time had come."[3] Nevertheless, the world of dance, the search for spiritual and physical renewal, and the urge for self-expression found a fervent exponent in this American dance pioneer.

Isadora Duncan, born in California and raised by an eccentric but educated mother, reached Europe in 1899, travelling with her family to London on a cattle boat. There she visited the British Museum and for hours at a time sketched the movements on Greek vases and tanagras, making them her own through inner concentration, and integrating these observed movements into her kinesthetic awareness. Most probably Isadora Duncan already had some knowledge of antiquity since, in the 1880s, Heinrich Schliemann's excavations of Troy had filled the newspapers, but it was in London that she absorbed Greek art work, predominantly of the Hellenistic period.

In 1900, facing some financial difficulties caused by their bohemian life style, the Duncans moved to Paris. There, in Auguste Rodin's sculpture garden, Isadora danced barefoot in her Greek toga for Rodin and his circle of friends. Walter Sorell comments:

> Today we may smile at the notion that bearded men wept when seeing Isadora dance. We can understand it only when we envision the setting in which these artists struggled with themselves and with a world to which they still bore witness, but against which they gave decisive, sometimes violent evidence. It was no longer a question of how to display one's creative abilities, but of how to disclose the inmost urge to make an artistic statement, how to discover and reveal the mystery of one's self. [4]

Duncan liked to say that she was influenced by "waves and wind"; she danced with the awareness that her body reflected nature. She also liked to think of her body as a temple enclosing the spirit of antiquity. She often appeared childlike to artists who admired her movement abandon, her "free spirit," which arose from an emotional source. Identifying with Greek philosophy and aesthetics, Isadora Duncan fit perfectly in the turn-of-the-century world of Art Nouveau. Her success in England and France came mostly from her striking personality, for, as much as her audiences were touched by Isadora, they held on to the concept of beauty of the classical ballet aesthetic which prevailed in Europe, and Duncan had no immediate intention of changing these notions. In 1904, the Duncans travelled to Italy and Greece. Inspired by the Parthenon, Isadora tried to find in her own body the feeling of weightiness that the architecture transmitted to her. At the same time, she read Nietzsche's *Birth of the Tragedy from the Spirit of Music*. The Dionysian notions espoused in the book broadened her perspective considerably, and she started to experiment with conflicting and dramatic movements which enriched her range. In this process of self-reflection she made the surprising discovery that her dance actually came from American soil. "We are not Greeks," she wrote, "and therefore cannot dance Greek dances. But the dance of the future will have to become again a highly religious art as it was with the Greeks." [5]

In 1905, when Duncan performed at the Imperial Theater in St. Petersburg, she met Diaghilev, Bakst, Benois, Anna Pavlova and Stanislavsky. Visiting the Imperial Ballet School in Moscow, she had harsh words for the stifling discipline of the classical training. Nevertheless, Russian audiences received her as a great American artist. Her free-flowing quality particularly impressed Michel Fokine and strengthened him in his efforts to modify the execution of classical ballet, giving it a smoother, more expressive style. Amazingly, in 1902, before they met, both commented in writing on "natural movement."

Duncan referred to movements in nature, such as waves, while Fokine, when he used the word "natural," meant a less formal approach to choreography, as he vividly demonstrated in the famous solo he choreographed in 1905 for Anna Pavlova. "The Dying Swan," a classically conceived dance, showed a new expressiveness within the classical form. Duncan inspired Fokine to explore new ways of choreographing for the ballet stage, but, ironically, she exerted her strongest influence indirectly on twentieth-century Russian ballet, which incorporated dancing " à la Duncan" into its vocabulary.

Duncan's greatest impact during her lifetime, however, was as a performer in Germany, the country which, since Noverre's years in Stuttgart, had produced no original dance tradition. It was in Munich, the German center of progressive artists and writers, that Isadora first found recognition. Her greatest professional success was in Germany; there, other artists perceived her as the great dancer of the future. Accustomed to a migratory existence, she enjoyed a relatively stable life in Berlin, where she opened a school in Berlin Grunewald, in 1904. By then, Duncan considered Germany her homeland, and she experienced her most fulfilling and harmonious years there. In Germany she met the stage designer Gordon Craig, and gave birth to their first child. Her personal and her artistic life seemed to have reached a point of balance.

The first Duncan school lasted for four years, from 1904 to 1908, functioning like a state-supported institution, without any tuition fees. A Swedish instructor taught gymnastics and Elizabeth Duncan, Isadora's sister, taught a dance class consisting of walks, runs, and leaps applied to simple polkas, mazurkas and waltzes. Occasionally Isadora gave an inspirational class, but because of her belief in spontaneity, she did not build up a methodical program. As much as Duncan loved the idea of her school in theory, in reality she was first of all a performer, and she failed to develop a firm foundation for dance.

In 1904, Cosima Wagner, the widow of Richard Wagner, invited Duncan to dance at Wagner's new Festspielhaus (Festival Hall) in Bayreuth. Duncan danced the famous "Bacchanale" from Wagner's opera *Tannhäuser* with Dionysian fervor before a highly eclectic audience of German conservatives. She was honored as the High Priestess of Dance, the "göttliche Isadora" (the godlike Isadora). Duncan appeared to the German audience as the embodiment of dance from the spirit of the music in Wagner's Bayreuther Festspielhaus, and she definitely embraced the quasi-religious ritual surrounding Wagner's shrine.

Hans Brandenburg, author of the now classic German book on Modern Dance, *Der Moderne Tanz* (third edition of 1921), was aware that Duncan's relation to music was not a genuine one: she basically used to "illustrate with soulful gestures moods created by the music."[6] He saw in Duncan a first pioneer of the new dance who had rediscovered the body and its natural expressive gestures and intuitively felt its harmony without being able to explain or teach it. Her art and person were inseparable and, thanks to her strong personality, she gained recognition as an artist. Brandenburg came to the following, most interesting conclusion:

> The recognition of the true relation between music and body movement,
> between sound rhythm and dance rhythm, between time-audible and time-
> visible order was not yet in her field of vision.[7]

Brandenburg pointed precisely to the problem that succeeding generations of dancers tried
to solve: Dalcroze, Nijinsky, Laban and Wigman all strove in their work to clarify the
relation between movement and music.

It was true that Isadora Duncan's field of vision was very subjective; her art arose
from intuition. She expressed herself in solo recitals. The next generation of "interpretive"
dancers followed her example, using the recital stage as an appropriate forum for women
to express their feelings. Accordingly, she speeded up the process of women's liberation
from social strictures and replaced the Victorian idol with her own self, which she
celebrated through her dances. To Duncan we owe the fact that the modern dancer
appears to the audience on stage basically as a nude figure clad only with a minimum of
clothing, the way Isadora looked in 1904, when Gordon Craig captured her youthful
charm in the Art Nouveau style.

The dances Duncan composed after the tragic drowning of her two children in
1913 changed to a more sombre color. Isadora had gained weight during a period of
withdrawal from performing, and she returned to the stage as a heroic mother figure.
During this period, she may have been influenced by Delsarte's ideas of expressing strong
emotions in movement. The Frenchman François Delsarte (1811-1871), a teacher of music
and drama, had ruined his voice by faulty instructions, but he had cured himself by
learning about human anatomy and recording data based on his own observations of how
people react to emotional stimuli. Recovered, he devoted his life to the discovery of
general laws and principles of expression. In the years following his death, many had
misinterpreted his ideas, since Delsarte himself had published very little. The American
dance pioneer Ted Shawn took it upon himself to reassemble what he considered the
authentic Delsarte method in his book *Every Little Movement*.[8] Shawn recognized as
fundamental to Delsarte's theory the Law of Correspondence: for each spiritual function
there is a corresponding body function. Delsarte also taught that gesture is more than
speech; it is the direct agent of the heart. These two fundamental notions, that inner
movement causes outer movement, and that human gesture directly speaks to the heart,
inspired Isadora Duncan, who consciously created dances such as "Marseillaise" (1917)
with these principles in mind. When in "Marseillaise" Duncan rose in revolt against
World War I, expressing her personal drama and her compassion for mothers in France
in gestures of monumental grief, she became a universal voice of European protest. She
used popular music, and wore a costume that was not considered to be in good taste, but
her gestures grew directly out of her own being, and showed the influence of Delsarte's
principles of dramatic motion. There was no longer any trace of Victorian propriety in
her; Duncan, a mature woman, made an abstract statement of dissent.

After World War I, Duncan's life became increasingly restless. She was obsessed
by the idea of establishing a large school for children. Somehow she wanted to give to
the world's children what she had not been able to do for her own. After a failed attempt
to establish a school in Greece, Duncan resumed her efforts to build a school in Russia.

Actually, this idea had been in her mind since 1908, when Konstantin Stanislavsky had proposed to bring her to his Moscow Art Theatre School. The way that Duncan now pursued her goal showed her romanticism and unshakable sense of mission. In 1920, in London, she met with an outstanding Russian diplomat, Leonid Krasin, and won his approval for her proposal, which he submitted to the Commissar of Education, Anatole Lunacharsky. Duncan proposed: "to found a school in Moscow where she would teach thousands of proletarian children, giving them the joy and beauty through free and uninhibited movement."[9]

In July of the following year, Duncan arrived in Moscow. In the conversation with Lunacharsky, the Commissar of Education, Duncan stressed "that she wanted to work, not for the theatre, but for everyday life."[10] Her ultimate goal was clearly educational. Amazingly, in spite of great financial and physical difficulties, Lunacharsky supported her proposal, and the state-supported school opened in fall 1921. The first concert, given in honor of the fourth anniversary of the Russian Revolution, at the Bolshoi Theatre, on November 7, 1921, presented 150 children. A year later, in 1922, the Duncan School was removed from the state budget and had to support itself. Simultaneously, some professional ballet critics pointed out the lack of spatial organization and structure in the school's demonstrations. Thanks to Irma Duncan's pedagogic help these problems were gradually solved. Irma Duncan also took the children on tour throughout Russia and apparently produced some skillful young performers. In 1924, Isadora Duncan choreographed "Songs of the Revolution" in memory of Lenin. Her last set of concerts in Moscow, titled "Civil Requiem," were tremendously successful. After this event, Irma Duncan became almost totally responsible for the school and she even travelled to China with a group of teenage Duncan students. Meanwhile, Isadora Duncan's life, travelling between Berlin and Paris, became increasingly restless. Her death in 1927 was just as eccentric as her life; it ended in a tragic car accident in Nice.

Amazingly, Duncan's vision of hundreds of children moving to music became reality in a way nobody could have imagined during her lifetime. After a number of very difficult years trying to survive, some of her former pupils who did not go on tour to the United States formed a new group and toured in Russia during the entire pre-war decade. When it was time for them to retire, they started to teach "artistic gymnastics" or "Duncan plastiques" in schools. Beginning in 1947, these forms became the foundation for the developing system of "Artistic Gymnastics." Thus, there is a direct line from the Duncan School to Soviet gymnasts such as Olga Korbut. Duncan's efforts and her dreams came to life in Russia and in all the Eastern European countries influenced by Russian cultural propaganda. Neither America nor Germany can claim such a direct line of influence.

To the Western world, Duncan's life might appear emotionally motivated and filled with vaguely shaped dreams, but she accomplished what she had set out to do for all her life; she laid the ground for Russia's artistic gymnastic, which combines physical skill with aesthetic principles. Duncan's school taught a whole generation of youth all over the world regardless of class.

While Isadora Duncan expressed her rebellion against societal restraints in her dance and retained a sense of her own mission as an artist in all the fluctuations of her eventful life, Emile Jacques-Dalcroze (1865-1950) had a very different relation to movement, one originating from a rational base. As a twenty-seven-year-old professor of music harmony in Geneva, he developed a method and theory to improve his students' rhythmic sense. Dalcroze had no previous training in movement. He was guided solely by Delsarte's theory, which divided the human body into three zones: the head and upper chest as the spiritual center, the torso as the location of the emotions, and the abdomen and hips as the physical center. Because Dalcroze considered the human walk as the base of all rhythmic activity, when he began each class he had his students march to his playing the piano, in order to develop an awareness of the pulse. With this accomplished, they then marched to the pulse of his playing and had simultaneously to indicate the musical rhythm in the arms against the pulse of the march. From this fundamental ability of the body to illustrate simultaneously the measure as well as the rhythm, Dalcroze gradually developed a more refined system in which movements exactly mirrored intricate rhythmic patterns. His method of translating sound into physical action, called "Eurhythmics," was purely functional in purpose, designed to help musicians develop a better motor memory, but Dalcroze gradually saw benefits beyond his original goal. Although intended to achieve the exact functioning of the sensory and movement center and help students develop a better sense of rhythm, his method also improved coordination among the different zones of the body. This discovery led him to a fundamental philosophy -- that rhythm both embodies the spiritual and spiritualizes the body -- a philosophy close to Duncan's theories of harmonizing the spiritual and the physical through dance without really having a knowledge of the body's full capacities. But since Duncan had not developed a structure for teaching her form of dance, Dalcroze's methodical Eurhythmic art education attracted many young females who, following the spirit of the time, craved exposure to the arts and inner harmony through self-expression in movement.

Growing up in French Switzerland, Dalcroze remembered from his youth "Festspiele," civic plays that nonprofessional people performed at patriotic occasions commemorating historic events. When he realized that some of his group sequences had aesthetic appeal in addition to their functional purpose, he extended some of these materials: he had his students participate in civic festivals in which they illustrated the text and the music in eurhythmic group arrangements he designed. He also began to hold demonstrations regularly at his studio. Both of these activities created a new theatrical experience for his students, and the audience responded very positively to Dalcroze's work. Even so, he continued to consider himself a musician, and not a man of the theater.

One of the visitors to Dalcroze's studio in 1906 was the stage designer Adolphe Appia, an innovator in the field of theater architecture. He experimented particularly with color and light in his effort to create an atmosphere; he felt that only light seemed to give "the inner nature of all appearance."[11] Appia was fascinated by Dalcroze's moving groups, and he visualized ways to apply his idea of abstract theater to Dalcroze's work. Between 1906 and 1909, Appia regularly frequented Dalcroze's studio, coming up with the idea of "rhythmic spaces," platforms on different levels that visually articulated rhythmic movement sequences. The two worked well together, and Appia as a theatre professional added a visual dimension to Dalcroze's material. Through their exchanges, Dalcroze's method of eurhythmics gradually reached far beyond the confines of the Conservatory of Geneva.

Dalcroze's method also started to have a profound influence on dance education in America through Ruth St. Denis (1880-1972). A self-taught dancer born in New Jersey as Ruth Dennis, she entered her stage career as a high kicking, acrobatic dancer. Dissatisfied with the commercial forms of entertainment, she changed her name to Saint Denis, and started to explore dances of the "Mysterious East". From 1906 to 1909, she toured Europe and showed her dances, inspired by the Orient, in Austria and Germany, where they were more appreciated than anywhere else in Europe. Her appeal was very different from Duncan's outgoing approach. To the German educated audiences, she appeared as an embodiment of the Indian poet Rabindranath Tagore's poems, which were popular in Germany during the first years of the new century. The Austrian poet Hugo von Hoffmannsthal was very moved by her naive, and at the same time theatrical and mystical, performance of an Indian temple dance, "Radha," which she danced "clothed with chains of metal and jewelled plaques."[12] Admirers of St. Denis were ready to build a theater for her in Weimar, but St. Denis did not want to commit herself to five years in Germany; she returned to the U.S. in 1909.

World War I eliminated her further hopes and plans. While in Europe, however, Ruth St. Denis had absorbed some of Dalcroze's ideas about the relation of music to dance movement. After she married Ted Shawn, they established the Denishawn School of Dance, and decided that their dance institute should have some "scientific" foundations. "St. Denis and I," Shawn wrote in his book *Every Little Movement*, "feeling there should be a closer "scientific" relationship between movement and music, invented what we called "Musicvisualization."[13] In retrospect, musicvisualization was not an invention, but an adaptation of Dalcroze's Eurhythmics. When Ruth St. Denis applied the principle of literally illustrating the structure of the music in her choreographic creations, this misinterpretation of Dalcroze's method caused a regrettable detour in the progress of the young American Free Dance.

In 1910, Dalcroze, by then one of the leading men in art education, was invited to become the director of the newly created Bildungsanstalt für Musik und Rhythmus (Educational Institute for Music and Rhythm) in the newly completed garden city of Hellerau, near Dresden. The founders of the garden city, the brothers Wolf and Harald Dohrn, were the artistic and financial leaders of a highly progressive project, which they started out of idealism and trust in the social reform movement. Their idea was to create a healthy environment for arts and crafts education in Germany, and they chose Dalcroze to direct this preparatory school for the arts. Dalcroze brought forty-six students from Geneva with him to the new progressive city near Dresden. It was the home of the Brücke artists, who had, in their exhibitions, already made a name for themselves as creators of a new approach to painting. Students came from all over Europe to study with Dalcroze and his collaborators. The new director proved masterful in setting up a tight curriculum for every student in the brand-new facilities, and he was highly aware that his institute was designed to demonstrate the effectiveness of reform ideas. His administrative style was characterized by the same kind of discipline and clear structure that had already proven successful in Geneva.

In the summer of 1912, the large Festspielhaus (Festival Hall), designed and built in the style of Art Nouveau by Heinrich Tessanow, was inaugurated with Dalcroze's dance drama *Echo of Narzissus*, followed by the scene in Hades from Gluck's *Orfeo ed Euridice*. According to Hans Brandenburg, Dalcroze placed groups of singers and dancers on series of stairs Appia had created. The chorus at first stormed toward and then retreated from Hades in strict adherence to Gluck's dramatic musical structure. Pictures taken of these plastic groups show that the group arrangements made good use of "living spaces" on different levels, but the performers appear frozen in Greek positions rather then moving. Brandenburg apparently made a similar observation: "the rhythm stood beside the motion, instead of being the soul of it, and the consciously accentuated stamping of the furies added a crude element to the music...the performers adhered to the metronome instead capturing the large, free breathing curve of a movement phrase."[14] It was Appia's light design that made this production outstanding by creating an atmosphere of antiquity. In combination with fresh ideas in scenic design, a total work of art was created "from the Spirit of Music." Thus, the production of *Orfeo ed Euridice* exemplified to many contemporaries, particularly in the field of music, the idea of "Gesammtkunstwerk" (Total Work of Art) in Richard Wagner's sense. Dalcroze reached the highpoint of his career with this production of *Orpheus*, which attracted the European artistic elite to the model city Hellerau.

Mary Wigman, at this time still Marie Wigmann, was one of Dalcroze's students at Hellerau. She was not altogether impressed with *Festive Orpheus* judging from a 1913 diary entry: "Music as foundation on one side, twenty vertically lined up gestures were solely connected by external reasons of form, missing any dynamic motivation. These gestures were arbitrarily used.... The music alone was expressive, since the expressiveness of the body itself was barely known."[15]

In the spring of 1913, Diaghilev, the great impresario of Les Ballets Russes, came to Hellerau with some of his collaborators, one of whom was Vaslav Nijinsky. The legendary male dancer of this company, encouraged by Diaghilev, was eager to try his hands at choreography, and Dalcroze, who was rehearsing a complete version of Gluck's *Orpheus* for his annual school concert in June 1913, very much impressed both Diaghilev and Nijinsky with his rhythmic chorus movements. Diaghilev had come with a purpose: he was seeking a way to prepare Nijinsky to choreograph Igor Stravinsky's *Le Sacre du Printemps*, which he planned to produce later the same year. Dalcroze recommended Miriam Rambach, who later became Marie Rambert, as assistant to the choreographer. The young Polish girl followed Diaghilev's company to Monte Carlo to familiarize the company with Stravinsky's complex score.

The period of Dalcroze's appeal, however, was short-lived. In the Spring of 1914, 500 students were enrolled at Hellerau, and branches of Dalcroze Schools were established in St. Petersburg, Moscow, Vienna, Prague, Frankfurt, Breslau, Nürnberg, London, Warsaw, and Kiev. While his method was apparently flourishing in all these branches, internal tensions were building up at Hellerau. Some students voiced the opinion that Dalcroze's method predominantly used the extremities of the body, without full knowledge of the inherent expressive qualities of the human body. Also, some young aspiring dancers felt that there was very little opportunity for individual movement exploration, and they left to join Laban. Other students complained that the predominant atmosphere was similar to a convent, based on a strict discipline of drilling for rhythmic precision.

It might have been that Dalcroze tried too hard, in fact, to prove that his institute provided exemplary art education. He was a diligent administrator, and the institute functioned in an orderly fashion even when he was sometimes absent. In the spring of 1914, however, when Dalcroze was in Geneva organizing another of his festivals, World War I broke out, and Dalcroze never returned to his institute. Three tragic events caused the abrupt end of his activities at Hellerau: the death of one of the founders, Wolf Dohrn, the outbreak of war, and Dalcroze's political opinion regarding Germany.[16] Hellerau was closed down, and the garden city, built to reflect the idealistic reform dreams of its founders, became a hospital. Overwhelmed by world events, Dalcroze abandoned his reform dreams of harmonizing society through Eurhythmics, at least in Germany.

In 1919, several former students of Dalcroze reopened a "School of Applied Rhythm" on the same grounds as the Hellerau institute and, in 1925, moved to Laxenburg castle in Austria, near Vienna. There Rosalia Chladek refocussed on the dance aspect of Eurhythmics, developing her own very refined method of body awareness and control far beyond Dalcroze (see Chapter VI).

RADICAL EXPERIMENTATION

Until 1913, the "Total Work of Art" in Richard Wagner's sense (as Synthesis of all the Arts) still remained a dream even in Dalcroze's production of *Orpheus*, since Dalcroze approached performance as a music educator, and not as a genuine artist. To Dalcroze, music was a given form that dictated an equivalent in movement patterns, and even Appia's abstract movement spaces and inventive platforms could not hide the fact that the music was dominant. Thus true fusion of the different medias did not occur. The world of music needed the genius of Igor Stravinsky to cut through to the heart of the matter. He approached the synthesis of all the arts in a radically new manner; breaking many academic conventions in music theory, he proved that rhythm does not have to stay in a conventional metric order, but can pulsate asymmetrically, when the composer wants to express the vitality of primal life in his music. Stravinsky's music did not sound like anything composed before. He created violent rhythm through displaced accents and polytonal chords, and his orchestral scores purposely broke established rules in order to manifest the elemental power of rhythm. Stravinsky explained his motivation in creating primitivism in music: "I saw in my imagination a solemn pagan rite: sage elders, seated in a circle, watched a young girl dance herself to death." Stravinsky said, "they were sacrificing her to propitiate the god of Spring."[17] The score for *Le Sacre du Printemps* was radically new, in the same sense that Picasso's paintings were radical. Stravinsky had come up with the concept for *Sacre* after he had successfully collaborated with

Diaghilev's first choreographer, Michel Fokine, on *Firebird* in 1910, and also on *Petroushka*, premiered in 1911. When Stravinsky explained his concept of the new ballet to Diaghilev, he suggested Nijinsky as choreographer for this apparently revolutionary work.

Nijinsky had already created controversy with his first choreography, *The Afternoon of a Faun*, a choreographic tableau in one act, composed to Debussy's *Prelude*. The piece was remarkable for more then one reason. Nijinsky choreographed straight lines and harsh angles to Debussy's lush legato music. The dance writer Edwin Denby wrote that the choreography for *Afternoon of a Faun* proved "Nijinsky's natural musical intelligence was of the highest order. For this was the first ballet choreography set clearly, not to measures and periods, but to the expressive flow of the music, to its musical sense."

Nijinsky's dancing, too, violated previous aesthetics of ballet, which asked for an even distribution of tension through the whole body. "Nijinsky does not dance from his feet; he dances from his pelvis. The legs do not show off. They have no ornamental pose."[18] Nijinsky's poetic portrayal of a faun, which did not follow the music but created dynamic tensions independently of the flow of the music, was unlike Isadora Duncan's dance, which was emotionally carried by the music, or Dalcroze's approach to movement, which reflected the structure of the music. To most people in the audience, Nijinsky's work was shocking; it was not representative, but intimate and psychological. Only his progressive artist friends understood Nijinsky's intent to characterize the innocence of the mythical creature, half man-half animal, in his role of the faun. Nijinsky's very own choreographic handwriting characterized *Afternoon of a Faun*, and also *Jeux*, the first ballet on sports to show, in Lincoln Kirstein's words, "love as a triangular tennis match."[19]

Thus, Nijinsky had developed an independent approach to music even before he started his collaboration with Marie Rambert. Still, he took over a very difficult task as choreographer of *Le Sacre du Printemps*. Being a Pole himself, he communicated well with Marie Rambert, but his dancers resisted her eurhythmic explanations. Trained by the Imperial Ballet to dance *Swan Lake*, they had absolutely no existing precedent to guide them. Moreover, Stravinsky's music was shockingly new even to professionally trained musicians. Stravinsky himself had made a fundamental breakthrough when he used rhythm as the motivating force of his music. He replaced regular measures that had characterized Western music since the Renaissance with irregular barring and propulsive rhythm. Nijinsky did not attempt to follow these complex rhythmical patterns literally; instead, he translated these directly into the bodies of his dancers and into the way he used his dancers in the stage space.

While the Russian painter Nikolas Roerich's scenery and heavy flannel costumes evoked the ethnic color of Old Russia, Stravinsky's concept was not really ethnic, but universal. Nijinsky worked in accord with Stravinsky's artistic intentions. His image of tribal behavior radically contradicted the aesthetic principles of symmetry, balance and beauty of line of the classical tradition in which he and his dancers were reared. The dancers had to move in large, convulsive groups, massed together in asymmetric motions, feet and knees turned in. Nijinsky insisted that they use weight: they had to stamp out and accentuate complex rhythms while they swept, in tightly connected groups, across the stage.   Nijinsky's use of space also was very different from traditional ballets. He conceived of space as an expressive element, and not as a formal, ordering element. In fact, the counter tensions within the dancers' bodies presaged characteristics of American Modern Dance that would develop twenty years later.[20] At the time, however, Nijinsky's choreography for *Le Sacre du Printemps* caused one of the most notorious riots in theatrical history at its premiere performance, on May 29, 1913. The audience reacted with outrage, aggravated by the harsh, dissonant sounds of the music as much as by the rawness of the dancers' movements. The ballet, as first performed, was lost after six performances; in 1913, the audience was evidently not yet prepared to accept dance as a primitive fertility rite.

As vehement as this riot was, *Le Sacre du Printemps* paved the way for twentieth-century rituals in dance. It became the pivotal work attracting leading classical and modern choreographers on both sides of the Atlantic Ocean. In 1930, one of Diaghilev's choreographers, Leonide Massine, staged his own version of the work quite successfully, and Martha Graham danced the role of the chosen maiden. One year later, Graham conceived *Primitive Mysteries*, a signature early work that inspired the American modern dancers of the thirties to explore their own pasts in dance rituals.

A similar move away from traditional theater aesthetics toward primitive ritual occurred in Germany, starting in the same year of the premiere of *Le Sacre du Printemps*. Rudolf Laban's early work and, to a greater extent, the work of Mary Wigman were deeply rooted in ritual. For quite a while during the early twenties, Wigman experimented with dance in silence. She shied away from choreographing to very complex, existing musical scores, creating her own sparse percussion accompaniment. But towards the end of her career, in 1957, she choreographed a very abstract version of Stravinsky's *Le Sacre du Printemps*. She staged this large-scale production after her move to Berlin. By this time a mature artist, she approached Stravinsky's score and libretto as a challenge. She wanted to prove that in post war Germany Modern Dance still had vitality. Two years later, at the Theatre Royale in Brussels, Maurice Bejart, a dominant figure of the French Ballet, staged *Le Sacre du Printemps* as a spectacular production for his Ballet of the Twentieth Century. Departing from Stravinsky's original libretto, Bejart's theme was the awakening of human love in its full physicality. Balanchine was said to have called it the best interpretation of Stravinsky's score. During the Sixties, several other choreographers followed. Pina Bausch created a sensation with her version danced by her Tanztheater Wuppertal (Dance Theatre Wuppertal). Setting the work in contemporary society, Bausch expressed the themes of painful isolation and the impossibility of genuine human intimacy, and focussed on the sacrifice of one young woman. Finally, Martha Graham presented her version of the work in 1984. Very different from Bausch's, Graham's *Rite of Spring* celebrated the beauty of youth, particularly of her male dancers, who seemed to be the dominant element, while the sacrifice of the female, although beautifully danced, was a very free treatment of Stravinsky's theme.

The diversity of all these choreographies created to the same Stravinsky score provides further proof of the tremendous influence of his music on the development of dance in the twentieth century. Expanding the scope of rhythm in music, Stravinsky helped dancers find internal rhythm. For the first time, a true fusion in a total work of art seemed to be possible, not by a dependency of one art form on the other, but by a free association of sound and movement, each developing its own rhythm. The premiere of *Le Sacre du Printemps* in 1913 marked a turning point for music and dance. That same year was significant in other art media as well. The Armory Show provided works from the major painters of the day, including Gauguin and Van Gogh, and Cubist painters like Picasso and Braque.

LABAN

In the area of the dance, it was Rudolf Laban who specifically worked to define the internal rhythm in dance movement. He and his dance students arrived in Ascona, Switzerland, in 1913, the year that *Le Sacre du Printemps* made its premiere. In Switzerland, he came up with his concept of "body rhythm," which was as fundamental to the new dance as Stravinsky's redefinition of rhythm was to contemporary music. In that same year, Mary Wigman (1886-1973), a contemporary of Nijinsky, finally left Hellerau, where she had studied under Dalcroze, to study with Laban. She wanted to learn how to express herself directly in dance movement, and she felt she could not accomplish this under Dalcroze.

The world into which Rudolf Laban (1879-1958) was born was the Hapsburg Empire. In the fourth quarter of the nineteenth century, the Hapsburg government was bureaucratic, but the general attitude toward life seemed liberal for its time. A closer look, however, reveals a society run by strict adherence to law and order achieved by censorship, and presided over by the old Emperor, Franz Joseph, an opponent of change. The middle-class values of progress, conformity to the standards of good taste, and preservation of a good reputation were generally prized. Particularly in lands that were ruled from a distant capital, such as Bratislava where Laban was born, the populace adhered to these values. Laban was the son of a military governor in the Austro-Hungarian Army. Once his father became governor of Bosnia, a province close to the Turkish border, Rudolf saw him only on his vacations, which he spent in "adventurous" frontier country. Early in his life, therefore, observing Moslems in their daily religious rituals, he became aware of differences in nationalities and social customs. In his autobiography, *A Life for Dance*, Laban described how he had experienced the magic power of dance in the ceremonies and exercises of the whirling dervishes. This experience constituted one of the most decisive memories of his younger years, and had strongly influenced his concept of dance. [21]

There was little emotional closeness between Rudolf and his father, whom he saw mostly as a uniformed officer astride a horse. Still, Rudolf unconsciously adopted his father's aristocratic manners. The father, an ambitious, self-made man, was born bourgeois, but was ennobled in 1897. There was no doubt in his mind that his eldest son, Rudolf, would follow him in a military career. To please his father, between 1899 and 1900 Rudolf did fulfill his military training, but the only highpoint for him of this year of army service was the cadets' festival, which he organized as a dance event, with men of different nationalities dancing together in their national costumes.

Having grown up in Bratislava, and later having attended school in Vienna, Laban danced at many social occasions during his teens; to dance was actually the most enjoyable form of socializing for him, and he arranged the cadets' festival with great enthusiasm. Thinking back to this event, he concluded in his memoirs that after this time, "The thought of the magic in dance held fast in my mind and my decision to give my life to the arts became irrevocable."[22] As soon as he was released from his military service, in 1900, Laban left for Paris, against the will of his father, to involve himself with drawing and painting, architecture, acting and dancing.

Around the turn of the century, Paris was vibrant with innovative artistic ideas, but trying to make a living there as illustrator, Laban experienced poverty. He took ballet classes and, between 1902 and 1903, became familiar with Francois Delsarte's principles of expressive movement through one of his former pupils, Monsieur Morel. Laban was fascinated by this first encounter with a theoretic approach to human expressiveness, and especially by Delsarte's definition of trinity: "the unity of three things, each of which is essential to the other two, each co-existing in time, co-penetrating in space, and co-operative in motion."[23] Laban later developed this idea of trinity, modifying it to the trinity of "Tanz, Ton, Wort" (Dance, Sound, Word).

Between 1900 and 1910, Laban was a wanderer, simultaneously trying to pursue his artistic interests and to earn a living. Munich attracted him for its artistic vitality and also for its Bohemian life style, which reached its climax annually in February, when Shrovetide was celebrated with elaborate festivities. Laban made a name as designer and organizer of carnival parades and costume balls with spectacular dance activities. His life became relatively settled when he married Maja Lederer, a singer, in 1910.

By this time too, Laban started to explore dance as an art form, not just as a tool to prepare a festival. He started to give classes in "Free Dance," a dance which neither illustrated music nor told a story, but arose from the inner rhythm of bodily movement that found its realization in spatial and dynamic components. In these pre-World War I years, the borderline between gymnastics and dance was not yet clearly defined, nor was the relation of movement to sound well understood. The Duncan School, directed by Isadora Duncan's sister Elizabeth, specialized in the education of young girls. In the lovely surroundings of a park with a new gothic castle, Elizabeth Duncan used music with her dance instructions, to convey, according to Duncan's philosophy, grace and harmonious movement flow. The music served solely as stimulus for expressiveness, not as a rhythmic discipline. Elsewhere, Dr. Bess Mensendieck's first gymnastic system for young females promised therapeutic benefits for the female body. It operated without music, since the class aimed to develop physiological rhythm. Rudolf Bode was a another teacher of gymnastics in Munich who, coming from Hellerau, had distanced himself from Dalcroze, whom he criticized for deriving the body's education from music instead of deriving music education from a physical source. Each system had a slightly different emphasis, reflected most clearly in its attitude towards the relationship between music and dance. Naturally, they competed with each other for students.

Duncan and Dalcroze were unquestionably closest to Laban in their aim to spiritualize the body. Laban certainly was highly aware of Isadora Duncan's influences.

"The main achievement of Duncan," he wrote,

> was that she reawakened a form of dance-expression which could be called dance-lyrics, in contrast to the mainly dramatic dance-forms of the ballet. There was no story behind her dances, which were, as she herself termed it, the expression of the life of her "soul." She awakened the sense of poetry of movement in modern man. At a time when science, and especially psychology, endeavored to abolish radically any notion of a "soul," this dancer had the courage to demonstrate successfully that there exists in the flow of man's movement some ordering principle which can not be explained in rationalistic manner.[24]

Laban, who had experienced magic in the whirling dances of the dervishes in his youth, valued the irrational element in Duncan's performance. He thought that her Greek-inspired dances, however, "had no other than external resemblance" to movement forms of Ancient Greece.[25] He also saw clearly the limitations of her teaching.

Although Laban expressed his opinion about Duncan very explicitly, he was reserved regarding Dalcroze. While teaching at the conservatory at Geneva, Dalcroze several times had been a patient at Monte Verita, taking water cures for his health and also participating in the intellectual life of this anarchist artist colony. He had come into contact with theosophy and mystical religions there without really engaging himself in the Monte Verita circle. During the summers, in fact, Dalcroze started to revive a tradition of civic plays commemorating historic events of French Switzerland; his movement groups served to confirm visually the spirit of order and tradition of the Swiss Republic. Dalcroze tried to instill these same values at Hellerau. He hoped to maintain a similar spirit of discipline and conservative bourgeois values in his educational institute for daughters of the educated European middle class.

The different approach to festivals reflected clearly the difference in personality and life style of Dalcroze and Laban. Laban's creations, particularly in connection with the Munich carnival, had a Dionysian character. Despite advanced planning, these events in the artist colony of Schwabing were spontaneous in nature, open to one and all, and designed as flamboyant extravaganzas in fantastic and often provocative costumes, where everybody danced on the street and enjoyed a week of total freedom from moral restrictions. In addition to making money, Laban delighted in the way his *feste* released man's Dionysian powers in this one week, while the Catholic Church officially looked the other way. These festivals had no particular political color, but they certainly provided opportunity for artists to comment on the morbid state of bourgeois society in humorous ways. While in Munich, Laban gave considerable thought to defining the distinction between dance and gymnastics and to clarifying the relation of dance to music and drama. In his studio for dance and performing art he placed increasing emphasis on the need for students to understand dance as an independent art form that relied for its expressiveness neither on music nor on dramatic structure derived from a story line. Out of this realization, Laban reexamined the interrelationship of dance, sound, and word, "Tanz, Ton, Wort," which originates in the body as gesture, song, and speech.

Because of the broad foundation in movement that Laban developed in Munich between 1910 and 1912, the leaders of Monte Verita, the mountain resort near Ascona, chose Laban as director of their newly opening "School of all the Arts of Life." This center was created to provide an alternative life style to people suffering from stress and cultural exhaustion. In July 1913, Laban brought his students from Munich with him to the newly opened "School of all the Arts" at Monte Verita, which offered facilities for sunbathing, gardening and outdoor living in addition to movement activities directed by Laban. It was here that Laban experimented with movement choirs, combining his students with the summer guests of Monte Verita. Laban translated the school's ideals of physical and spiritual renewal into dance action, and in this process he became the leader of the "New German Dance." In the Fall, he returned to Munich where he consolidated his own school for dance, sound and word, also adding a performing group. In the following summer, Laban and Wigman returned to Ascona for the second season of teaching. Unfortunately, by July 1914, World War I broke out, reducing the circle of summer students at Monte Verita. After the closing of the summer's activities, Laban and Wigman remained at remote Monte Verita to do their most intense movement research while World War I continued.

Laban was not oblivious to the war, but, because of his father, he deeply objected to militarism in any form. He became a pacifist while at Monte Verita. Politically, he was very naive, which certainly became apparent in his dealings with Dr. Goebbels between 1933 and 1936 (see Chapter V). Laban honestly believed that he could bring about social changes by his innovations in movement. This gave his movement research urgency and relevance in his eyes. He saw dance as a way to heal the ailments of the past century. During the summers of 1913 through 1917 at Monte Verita, he experimented with movement as therapy for people tired of conventional life styles. His most famous innovation during this period was "movement choirs," choral arrangements of "Free Dance," in which people without formal training could celebrate the joy of moving in fresh air with a minimum of clothing. In this phase of his life, Laban was the great guru, whose experiments and improvisations aimed at liberating his students from the constraints of modern civilization:

> The movement choir is a creation born out of the compulsion and joy of movement of our present time. The movement choir has nothing in common with the mechanism of the previous "Corps de Ballet" and is also not comparable with choral dance ensembles in Modern Dance. The movement choir is an independent organism, whose task is to mediate between true dance as an art and the joy of movement of the dance-loving amateur. The movement choir is the logical form of layman dance.[26]

Working with amateur groups, Laban used body rhythm rather than musical meter as the impetus for movement. Just as singing groups performed for the love of music, the movement choir performed for the love of group motion. Laban gradually developed larger and more structured choir festivals in order to channel the immense demand for an emotional outlet into a performance experience: "Thousands of people," he wrote in *A Life for Dance*, "can now experience the benefit of the rhythm and flow of dance, not only as spectators, but also as active players."[27]

Laban was at a very good point in his life at Monte Verita. In his middle thirties, he was tall and handsome, full of energy, and apparently very successful with women. The seemingly contradictory trends of his character had reached a counter balance: a Bohemian at heart, he flourished in this anarchist artist colony; at the same time his inborn ambition to be outstanding drove him restlessly forward. He loved nature, and gave his movement instructions outdoors on the grass, directly relating to the landscape around him. He used to say that living a simple life with the fewest possible wants was one of the most important sources of happiness because "one needs to have all one's energy and time free to devote to festive exaltation."[28] His contagious enthusiasm brought out the charismatic side of his personality. He truly lived according to this philosophy, alternating between outdoor dancing, thinking about the function of dance in society, and living a quite adventurous amorous life. He also was very fortunate to have two women at his side sharing his artistic and personal voyage.

Suzanne Perrottet was a young Swiss teacher at Dalcroze's institute in Hellerau. After meeting Laban only once, she left her first mentor, Dalcroze, in order to join Laban. Perrottet admitted that she had learned a great deal as a teacher under Dalcroze, but, as she explained in a taped interview, she was "looking for dissonance in order to express her character," and evidently, that was not possible with Dalcroze's altogether "harmonious structure."[29] She certainly had to face a great deal of dissonance working and living with Laban in the following years at Monte Verita during the summers, and in Zurich in his newly established studio during the wintertime. Her dedication in teaching his approach to dance and her expertise in music served Laban well, since she was also able to compose some of the musical scores for his productions when he occasionally worked with sound.

Mary Wigman was the second young female dancer to join Laban. She found her way to the master by climbing up the steep hill to Monte Verita in the afternoon heat of a summer day in 1913. Wigman described how she followed the sound of a drum that led her directly to a clearing in the forest where Laban directed a group improvisation which she immediately joined. She knew then that this was where she belonged.

Mary Wigman came to dance relatively late. She was born in 1886 in Hannover, Germany, and she grew up as Marie Wigmann, in a well-to-do middle-class family in the sewing machine business. As was also the case for Martha Graham, the family, though well educated, had no particular interest in the arts and resented the fact that their daughter Marie wanted to choose an artistic career. As the daughter of a good Wilhelmian (Victorian) house, she had instruction in piano and voice. She was also sent to a boarding school in Folkestone, England, and, for language studies, to Lausanne, Switzerland, for several months, but all these activities left Marie Wigmann unsatisfied; she felt that her life had no direction. Back in Hannover, she attended a concert of the three sisters Wiesenthal at the Hannover Opera house. The Viennese Grete, Elsa, and Bertha Wiesenthal, contemporaries of Isadora Duncan, toured as a most popular trio dancing Johann Strauss's Waltzes. There she was absolutely spellbound by the expressiveness of their hands and the smooth flow in all of their dances, and it was this experience that made her decide that she, too, wanted to dance.

In 1910, at age twenty-three, Marie Wigmann heard of Jacques Dalcroze's move to Dresden Hellerau. Since she had taken private piano and voice lessons for years and had apparently a very good ear, she was able to convince her mother to let her sign up to study for a diploma as a teacher of Eurhythmics at the newly established Dalcroze Institute. Once at Hellerau, Marie's life became focussed; she took her music studies very seriously. Although she made excellent grades, she knew that she had come to Dalcroze not to learn music, but to learn to speak directly through her body.

The highly structured curriculum filled her days with classes in piano, voice, and music theory, but her favorite class was when Dalcroze was sitting at the piano and she could improvise movements. These classes seemed to Marie always to end too soon, and very often she improvised at night for herself, without music, in her small attic. Occasionally she also posed for the painter Emile Nolde, especially for his "Candle Dancers" of 1912, and it was Nolde who first discovered her affinity to Laban. One night when she was improvising for him, Nolde told her: "You are moving like Laban, he also dances without music, you should see him." [30] As soon as she completed her diploma, Marie left Hellerau to find Laban.

Like Suzanne Perrottet, Wigman went from Dalcroze's meticulously orderly curriculum to complete freedom of experimentation with Laban. In contrast to Dalcroze, Laban did not stop Wigman when she followed her intuition and gave herself passionately to the movement, without trying to control it for aesthetic reasons. In her diaries of 1913, Wigman called Laban a "magician" and "irresistible." During her first summer with Laban she experienced a sense of complete liberation and, regardless of tensions which later developed between them, she remained grateful to him throughout her life. It was at Laban's suggestion that Marie changed her name to Mary Wigman, and thanks to Laban she broke through to that unique artistic personality we connect with this name.

After that first summer, Mary Wigman joined Laban and Suzanne Perrottet in Zürich, teaching and helping Laban in his movement research, which increasingly engaged her time and energy. The following summer, she taught at Monte Verita as Laban's assistant. As student, devoted assistant and trustworthy collaborator in Laban's most experimental years, Wigman shared his movement investigations in Zurich and at Monte Verita from 1913 to 1917. However, although it was typical of Laban to run three projects simultaneously, Mary Wigman chose to pursue the only goal that had brought her to Laban: learning how to dance. In *The Mary Wigman* book, edited and translated by Walter Sorell, Wigman vividly described one morning session when she demonstrated Laban's swing scales:

They were most exactly tested for their relationship to each other, to be later demonstrated in their unshakable oneness of force, time, and space. The first of these scales consisted of five different swinging movements leading in a spiral line from downward to upward. The organic combination of their natural three-dimensional qualities led to a perfect harmony. The different movements not only flowed effortlessly from one to the other, they seemed to be born of each other. It also was hard for me. Every movement had to be done over and over again until it was controlled and could be analyzed, transposed, and transformed into an adequate symbol. I have always had a pronounced sense for rhythm and dynamics, and my belief in living a movement and not just doing it was strong. Therefore my individual way of expression and reaction must have been as much torture to Laban as his indefatigable attempts to achieve objectivity were to me.

To point out the dynamic value of these movements they were given by him names like pride, joy, wrath, and so on. I needed little more than to hear the word "wrath" and I immediately threw myself into a colossal rage. The swinging virtually exploded in space. The endlessly repeated movements became more or less mechanical. I was simply delighted to do them once in a different, more personal way. Laban's wrath was even more vehement than mine. He jumped up as bitten by a tarantula, hammered with his fists on the table so that the papers whirled around the room. He shouted: "You clown, you grotesque monster, with your terrific intensity you ruin my whole theory of harmony!" He was furious about what he called my super-self-expression, declaring that the movement itself was wrath and needed no individual interpretation.[31]

Wigman's diaries from 1913-1917 give a very thorough account of the relation between her and Laban; they delineate her debt to him. Collaborating with him, she found her roots; she also deepened her body awareness when she intuitively filled Laban's theoretically constructed movement sequences with life. Her technique became stronger and her coordination improved.

However, the clash of temperaments between Wigman and Laban gradually made their relationship impossible to continue. Eventually, Wigman felt that she had absorbed what Laban was able to give at that time, and she left him in 1917. Reflecting on his work, she more clearly saw her own artistic direction:

Undoubtedly one of his strongest talents was his gift for improvisation. He was able to fashion a fascinating event out of a completely insignificant happening. But he never tried to hold on to it and give it artistic form. It remained vague. As a matter of fact, he always needed people who would take up his ideas and put them to practical use. He always found them, too, all his life.[32]

Laban's mercurial nature was increasingly disturbing to Wigman, who always pursued whatever she began, to the last detail, often with painful perseverance. Because of these characteristics she held on to Laban's use of improvisation and to his basic theory of the three elements--force, space, and time--which became clearly recognizable components of her dance compositions and fundamental to her teaching. Wigman also adopted

Laban's metaphysical idealism, using space as a metaphor for cosmic order. By nature more inclined to Dionysian thinking, however, she stressed space in its dramatic aspect: she made it an imagined, dramatic partner, or she conceived the surrounding space as a living volume, as water or clouds. She used images from nature to arouse tactile sensitivity, not just peripherally or in the extremities, but as a specific translation of the tactile experience of hands or feet into the whole dance instrument. Studies in different textures formed an essential part of her improvisation classes: the texture of wood compared with the feel of a metal gong, or the tactile sensation from wax as a particular heavy flow quality. This approach departed considerably from the practice of simply providing students with visual images (the over-used "awakening flower" or the "tree in the wind"). Wigman's vision was first of all tactile.

By the time she left Laban, this boundless physicality had already made her an incomparable teacher and performer. Laban knew that Wigman was a powerful dancer, the type he had always wanted. Wigman understood him intuitively and shared some of his most secret dreams with him, such as his interest in dances of religious cults. For both of them dance arose from ritual, from their own undefined nonsectarian form of Dionysianism, inspired by Nietzsche. I myself experienced traces of this call to the unconscious when Wigman taught us "Dervish turns," in Leipzig in 1943. Wigman stepped to the center of the studio and executed these hypnotic, monotonous turns for a length of time while we students held on to the walls, observing through the haze of dizziness our fifty-seven-year-old teacher obviously enjoying our defeat. I understand today that this was an outbreak of her "Dionysianism," which made her blue eyes shine even brighter in hypnotic ecstasy. Wigman believed that the student had to reach this level of trance in order to connect to his unconscious roots, similar in thought to Carl Jung's collective unconscious. It was in this realm that Wigman conceived dance ritual, a direct outgrowth of her collaboration with Laban on the dance ritual "Song to the Sun" (*Sang an die Sonne*), in 1917.

This elaborate dance drama opened with a solemn ritual greeting to the sun, that placed the dancers on different hills surrounding Monte Verita. The second part, played at midnight, brought all the grotesque creatures of the night into wild play, while the third part, played at dawn, effectively used the rising sun as it gradually appeared over Ascona's mountains to celebrate the coming day. This piece aroused quasi-religious feelings in some observers; others took it as a political metaphor, since the piece protested the horrors of World War I at a time when numerous invited guests had come to Monte Verita to attend an international pacifist meeting. Mary Wigman led the celebration for the sun; it turned out to be the swan song of her Monte Verita period for shortly thereafter she left what Laban called his "dance farm," the place where she had found herself. She now had to concentrate on her own work.

Laban, too, left Switzerland after World War I and moved to Stuttgart, Germany, to start a new phase of his life, with another female dancer, Dussia Bereska, an attractive Russian German who had joined Laban's circle in 1916. Laban's departure from Monte Verita followed the disclosure that he had taken part in establishing a "free-masonic" Lodge for Women at Monte Verita which included his dancers as members. His dance farm dissolved, and Monte Verita changed its format under new leaders.

Susanne Perrottet directed the school in Zürich, following Laban's concepts, through the postwar period. The years of adolescence of the new dance had passed at Monte Verita, and, during the twenties, Wigman, Laban and Jooss shifted the scene of dance to Germany, creating the European Modern Dance.

NOTES FOR CHAPTER I

1. Reidemeister, Leopold (1983) *Brücke*, Catalogue of Brücke Museum, p. 2. Berlin: Hartmann

2. Kandinsky, Wassily (1977) *Concerning the Spiritual in Art.*translated by M.T.H. Sadler, pp 29 and 35. New York: Dover Publications

3. Martin, John (1965) *Introduction to the Dance*, p. 225. Republication of the original edn, first published in 1939. Brooklyn: Dance Horizons,

4. Sorell, Walter (1981) *Dance in its Time,* p. 318. Garden City, N.Y.: Anchor Press-Doubleday

5. Cohen, Selma Jeanne (1974) *Dance as a Theatre Art*, Source Readings in Dance History p.127. New York: Dodd, Mead & Co.

6. Brandenburg, Hans (1921) 3rd edn, *Der Moderne Tanz*, p. 28. München: Georg Müller

7. Ibid.,p. 29. Translation by I.Bergsohn

8. Shawn, Ted (1954) *Every Little Movement*. Pittsfield, Ma: Eagle Printing & Binding Co.

9. Roslavleva, Natalia (1975) The Isadora Duncan School in Moscow. *Dance Perspectives* 64, **Vol** 16, 7

10. Ibid., 8

11. Sorell, Walter (1981) *Dance in its Time*, p. 307. Garden City, N.Y.: Anchor Press Doubleday

12. Shawn, Ted (1954) p. 84

13. Ibid., 85

14. Brandenburg, Hans (1921) p. 106

15. Wigman, Mary (1913) Notes from her 1913 diary. Wigman Archive, Berlin: Academy of the Arts

16.   Welzien, Leonore (1990) From Rhythm to Movement, From Movement to Dance, interview with Rosalia Chladek. *Tanzdrama*, 2, Vol. 11, 1990, 19. Translation Bergsohn. According to Welzien, Dalcroze had signed a document together with other concerned Swiss citizens which protested against the bombing of Reims. Because of this document, Dalcroze was discriminated against in wartime Germany and could not return to Hellerau

17.   Sorell, Walter (1981) p. 370.

18.   Magriel, Paul (1977) *Nijinsky, Pavlova, Duncan*, 18,19. New York: Dacapo Paperback

19.   Kirstein, Lincoln (1970) *Movement and Metaphor*, p. 202. New York: Praeger Publishers

20.   These impressions I received at a film showing of reconstructions by Millicent Hodson of some of the group scenes of *Le Sacre du Printemps*, Essen, Germany, in June 1988

21.   Laban, Rudolf (1975) *A Life for Dance*, p. 50. London: MacDonald & Evans

22.   Ibid., p. 56

23.   Shawn, Ted. (1954) p. 30

24.   Laban, Rudolf (1948) *Modern Educational Dance*, p. 5. London: MacDonald & Evans

25.   Ibid., p. 5

26.   Laban, Rudolf (1927) Tanztheater und Bewegungschor (Dance theater and Movement Choir). Journal Article in *Tanz und Reigen,* ed. I. Gentges. Berlin: Bühnenvolksbundverlag, pp. 72-79

27.   Laban, Rudolf (1975) *A Life for Dance*, p. 184.

28.   Ibid., p. 109

29.   Green, Martin (1986) *Mountain of Truth,* p. 96. Hanover and London: University Press of New England

30. Sorell, Walter (1986) *Mary Wigman: Ein Vermächtnis*, p. 35.

31. Wigman, Mary (1975) *The Mary Wigman Book*, edited and translated by Walter Sorell, pp. 38, 39. Middletown, Ct: Wesleyan University Press

32. Ibid., p. 33

CHAPTER II: THE FORMATIVE YEARS: THE TWENTIES.

Although the entire generation of postwar Europeans sought radical change, nowhere was "the break in historical continuity more palpably felt"[1] than in Germany, whose artists spearheaded a major revolution in the visual arts, music, theater, and dance. World War I itself, and especially Germany's defeat, toppled the Wilhelmian monarchy, with all the nineteenth-century bourgeois aesthetics and values it had represented. Years in the trenches finally broke down the rigid class distinctions of Wilhelmian society, at least for the younger generation. Unlike previous generations of students who had grown up isolated within their social class, veterans returning from the war retained a sense of camaraderie with their fellow man that transcended educational background.

The young men and women of post-World War I Germany, in search of a new way of life, embraced the ideas of the Neo-Romantic reform movements that had predated the War. These radical visionaries in the first decade of the twentieth century had planted the seeds for far-reaching changes that sprouted in the nineteen-twenties. One of the earliest progressive groups, the Brücke artists (Ernst Ludwig Kirchner, Erich Heckel, Fritz Bley and Karl Schmitt-Rotluff) were especially attractive to German youth. Inspired by primal art, the Brücke artists had revolted against academic regimentation as early as 1905. Using vivid colors, they strove for spontaneity and expressiveness, and they celebrated the human body as free and in harmony with nature.

Influenced by this image, young people after the war organized themselves into various groups to promote Neo-Romantic ideals. Some called for a return to a simpler, more natural way of life, outdoor living, hiking, singing and folk dancing. Others took an aggressive stand against the mechanization of society and concentrated on improving the environment. They shared the ideal of an active, uninhibited body, and they tried to create a new world in which this ideal could become a reality. Thus, the aesthetic principles of a small elite group of artists from the prewar period became the mainstream values of German youth of the twenties. As museums began to organize exhibitions of Brücke artists, "Yesterday's outsiders became the new insiders."[2]

The diversity of artistic styles and philosophies that flourished under the Weimar regime demonstrated that creative development in the arts was possible even in times of extreme political struggle and economic crisis. German artists shared the desperate hope of overcoming Germany's defeat by forging a true twentieth-century art freed from the spirit of the nineteenth century. It was this quest that led to the emergence of the first abstract German painters, the Blue Rider group. The outstanding theorist Wassely Kandinsky wrote in his famous book, *Concerning the Spiritual in Art:* "Every artist, as a creator, has something in him which calls for expression. Every artist, as child of his age, is impelled to express the spirit of his age."[3] Kandinsky's work exerted a tremendous influence on his era: it opened the door to abstract modes of expressing the artist's life. This approach looked upon the creative process and the personal integrity of the artist as the legitimate source for art. In the visual arts, the postwar generation found the most distinct articulation in the German woodcuts of the twenties. In the performing arts as well, the urgent need for expression of the inner world stimulated a period of intense experimentation.

It was the realm of dance, however, which, perhaps better than any other art form, fulfilled the needs of enthusiastic young people striving to express themselves in a direct and unconventional manner. The need for free expression in movement had been an essential aspect of the twentieth-century revolt against the spirit of the past. After World War I, this craving for free expression in movement and human contact led to a public dance craze. A flood of social dances with close body contact rapidly emerged. Women as well as men now enjoyed gymnastics for self-improvement. Direct body action, unstifled by an antiquated vocabulary, was the way young people, as a group, expressed the new way of life.

This enthusiasm for physical movement, combined with the artistic concepts articulated by both the Expressionists and the first abstract painters, helped pave the way for the emergence of European Modern Dance. The "New Dance," or "Ausdruckstanz" (expressive dance), of the nineteen-twenties broke away from the formalism of classical dance, branching out instead into exuberant explorations of personal experience. Isadora Duncan already had thrown away restrictive clothing for the female and established the right to self-expression in dance in the beginning of the twentieth century. This newly granted freedom, at its best, led to a kind of metaphysical transcendentalism; at its worst, it justified purely emotional outbursts.

Out of the bewildering confusion, Rudolf Laban emerged as the first European dance artist to develop a clear concept of dance movement as an art form separate from free movement, different from gymnastics, and independent of music. His slogan "Tanz, Ton, Wort" (Dance, Sound, Word) placed dance clearly on the side of music and drama in the trinity of performing arts.[4]

RUDOLF LABAN

At Monte Verita near Ascona, Switzerland, Laban had originally experimented with choral group forms in order to serve the expressive needs of an eccentric anarchist colony of intellectuals and artists, outsiders to society's mainstream. After two successful summer school seasons, in 1913 and 1914, and after intensive research with Mary Wigman, in March 1915, Laban had opened a "Schule der Bewegungskunst" (School of Movement Art) in Zürich; he tried very hard to establish himself permanently in Switzerland. There, Laban had developed the so called "Laban scales," movement sequences based on spatial relationships parallel to harmonic relationships in music, which gave the students a sense of phrasing while moving through space. He had started to define space by developing a terminology, which became the foundation for his later dance notation system. In the summer of 1917, his movement choir work also tended to exhibit greater structure. The giant outdoor ritual he produced had raised questions in Laban's mind. He worried whether he would be able to create an alternative form of participatory theater at Monte Verita with performers of so limited training. There were personal reasons too that he could not continue his work in Switzerland (the disclosure that he had taken part in establishing a "free-masonic" Lodge at Monte Verita, as discussed in Chapter I). Therefore, in 1920, after a period of serious illness, Laban moved to Stuttgart, in Germany.

Considering the German artistic awakening of the nineteen-twenties, Laban's move occurred at the perfect time; his movement choirs flourished in the Weimar Republic. His belief that active participation in the movement choir generated a festive spirit and created a kind of contemporary ritual, found good response in Germany's youth movement. The young Germans embraced an alternative to conventional theater performance, which, in Laban's opinion, had declined into shallowness and triviality. "The changing destiny of our race," Laban wrote in 1919, "is its awakening to dance. We dancers are the pioneers of a new dawn in art."[5] In an article entitled "Festive Will and Festive Culture," he voiced reservations about the state of the contemporary theater, describing his vision of a magnificent ritual celebration of world dimensions that would unify people in a harmony of space and time.[6] The German youth movement adopted Laban's enthusiasm for outdoor living and ritual celebrations, and some of their group rituals had political connotations.

In the nineteen-twenties, Laban entered a new phase of his life. After moving to Stuttgart, he started to work on his first book, *Die Welt des Tänzers (The Dancer's World)*, published in 1920. In this book, Laban articulated his concern that dance was often regarded merely as a diversion instead of being comprehended in its body-mind complexity. "Much of what is called dance is unartistic gymnastic, acrobatic, fictional pretension, eroticism and more of this nature. We are just starting to understand the deeper contents of this art."[7] Mary Wigman, his collaborator during his Swiss years, described Laban's evolving vision of dance:

> He understood that a work of art, conceived in a unified way, could only be done by people trained in this way. He had to form his own great instrument--the dance group--by finding a language which could be learned by all, and by establishing laws which could, in their clarity and simplicity, unite most varied dance talents on a common basis.... The human orchestra had to be educated not only to dance, but to also understand the dance.[8]

To fulfill his vision of future dance in the theater, in 1920 Laban established the "Tanzbühne Laban" (Dance Theatre Laban) in Stuttgart, an independent performing group. Laban used this group as an instrument for accomplishing his goal of reharmonizing body and soul through the implementation of his complex theories of dance. The seemingly different directions of Laban's activities sprang from one root; the movement choirs of amateurs and the newly established dance ensemble both originated in his desire for harmonization. By 1920, however, Laban knew that he had to educate dancers carefully in order to reach his goal.

The Tanzbühne Laban, under the direction of Laban and Dussia Bereska, assembled such outstanding students as Hertha Feist, Jens Keith, Albrecht Knust, and Kurt Jooss. All of them later carried on Laban's ideas, each developing some particular aspect of his concepts. By this time he had already developed his fundamental definitions of harmonious and disharmonious relationships in space. The daily classes, which were often given outside on the lawn, consisted of twenty-four dancers, seven of them males, moving through set sequences of body swings, composed by Laban, that focussed on clear spatial articulation. The group was divided into high, middle, and low dancers, according to their natural movement proclivities. They were free to use the given sequences on any of the these three spatial levels. Improvisation was still encouraged, and occasionally group studies centered on ensemble awareness. "Dance was definitely an art form," said Sylvia Bodmer, one of the original members of the Tanzbühne Laban, "and the company worked in this spirit."[9]

The early twenties marked the beginning of Laban's more methodical work. His study of dance and his choreographic experimentation went hand in hand. The choreography itself grew out of the combined efforts of the choreographer, the dance director, and the actively contributing dancers. Laban's main interest lay in the creative process itself, and very often he left details to be worked out by his collaborator, Dussia Bereska, who co-directed the company in Stuttgart and also took care of the company on tours. The strength of Laban's process-oriented rehearsal approach lay in the interplay among members of the closely-knit ensemble and their absolute dedication. For this reason very few of his early works were transmitted to later generations, since he built works like *Die Geblendeten* (*The Deluded*) and *Himmel und Erde* (*Sky and Earth*) on the particular movement characteristics of his dancers.

In 1921, Laban accepted the ballet directorship of the National Theater in Mannheim for the production of his version of the Bacchanalia of Richard Wagner's opera *Tannhäuser*. Combining the twenty dancers of the Tanzbühne Laban with members of the opera ensemble, he staged a theatrical event of gigantic proportions. Ironically, the work placed Laban in the forefront of the established German theatrical profession that he had previously criticized as morbid and decadent. He was now professionally recognized as the leader of the new art form, recently termed Modern Dance.

After this success Laban, in his early forties, returned to his work as an independent choreographer. In 1923 he made Hamburg the new base of his operations, and founded there, with Dussia Bereska as his collaborator, the Kammer-Tanzbühne Laban (The Chamber Dance Theater Laban) and the Zentral-Schule Laban (Central School Laban), under the direction of Albrecht Knust. Laban's work after this time projected itself in three directions: the movement choir, choreographic activity with the new Chamber Dance Theater, and the creation of a system of movement and dance notation. This last endeavor preoccupied him from 1926 to 1928, when he published *Schrifttanz,* in which he described the dance notation system that he named "Kinetographie Laban," now internationally recognized as Labanotation.

To Laban, the development of movement and dance notation was of crucial importance. He saw that an art form based solely on oral tradition had no chance to develop "as an equal among the arts" of poetry and music. In *Des Kindes Gymnastik und Tanz,* Laban wrote that the "entire history of the art of movement is also the history of striving for a dance notation in which the dancer sees more than a useful tool for his professional education. If this art would have been practiced in previous centuries we would have today an insight into earlier movement forms and endeavors in our field."[10] To Laban, the word "movement" (in Greek *kinein*) had to be in the title, since he had struggled for about thirty years with the problem of how to document movement. eighteenth- and nineteenth- century ballet notation systems existed, but in Laban's eyes they were static, documenting positions and floor patterns, but not the flow of the movement. What was so new about *Schrifttanz* was that Laban's method broke up movement into different elements and indicated them by symbols. In 1928, in a special issue giving explanations of *Schrifttanz,* Laban used the term Kinetographie Laban for the first time. In Germany and certain other European centers the notation system still bears that name.

As varied as Laban's activities appear during the twenties, they all arose from the same motivating force: his determination to elevate dance to an equal standing among the other arts. His most decisive step in this direction was the establishment, in 1926, of the Choreographic Institute, a research center for advanced studies in "choreology," the study of the grammar and the syntax of the language of movement.[11] Accepting the invitation of the City of Würzburg to establish there the prestigious institute, Laban and his collaborators laid the groundwork for dance research with this center, moving it two years later to Berlin. They organized their work into three disciplines. The first, which Laban called "choreutics," focussed on the actions of the body in space. The second, a detailed study of dynamics and rhythm, which was undertaken by Laban and Bereska, was termed "eukinetics." The third discipline, dance notation, was taught by Gertrud Snell. Laban's dance notation, Kinetographie Laban, was in fact a team effort, the two closest collaborators being Albrecht Knust, one of Laban's first students, and Dussia Bereska, who had, according to Laban, a strong influence on the development of the notation system. Albrecht Knust tested Laban's system in practical applications; he introduced further refinements in his first notation center, in Hamburg, in the thirties, and while teaching Kinetographie Laban at the Folkwang Schule in Essen, Germany, beginning in 1949. Ann Hutchinson, a former student of the Jooss/Leeder School, along with Helen Priest (Rogers), Eve Gentry and Janey Price (Goeb) opened the Dance Notation Bureau in New York City in 1940. In 1954, after coming to Essen, Hutchinson published *Labanotation,* her book on dance writing.[12] In noteworthy meetings between Hutchinson and Knust, the notation system was reviewed and clarified, and today, under the name of Labanotation, it serves as an objective tool for the preservation of twentieth-century dance works, as music notation serves to preserve music.

With the rise of National Socialism in the nineteen-thirties, Laban's Choreographic Institute became a victim of politics. However, Laban's organization of dance materials reached the United States through the work of the Dance Notation Bureau in New York and through Effort/Shape Notation, later called Laban Movement Analysis, which was developed by Irmgard Bartenieff from her work with Laban. She and several other original Wigman students in the United States applied Laban's concepts to movement therapy and contributed the essential groundwork for the new field of Dance Therapy, which reached contemporary Germany as an American creation. Labananalysis, the combination of Labanotation and Laban Movement Analysis, is now clinically used to document movement characteristics of patients who cannot express themselves verbally. Both systems are also part of instruction in dance in American colleges and universities and helped develop a more objective perspective in the teaching of movement.

From the thirties through the fifties, American Modern Dance was taught with a studio approach, based on the work of the leading artistic personalities, Martha Graham, Doris Humphrey and Charles Weidman. The student came with the idea of learning the particular dance vocabulary of one of these American pioneers and, training in their style, hoped to become a member of a company. This attitude gradually changed with a growing knowledge of anatomy, kinesiology and Labanotation. Thus, although Laban himself is little known in the United States, his thinking had a great influence on the development of dance in the United States. Laban provided a vocabulary for describing movement that is not bound to a particular artistic personality, but applicable to any body movement. This became important when the contemporary American dance strived for more abstract forms of movements no longer derived from a single artist's work.

Independently of Laban, the New Dance in Europe had also been set in motion in Vienna by the Wiesenthal sisters, who combined free swinging motions with some classically inspired dance forms, and by Ruth St. Denis, recreating oriental dances in a spirit of fin-de-siecle mysticism. Alexander Sacharow and his wife, Clotilde von Derp, of the same generation as St. Denis, drew further inspiration for strongly pantomimic partner dances from images from the visual arts. Simultaneously, diverse systems of gymnastics competed with one another to offer the most effective method of freeing the female body; Rudolf Bode, born 1881, was the first European gymnastic teacher to separate gymnastics from music and military exercises. The German composer Carl Orff took an opposite approach; having experienced the fundamental ties between physical and musical rhythm as a conductor, he joined with the German dance writer Dorothee Günther to found, in 1924, the Günther Schule in Munich. His research as music educator focussed on how to stimulate a rhythmic response on the most elementary level with young children. Familiar with Mensendieck's gymnastics as well as with the work of Dalcroze and Laban, Orff, together with Günther, made one of the first attempts to educate a new type of performer trained equally in both movement and music. Instead of offering one method of movement education, it united three branches of movement studies: gymnastics, rhythmic movement, and expressive dance. Carl Orff broke new ground developing a pedagogical method of teaching elementary rhythmic education as the foundation for all three areas. In numerous publications, the most well known his book *The Schulwerk,* Orff describes percussion instruments which have consequently been widely used in primary education and in dance.

Orff commented on the impact that Mary Wigman's dances had on him in the early twenties: "The art of Mary Wigman was very significant for me and my later work. All her dances were animated by an unprecedented musicality, even the musicless witches dance. She could make music with her body and transform music into corporeality. I felt that her dancing was elemental. I, too, was searching for the elemental, for elemental music."[13] The closeness of their artistic goals became apparent much later, in 1943, in their first true collaboration, when Wigman choreographed Orff's *Carmina Burana* for the Leipzig Opera House (Carmina Burana will be discussed in Chapter V).

MARY WIGMAN

Mary Wigman's unique approach to movement led quite naturally to her experiments with "dance in silence" or "absolute dance." The term "absolute dance" had appeared first in 1917 in a performance art dance piece, when Sophie Taeuber (wife of sculptor Jean Arp), Laban, and Wigman were working together at the DADA Gallery in Zürich. Dada's credo was "absolute poetry, absolute art, and absolute dance." Although Dada in poetry and theatre was short-lived, Mary Wigman pursued to its ultimate consequence Laban's original idea of the independence of dance from music: the dance in silence. Wigman claimed absolute dance as her particular creation. She did not go as far as Cunningham in his denial of any structural relation between dance and music, but she gave dominance to dance. Whenever she used sound, it was composed after she had completed her choreography.

After 1917, Wigman shifted her focus solely to kinesthetic events, which occurred without any scenery in front of black curtains, completely independent of the music, similar to puristic tendencies in other arts of the early twenties in Europe. The titles of her solo dances, such as *Temple Dance* from the suite of *Ecstatic Dances,* indicated Wigman's attraction to mystic ritual. On each program she performed at least one dance without any musical accompaniment. She did not seem to need music in her trance-like, mesmerizing turns or in her majestic walk; she was carried by her profound body-rhythmic sense. The audience, however, very often failed to understand her dances. Only a few dance writers, Hans Brandenburg for one, appreciated her work:

> The unique characteristics of Wigman are that her dance is completely
> without any trace of pantomime, truly "absolute", based solely on themes
> of motion and architecturally structured: it is based purely on laws of form
> caused by a kinesthetic logic.... This dance draws from no tradition, but
> will be instrumental in creating a new tradition.[14]

In 1918, Wigman's work was temporarily interrupted by a bout with tuberculosis, which confined her to a sanatorium. The World War I years, and the summers at Monte Verita, with irregular meals and excessive dancing in a spartan surrounding, caught up with her. When she reentered the German dance scene on her own, she encountered rejection and ridicule. However, strengthened by months of solitary convalescence in a mountain retreat, she was now sure of herself, and gradually the tide of public opinion began to change. Her first performance in the large Dresden Concert Hall in November 1919 turned out to be an overwhelming success for her and her dancers, Gret Palucca and Berthe Truempy. The audience response made such an impression on her that she decided to make Dresden her home.

One of Wigman's oldest dreams was to have her own school in an active center where she could compose her dances and simultaneously build up her group of dancers. The Wigman School, opened in 1920, and later called the Mary Wigman Central School, became this refuge. Between journeys she always returned to work in her beloved "yellow room" and to recharge her creative energies. The "yellow room" was a large studio with a beautifully kept wooden floor. Every day at noon Wigman met there with her pianist to improvise and to find some new material for her compositions. The move to Dresden was a decisive step for Wigman. For years she had shared Laban's unstable life. Now, settled at last, she began establishing her own work and her own circle of associates. A young high school teacher named Will Grohmann, fervently interested in her work, became her friend for life. The Brücke artist Ernst Ludwig Kirchner spent many hours sketching while Wigman was rehearsing, and many friends visited whenever they came to Dresden. Composer/pianist Will Goetze joined as musical director in 1921, experimenting with new kinds of dance accompaniment. According to Carl Orff, Will Goetze was "an outstanding musician and extremely gifted with a sympathetic understanding for dance.... He accompanied Wigman on the piano, and for her dances he wrote music, including percussion, that was original and that caused a sensation at the time."[15] Wigman preferred single sound or sound clusters to melodic patterns and thus introduced new ways of using percussion instruments as accompaniment for the modern dance class. She particularly favored a new kind of drum, a small dance timpani used by Paul Hindemith in his violin concerto. Wigman also used it in the accompaniments for her group dances. Elizabeth Wigman, her younger sister, who came to help teach children's and laymen's classes, was introduced to these new ways of using sound and developed into a fine pedagogue. The Wigman School grew rapidly, while Wigman experienced her most productive and fulfilled period, participating actively in the exuberant artistic life of the blooming city of Dresden, surrounded by avant-garde artists of the twenties.

An amazing combination of highly talented students made up Wigman's first class: Hanya Holm, Harald Kreutzberg, Gret Palucca, Yvonne Georgi, Max Terpis, and Margarethe Wallmann. Each of them became well known representatives of various aspects of the "Ausdruckstanz," the new dance of the Expressionistic period in Central Europe. In teaching the new dance, Wigman emphasized improvisation; as she often said, "a pedagogic method did not yet exist."[16] But she gradually found unique ways to awaken in her students the sense of their body rhythm. She also tried to sharpen their sense of form, something she found not fully satisfactory in her own early instruction from Laban. Thus, Wigman gave to this remarkable first generation of students the technical means and spiritual impetus to further their creative work.

Wigman's students all were successful in various fields. On her recommendation, Max Terpis left first in fall 1922 to become balletmaster at the Hannover Opera, where he engaged Kreutzberg as soloist. Later, Kreutzberg became the great European solo performer of the Ausdruckstanz; his *Gardener in Love* to Mozart's music provided delightful proof that the new dance did not have to be without humor. Gret Palucca struck out on her own in 1923. After having performed in Wigman's first small group, she felt a need to pursue her own solo works. Palucca's physical exuberance made her one of the most admired modern dancers of the twenties and thirties. A favorite model for artists such as Wassily Kandinsky, Paul Klee and Ernst Ludwig Kirchner, Palucca performed dances that were purely kinesthetic; her ability to jump was legendary. During the Third Reich, Palucca held one of the leading positions in the Meisterstätten für Tanz (Master Institute for Dance), run by the Ministry of Propaganda. In 1939, however, her school was closed by the Nazis because of her friendship with artists of the Expressionistic period, whose works were now called "degenerate art." She continued as a solo performer through the thirties and forties in Germany. She returned after World War II continuing her performing career and reopening her Palucca School in Dresden in 1954.

Other Wigman students also achieved prominence on their own. Margarethe Wallmann, after directing the Wigman School in Berlin in the twenties, worked as the first female stage director of the operas in Buenos Aires, Vienna, Salzburg and Milan. Yvonne Georgi consolidated modern dance within the German theater, first as partner of Harald Kreutzberg, and later as main balletmistress of the Opera in Hannover, which became a stronghold of Modern Dance. Most of Wigman's students pursued their own independent careers, with the exception of Hanya Holm, Wigman's faithful assistant, who, in 1931, came to New York to direct a Wigman School. Hanya Holm successfully transplanted the Wigman tradition to the United States, where Wigman's philosophy of dance became widely known and bore fruit in the following generations of American Modern Dance.

During the twenties, Wigman shifted the emphasis of her choreographic work from solo dances to group compositions. The first Chamber Dance Group, attached to the school, performed Wigman's *Seven Dances of Life* in 1921 with her as soloist, rendering this dance poem in an Expressionist style that combined words and movement. Although inflation made touring increasingly difficult economically, Wigman enlarged her group to fourteen dancers in 1923, and by 1924, her production style had crystallized. *Scenes of a Dance Drama,* presented by the extended group in 1924, constituted Wigman's first completely composed modern group work and showed how far she had come from Laban's movement choirs. An overall design was clearly apparent in the strongly geometrical group formations and composed interactions between soloists and groups. Looking at Ursula Richter's photographs of the dancers, one sees that Wigman had achieved a complete choreographic orchestration in which the single dancer followed the overall design like a musical instrument. *Scenes of a Dance Drama,* completely unified by the choreographer's vision, represented an early landmark in the history of Modern Dance.

Wigman's shift from the subjective, artistic expression of the earlier twenties to abstract, stark and highly stylized movements reflected trends evident in the other arts, particularly in German architecture and painting of the mid-twenties. This stylistic change to geometric structure might have been influenced by her artist friends Ernst Kirchner and Wassily Kandinsky, or it may have represented Wigman's assimilation of a changing cultural climate. A reaction to the excesses of Expressionism was occurring under the name of Neo-Realism, and although Wigman was not a realist, aspects of the new trend appealed to her. Moreover, she was disturbed by the dilettantism of some of the so-called Ausdruckstänzer, who displayed only their personal feelings to an accepting and undiscriminating audience.

Wigman's choreographic output between 1926 and 1928 brought her, as she approached forty, to the climax of her artistic career in Germany. In this period she experimented with masks, concealing the performer's facial expression. Undoubtedly influenced by Japanese No theater, Wigman created magic with masks. Her visionary dances, *Ceremonial Figure, Dance of Death*, and *Hexentanz II* (Witch Dance II), expressed the inner experience in a most restrained form. By the end of the nineteen-twenties, Wigman had achieved a distinctive style and philosophy of dance, which she tersely summed up in eight words in her dance theory class (where I first heard it): "Without ecstasy no dance, without form no dance."

DANCE IN THE GERMAN THEATER IN THE NINETEEN-TWENTIES

The first generation of modern dancers regarded themselves as revolutionaries, creating a new world. Trained largely in various gymnastic schools, at the Dalcroze Institute, and by Laban at Monte Verita in an era of Free Dance, they avoided conventional theatrical settings for their celebrations in dance, because in their eyes, the theater preserved societal cliches. European theater, however, had undergone its own fundamental changes since the beginning of the century, and these new trends eventually influenced the course of Modern Dance, especially under the leadership of Kurt Jooss.

After the first World War, one of the major reform trends in German theater aimed at establishing a closer relation between the audience and the performer. German architects designed theater buildings to implement Antonin Artaud's original idea of facilitating communication between the two. Thus, the Great Theater in Berlin (Das Grosse Schauspielhaus), built in 1919 by Hans Poelzig, featured a stage enclosed by an elongated frame; platforms served as an extension of the stage. Max Reinhardt (1873-1943), the great Austrian-born director and the strongest force in the German-speaking theater in this period, took advantage of the new spatial relationships on this stage to produce theater events that integrated singers, actors, and chorus members into one dynamic force.

Elsewhere, Walter Gropius, the director of the German Bauhaus complex for architecture and applied arts, established an experimental Theater Stage workshop that originally grew out of the creative play and was used to entertain guests at Bauhaus parties. Students and professors performed parodies and sketches similar in spirit to Dada events. In 1927 Gropius provided an example of a workable experimental stage space when, for Erwin Piscator's "total theater," he designed an elliptical amphitheater that could be transformed into a circular platform similar to the Greek orchestra, simply by removing some of the seats.

Other examples of innovative staging include the work of painter/designer Oskar Schlemmer. When Schlemmer became director of Gropius's experimental theater stage workshop in 1923, he started a systematic investigation of the stage as space for physical action and even attempted to establish a grammar of stage actions. Schlemmer was mainly interested in transforming the actor/dancer into a mechanical object through the use of costume. His model was the marionette, a mechanical figure that could display movements beyond the human range. The closest he came to achieving his vision was the *Triadic Ballet*, performed first at a Bauhaus party in 1922 and restaged during Bauhaus Week in 1923 and also in 1926. (The word "triadic" referred to three concealed dancers, but also alluded to the fusion of motion, geometrically shaped costumes, and music, written by Paul Hindemith, for player piano). In 1977, the German modern dancer and independent choreographer Gerhard Bohner revived the *Triadic Ballet* with his own new version at the Berlin Akademie der Künste (Berlin Academy of the Arts). He utilized the original costumes, which gave a good idea of Schlemmer's design concepts in his experimental theater stage workshop at the Bauhaus in Dessau. In the nineteen-fifties and sixties, artists such as Alwin Nikolais furthered this vision of the interaction of moving shapes, colored light and music to create a whole new theater of motion, light and sound.

Germany also produced ingenious directors in the nineteen-twenties. For a while, Berlin was the capital of the theatrical world. Innovative artists such as Max Reinhardt, Karl-Heinz Martin, Heinz Hilpert, Erich Engel and Leopold Jessner turned away from literal, traditional theater in order to concentrate on color, light, and structured movement. These innovative efforts extended to the Berlin opera, which, owing to municipal support, had been the most hidebound of all theatrical forms. Producers now demanded performers with movement training and refused to make use of the traditional opera ballet, a residue of the nineteenth-century stage convention, since its classical vocabulary did not match their new, progressive production style. The experimental trend in theater was not limited to Berlin alone; many of the most progressive plays were first seen on municipal theater stages.

In 1921, Dr. Hanns Niedecken-Gebhard (born 1889), an innovative personality in the field of opera, became the stage director at the State Theater of Hannover. After studies at the Universities of Lausanne, Leipzig, and Halle, Niedecken-Gebhard had completed his doctoral degree with an outstanding paper on the eighteenth-century choreographer Jean-George Noverre, who had coined the slogan "ballet d'action" (dramatic ballet) in his famous *Letters on Dancing*. As the new stage director of opera, Niedecken staged operas in accordance with Noverre's dramatic choreographic concepts, translating the eighteenth-century Swiss choreographer's ideas into twentieth-century theater. Niedecken-Gebhard invited Wigman and her Chamber Dance Group to perform *Seven Dances of Life* at the State Theater in Hannover, her home town. Impressed with this work, he also asked her to choreograph her first opera for Hans Pfitzner's *Rose vom Liebesgarten (The Rose from the Garden of Love)*. Thus began a friendship that lasted over thirty years. Niedecken-Gebhard soon discovered that modern dancers understood his dramatic stage directions more easily than classically trained dancers, and through his leadership, the Theater of Hannover became a stronghold of the young Modern Dance movement throughout the twenties and thirties. In 1922, Niedecken-Gebhard hired Max Terpis, whose classical background had been augmented by a year of studies under Wigman, to be the first balletmaster. A year later, Terpis brought Wigman-trained Harald Kreutzberg and Yvonne Georgi to Hannover as solo modern dancers.

Niedecken-Gebhard left Hannover in 1924 to accept the artistic directorship of the Theater of the City of Münster, a middle-sized town in Westphalia, where the musical director, Rudolph Schulz-Dornburg, had pioneered innovative music productions. Niedecken-Gebhard engaged Frederic Alexander Cohen, most famous as the composer of the music of *The Green Table*, as opera conductor. Stage designer Hein Heckroth was in charge of all opera and theater productions. Recognizing the need for a movement specialist, someone trained to deal with the various tasks that his progressive style demanded, Niedecken-Gebhard in 1924 hired Laban's talented assistant, a young man named Kurt Jooss. Jooss, whom Niedecken-Gebhard had met while Jooss was on tour with the Tanzbühne Laban two years earlier, was engaged to fill the new position of "movement director," created especially for him. In addition to assisting with opera and drama performances, Jooss was offered the chance to direct the first independent dance group within the Theater of Münster, in the summer of 1924.

KURT JOOSS

The first generation of European modern dancers had criticized theater for being too conventional. As a member of the second generation of modern dancers, Kurt Jooss saw theater in a very different light. The theater that Jooss encountered actually reflected the reformist spirit of the new age. Trained by Laban and experienced in performing, the young Kurt Jooss was one of the first to recognize that the Modern Dance could and should find its place in the contemporary theater. Jooss directed his energies towards making this happen.

Born in 1901, Kurt Jooss grew up on a farm in Württemberg. At his parental home the family practiced music together in the evenings, and Kurt recalled later how his little grandmother had taught him to dance a waltz. This musical family, however, was not accustomed to thinking of dance as an art form or as a medium for expressing feelings. They were astonished when, at the age of fourteen, Kurt composed his first dance, inspired by an Indian poem, and performed in the family's living room to the Schubert song *Leise flehen meine Lieder*.

Since Kurt had a good voice and was artistically inclined, the family permitted him to enter the Stuttgart Academy of Music as a student of piano and voice, when he turned eighteen. Kurt was not satisfied with his study of music. However, when Rudolf Laban moved to Stuttgart, he went to the famous artist's home. That first meeting with Laban set the tone for their relationship for years to come:

> One Sunday afternoon in 1920, I had the courage to ring his [Laban's] doorbell. A servant in black opened, listened to my request and disappeared for about ten minutes. Returning, she announced formally: "Count von Laban is ready to receive you." After climbing a flight of stairs, I entered a sparsely furnished room where Count Laban was enthroned in the center of the room, dressed in a red velvet cape. I confessed that I had come to be instructed by the master in his art. An audition followed. Taking off my shirt, I moved around the living room performing for Laban my dance inspired by the Indian poem, "Indian Prayers." Laban consented to teach me under one condition: I had to return with five healthy males to constitute a class. I returned with all my friends from my nearby hometown, and those young men built the nucleus of Laban's ensemble work in Stuttgart in 1920.[17]

This audition decided Jooss's career. He dropped his studies of music and entered the world of dance. In his biographical notes he confessed that "a complete change overtook me. I became deeply involved, my body changed, and my whole being gradually became part of this art."[18]

The decision to study dance was not an easy one for Jooss to make. He struggled unsuccessfully for four months, trying to combine farming and dance. In the end, choosing dance, he disappointed his family, who expected him to follow in his father's footsteps. Laban's magnetic appeal was irresistible; the young farmer's son saw in Laban an authoritative master of the art form he chose for his life's work.

By the time Jooss met Laban, the master had changed from the magician who confronted Mary Wigman at Monte Verita to the scientist of movement. The swing scales, which Laban had worked out with Wigman, had shown a rhythmically harmonious progression of the body's action in the interplay of the three dimensions (height, width and depth). In his Stuttgart years, Laban's spatial research encompassed a wider field of movement; his attention focussed on three dimensional movements. The space diagonals that cross the center of the body require three nominators, for instance, from high, right, back to low, left, forward. Laban had tested this material on which he based his class instructions, and it appeared to his students as objective knowledge. Irmgard Bartenieff's *Body Movement Coping with the Environment* gives a detailed description of Laban's choreutic practices.[19] To Jooss, the farmer's son, Laban's reference to the organic world made sense: "What Laban brought us was not invention, but finding. Which means he did not invent anything, but he looked at nature and found a solution."[20]

In the following four years with Laban, Jooss laid the foundation for his own life work. He saw and respected Laban first of all as dancer and artist. He worked under him as student, dancer and assistant, and he agreed with Wigman's assessment of Laban's mercurial nature:

> His marvelous method was not to tell anything, but to take away everything which might be in our way to penetrate deeper into the realm of dance. One of his very effective pedagogic means was destruction. He was able to destroy a lot in us to make space for good things to come.[21]

Training the body was just one of several aspects of Laban's approach. Exploring where and how to move through space in a given movement sequence and becoming aware of dynamic changes were equally important exercises. John Hodgson and Valerie Preston-Dunlop explained Laban's training methods in their book, *Rudolf Laban*:

> For many, dance technique means acquiring a finite and established pattern of skills which are regularly practiced and maintained. These, then become the vocabulary of the dance work. Laban's approach was almost the reverse of this for his aim was to give access to a vast and versatile vocabulary which could be brought to the creation of a dance, each individual contributing as genuine artist within the overall shape of the given choreographic idea.[22]

Jooss danced the male lead in the company's first production, *Die Geblendeten* (*The Deluded*), only a few weeks after joining Laban. As he explained in his memoirs, "At that time, for the Expressionistic Dance in Germany one did not need great proficiency: strong intensity was enough." [23] In 1921, when Laban was asked to choreograph the Wagnerian *Tannhäuser Bacchanal* for the National Theater in Mannheim, he combined his Stuttgarter students, among them Kurt Jooss, with the dance ensemble of the theater. From then on, Jooss toured with the Tanzbühne Laban as performer and later as Laban's assistant.

In 1922, Jooss and another Laban dancer, Aino Siimola, followed the master to Hamburg, where Siimola, a beautiful Estonian dancer who had been a member of the Tanzbühne Laban in Stuttgart, became solo dancer of the newly established Chamber Dance Theater Laban. Aino became Kurt's closest associate in work as well as in life: the two married in 1929.

Also in Hamburg Jooss met another dancer who became important to his artistic career. Sigurd Leeder, born in Hamburg, was six months younger than Jooss. Beginning in 1924, Jooss and Leeder prepared a joint dance program, entitled *Two Male Dancers*, which marked the start of their association as artists.

Despite these promising opportunities, by 1924 Jooss felt the need for independence. Still, he left Laban's Tanzbühne "with great pain," knowing he had irritated his mentor.[24] Jooss did not discuss the reasons that led to this decision. Unlike Wigman, who kept a detailed record in her diaries of her own creative process and her changing relation to Laban, Jooss was not inclined to write down his inner thoughts. In personal matters he was very private. He left countless small notes on movement ideas, often scribbled on an old program or even a railroad ticket, but his writings are relatively sparse. The opening words of his autobiographical notes admit that,"By nature my talents are practical, but ever since I have been able to think clearly for myself, my strongest wish has been toward philosophy and the arts."[25] He left large gaps in his memoirs, covering barely the most important events in his life. Still, we can assume that his decision to leave Laban's company, like his decision to leave his father's farm, was a difficult one. Laban had opened up the world of dance for him, and for this Jooss was grateful throughout his life, but Jooss instinctively knew when the time to leave had come. Relations between the two men were strained by the separation; it took three years before Laban recognized Jooss as a colleague. During that time, Kurt Jooss gained valuable experience as Movement Director at the Theater of Münster.

In many ways Jooss encountered an ideal environment at the Theater in Münster. He enjoyed the support of the theater's musical director, Rudolf Schultz-Dornburg, and he had fine collaborators who formed the nucleus of his team: the musician Frederic Cohen; the designer, Hein Heckroth; Aino Siimola; and Sigurd Leeder. Jooss still felt committed to Laban's work, which closely combined dance for the theater with pedagogic ideals. In fact, during the spring of 1925, Jooss and Leeder developed plans for a professional School of Dance to be based on Laban's "Tanz, Ton, Wort" (Dance, Sound, Word) ideas. In the fall of the same year The Westphalian Academy of Movement, Speech and Music was established, with Rudolf Schultz-Dornburg as director, and three departments: Dance, Speech, and Music, headed respectively by Kurt Jooss, Vilma Moenkeberg, and Hermann Erpf.

Simultaneously, Jooss started rehearsals with the Neue Tanzbühne, his dance group of three male and four female dancers, some of them his colleagues at Laban's previous group. Jooss complemented the small dance ensemble of professional dancers with a Laban-styled movement choir. Actors and amateurs, trained in the movement choir, participated in dramas, operas and dance comedies, carrying out Laban's belief, shared by Jooss, in the unity of the arts. This goal challenged dancers to the utmost. They had to stretch themselves in three different directions to cover the various movement needs of progressive drama and opera productions while also consolidating their own independent work.

Jooss's pedagogic work went hand in hand with his choreographic productions, which blended well with the production style practiced by Niedecken-Gebhard. Jooss's choreographic record was impressive. Between 1924 and 1926, he created five major works: in 1924, *Persisches Ballett* (music by Wellesc); in 1925, *Der Demon* (music by Hindemith) and *Die Brautfahrt* (music by Rameau and Couperin); and in 1926, *Larven and Tragödie* (music by F. Cohen). In the winter of 1926/1927, Kurt Jooss and Sigurd Leeder started on tour with a full evening's program, including four duets and four solos each, but unfortunately, Jooss seriously injured his knee, and his theater career was temporarily interrupted. However, the program with Leeder laid the ground for a friendship and close collaboration that would endure over the next twenty-three years. The joint program remained Kurt Jooss's single attempt to work as solo performer in an expressionistic style.

Despite the excellent progress Jooss made in the first two years as movement director in Muenster, he was not completely content. While recovering from his knee injury he had a chance to reflect more clearly on his priorities. He realized that he had to find a method to train dancers for his contemporary dance ensemble in an objective movement language. This recognition led him back to Laban's circle. Jooss and Sigurd had heard of Laban's most recent research, which focussed on a definition and systematization of qualities of movement. Whenever Jooss had a chance to leave Münster, he and Leeder went to Hamburg to work with Dussia Bereska, who introduced them to this new development, called "eukinetics." Eukinetics might be described as the theory and practice of movement expression. It deals with temporal and dynamic values and the manner in which movement extends into space. The fusion of these three factors, time, force and attitude toward space, define the particular movement expression. From the combination of these basic elements eight qualities were derived, each containing all three basic factors.[26]

The new eukinetics were fascinating to Jooss and Leeder. Jooss immediately saw the possible benefits of systematically applying qualitative aspects to the training of his future dance ensemble. However, he needed to do further movement investigations in order to pursue his vision of a contemporary dance theater; so he and Leeder went to Vienna and also to Paris to study the classical dance. Though barely documented, these studies must have had a decisive influence on Kurt Jooss, clarifying for him his ideas about contemporary theatrical dance and also helping to crystallize principles for preparing dancers for his contemporary ensemble style. By fall 1927, fully recovered from his knee injury and revitalized by his dance studies, Jooss reentered the German dance scene as a promising choreographer at the first Dancers' Congress, held at Magdeburg in May 1927. The Congress assembled leaders of the dance world to discuss the situation of the dancer in the German theater. It was a topic that deeply interested Jooss and his contemporaries and that generated considerable debate between Wigman and Laban. As the two leading authorities on Modern Dance in Germany, Laban and Wigman were invited by *The Magdeburg Daily Newspaper* to express their views on the position of the dancer in German theater. Wigman wrote an essay, published in the May 15, 1927, issue, in which she recognized two essential types of creative dance: the "absolute dance" and the "stage dance." The latter, according to Wigman, was in a state of confusion and compromise. Dance in theatrical productions alternated back and forth between classical and pantomimic elements, resulting in an unfortunate mixture of styles. Wigman ended with a plea: "Our dance is born of our age and its spirit; it has the stamp of our time as no other art form has. I wish that our contemporaries would become fully aware of their responsibilities toward their own and most alive creation, the modern dance."[27]

Laban's views were considerably less exclusive than Wigman's. In "The Dance as a Work of Art," a lecture delivered to the Congress, he proposed an alliance of all dancers under his direction. In obvious confrontation with Wigman, Laban looked to Jooss as a strong ally in his efforts to unify disparate modern dance groups, including movement choirs, and also to give modern dance a place in the German theater. The two men resolved the tension between them, and Laban now accepted his previous student as a valuable ally in the move to promote "stage dance."

The differences in point of view between Wigman on the one hand and Laban and Jooss on the other were graphically revealed to Congress participants when their works were performed as part of the Congress program. An early pupil of Mary Wigman, Vera Skoronell, presented her own dance group performing a highly abstract work entitled *Mysterium der Form* (*Mystery of Form*). In contrast, Kurt Jooss's *Kaschemme* (*Pub*), danced by the Neue Tanzbühne Münster, and Laban's *Narrenspiegel* (*Fool's Mirror*), danced by Laban and Bereska with the Chamber Dance Theater Laban, clearly exemplified how modern dance could function as part of contemporary theater, working with characterization, humor and irony. The first Congress spotlighted theater dance and made it a part of the ongoing dialogue on the future of dance in Germany. Very soon afterward, Kurt Jooss and Sigurd Leeder participated in a summer course of Laban in Bad Mergentheim. Jooss, reconciled with Laban, found himself in the forefront of the dance world, as one of the leading exponents of the new performing art form.

THE FOLKWANG SCHOOL

In 1927, after the First Dancers' Congress, Rudolf Schulz-Dornburg asked Kurt Jooss to serve as co-founder of the Folkwang School in Essen. The school continued the earlier efforts of the two men to establish a general academy of the arts. Parallel in spirit to the Bauhaus in Weimar and later Dessau, the Folkwang School, like the Westphalian Academy, attempted to implement Laban's ideals, expressed in his slogan "Dance, Sound, Word" (Tanz, Ton, Wort). Education in dance, music, and speech was offered in the School for Expressive Arts, and another division, the School for Design, provided education in applied visual design. Jooss became the director of the department of dance.

Schulz-Dornburg's offer came at just the right time for Jooss, who, together with Sigurd Leeder, had already developed a model for the comprehensive study of contemporary dance as an art form. In the fall of 1927, just before the Folkwang School officially opened, Jooss published an article "Tänzerziehung in der Folkwang Schule" (Dance Education at the Folkwang School), that clearly articulated the distinction between dance and gymnastics.[28] Accordingly, the central goal of the dance program of the Folkwang School was "to create a place where dance was comprehended and taught as an art discipline." Jooss further stressed that the instructors would be artists, and that the work of the dance department would be based on the life work of Rudolf Laban and his choreographic space principles. At the same time, dancers had to grasp a new understanding of the classical style, especially after the Ausdruckstanz had vehemently denied any value in ballet.

Out of these considerations grew the Folkwang School's comprehensive program of studies for the future professional dancer, a program that included a modified form of classical training (barre, adagio, allegro, but no pointwork or batterie) as a supplement to the modern technique. Modern technical instruction was enhanced by the analysis and practice of expressive dynamics (eukinetics) and the theory and practice of form in relation to space (choreutics). In addition, the dance curriculum offered improvisation and composition, Kinetography/Labanotation, as well as music, anatomy, and dance history.

The Folkwang School opened on October 1, 1927. Lisa Ullmann, a former student of Laban, was hired as an additional modern dance technique teacher, and Gertrud Snell joined the faculty to give classes in Laban's movement theories. Jooss and Leeder devoted most of their energies to their pedagogic work, which both enjoyed deeply. Jooss was patient and understanding, explaining particular assignments to students, but uncompromising in demanding concentration in the rehearsal of his choreography. Leeder complemented Jooss very well. He developed the idea of the modern etude, a combination of movements in contemporary style focussing the student's attention on performing qualities in class. When Jooss was working choreographically, Leeder provided continuity of the pedagogic process.

Other collaborators from Jooss's Münster days also joined him in Essen. Frederic Cohen, the composer, Hein Heckroth, the designer, and Aino Siimola had moved there to join the Opera in Essen in 1927. The City of Essen raised some municipal funds to support a performing unit connected to the Opera and called it the Folkwang Dance Theater Studio.

In many ways the years in Essen brought Kurt Jooss to artistic maturity. Bolstered by the support of the City of Essen and his long-time associates, by the end of the nineteen-twenties, Jooss finally achieved his goal: the combination of a professional school of dance with a dance ensemble capable of realizing his artistic vision. Under these nearly ideal conditions, Jooss not only implemented Laban's movement principles, but more fully developed his own idea of dance drama as kinetic dramatic action.

THE SECOND DANCERS' CONGRESS

In June 1928, Jooss organized a second German Dancers' Congress, this time in Essen, for the purpose of continuing the discussion of the place of dance in German theater institutions. In his opening address, Jooss set the agenda of the four-day Congress: through an exchange of ideas and live performances, Congress participants would investigate the two main forms of contemporary dance in Germany, "absolute dance" (dance as an independent art in itself) and "theater dance" (dance serving a theatrical production). Jooss put the question bluntly: Did the future of dance lie with Ausdruckstanz, which repudiated classical ballet altogether, or with dance drama, in which the Second Dancers' Congress incorporated aspects of ballet and Laban's expressive movement principles to create a new entity?

Once again, Wigman and Jooss could not agree. Wigman spoke as an exponent of Ausdruckstanz. A member of the first generation of modern dancers, Wigman continued to rebel against theater, labeling it hidebound and conventional. Typical of Expressionist artists, she wanted to assure the unrestrained freedom of the individual's artistic development. She regarded dance within a theatrical production as a specialized form of dance that only dancers with a good general foundation could master. "Without the experience of the absolute dance for its own sake, the dancer is not able to specialize."[29] In Wigman's eyes, absolute dance seemed to be the only path to a true dance art of the future.

Wigman differed from both Laban and Jooss not only in her antipathy to theater, but in her rejection of classical ballet. Whereas Laban had considerably revised his opinion on ballet as the result of his research on movement principles done in the early nineteen-twenties, Wigman steadfastly held on to her opinion of ballet as outmoded, sterile formalism. Furthermore, her view of dance ensemble, which she developed independently of Laban, derived from the Greek model of ritual chorus. Wigman used her dance group in an archetypal context, with increasingly abstract stylization. The future of dance, in Wigman's eyes, lay in the revival of the ritual origins of dance. Wigman thus remained fundamentally opposed to Laban and Jooss, who saw dance with dramatic action, which they called "dance theater," as a truly revolutionary, artistic form of contemporary drama. Both feared that the Modern Dance would be lost altogether unless it was linked to dance drama in a renewed German theater. Hans Brandenburg, sharing Laban's view, commented that Laban had freed contemporary dance from the excessive individualism of the Ausdruckstanz by choreographing ensemble works. Also, his theoretical dance writings fostered a more wide-spread appreciation and understanding of movement.

Opinions clashed even more when the question of dance pedagogy became the focus of the discussion on the third day of the Congress. Laban and Jooss presented a plan for a German Dance Academy that very much reflected the Laban tradition. Since the spring of 1925 the goal of Jooss's movement research was to implement Laban's concepts into a training method which could equip professional dancers to meet the needs of the contemporary stage. Jooss's goal of integrating elements of the traditional, classical system with elements of the new modern dance was, however, opposed by the panel's majority, which consisted of Hanya Holm, Gret Palucca, Max Terpis, Gertrud Snell, and Sigurd Leeder. The question was: who should create the German Dance Academy, and what should be the content of its curriculum? Rivalry between Wigman, who considered herself Germany's first dancer, and Laban, her teacher, threatened the harmonious settlement of this question, which never was solved.

By this time, Laban's Choreographic Institute, the Central School Laban, and the Tanzbühne Laban had all been moved to Berlin. Meanwhile Mary Wigman, who had just enlarged her school in Dresden, had named the renovated building the "Academy of Dance". Not only did the two artists disagree on basic principles of dance, but they both faced strained financial circumstances that only exacerbated the tensions between them. Indeed, on the closing day of the Congress, Wigman shocked her audience by announcing that she was forced to dissolve her dance group because of financial difficulties. However, despite their disagreements and rivalries, shortly after the Congress, Laban and Wigman managed to reach at least a tentative agreement about the need for a German Dance Academy, though they specified that their individual artistic intentions and pedagogic goals would be "untouched." The German Dance Academy remained a dream.

Once again, as at the First Dancers' Congress, performing artists at the Second Congress vividly conveyed the differences separating Ausdruckstanz from Laban and Jooss and all three from classical ballet. At the end of the first day's Congress, the State Opera Berlin performed Max Terpis's *Der Letzte Pierrot (The Last Pierrot)*, and the State Opera Munich presented Heinrich Kroeller's *Pagoden (Pagodas)*. These two opera companies still set the standards for ballet in Germany in the nineteen-twenties, an era when international dance companies had not yet toured the country. On the second evening of the Congress, leaders of the younger generation of Ausdruckstanz, solo performers including Rosalia Chladek, Edgar Frank, Yvonne Georgi, Harald Kreutzberg, Gret Palucca, and Vera Skoronel, presented a chamber dance recital. These six represented the most prolific younger creators of the solo dance in the twenties. Mary Wigman illustrated her artistic credo on the third night of performances with *Die Feier (Celebration)*. Her first evening-long dance composition was performed by fourteen female dancers well trained in Wigman's style. They gave a superb presentation of this core work in the Wigman repertory before twelve hundred dancers from all over Germany and several international guests of the dance profession. Wigman's choreography was not only the highpoint of the Congress, but also a climactic event in her artistic life. *Die Feier* showed Mary Wigman's choreographic style in its uncompromising strength. Performed on the eve of her first American tour, it was, in retrospect, her summation of Ausdruckstanz. Wigman, at forty-two years old, had reached the summit of her career.

The Second Dancers' Congress captured press attention not only in Essen, but also in newspapers all over Germany. The Congress made history for more than its controversial debate over the future of dance in Germany, however. On the second day of the meeting, Laban presented a lecture-demonstration on the development of Kinetography Laban, officially recognized for the first time as the most comprehensive method of writing dance. Known in America as Labanotation, the Laban system of notation "has proven to be the first practical method devised to meet the complex problem of recording human movement."[30] The Congress also marked the culmination of Laban's theoretical writings. Since 1924, he had worked consistently to give dance a theoretical foundation. *Choreography*[31] and *Gymnastik und Tanz*,[32] both published in 1926, attested to his meticulous observations of human movement. At the Congress he presented the booklet "*Schrifttanz*," which can be seen, according to Vera Maletic, as part two of *Choreography*, in that "it presents the final version of the notation and marks the birth of Laban's system." [33] (*Schrifttanz* was actually published in 1928 by Universal Edition, Vienna, with Alfred Schlee as the first editor.) The major significance of the Second Dancers' Congress thus lay in the official recognition of Laban's notation system and in the theoretical foundation he gave to dance. In addition, Kurt Jooss's planning of the Congress and his thoughtful outlining of the topics most ripe for discussion showed that this ally of Laban, now more than just a protege of the master, had become one of the most aggressively striving young choreographers in Europe.

LABAN'S FIFTIETH BIRTHDAY

In 1929, half a year after the Second Dancers' Congress, Jooss proposed to Laban a merger of the dance department of the Folkwang School with the Central School Laban and the Institute of Choreography at Essen. This would make Essen the center of all Laban Schools. Laban agreed to this plan, and moved various areas of his work from Berlin to Essen. Jooss, together with Sigurd Leeder, further integrated Laban's concepts into the curriculum of the dance division of the Folkwang School and simultaneously used the same training basis to elevate the Tanzbühne to the level of international professional standards.

Approaching his fiftieth birthday in the same year, Laban reached the peak of his career in German theater. After Max Terpis resigned from his position as ballet master-in-chief of the State Opera Berlin, Laban replaced him and became the director of Movement and Dance for the State Opera, a position for which Wigman had also vied. It speaks well for Mary Wigman that, on the occasion of Laban's fiftieth birthday, on December 15, 1929, she rose above personal and professional rivalries to join with Jooss in honoring Laban's contribution to the creation of the new Modern Dance. In an article on Laban that she and Jooss wrote for the December 1929 issue of *Singchor und Tanz*, Germany's dance magazine, both attempted to assess Laban's place in the history of German dance. Wigman gave a very generous assessment:

> Laban's work is no longer bound to Laban's person; it has became the common basis for the modern dance. The dancers of today honor in the name "Laban" the beginning of a new epoch in the history of the European dance. Laban was the great inventor and stimulator. He gave us dancers a foundation. He taught the nature of tension, the harmonic relations of swing sequences, and the unity of body and space. Laban freed dance from its reliance on music and returned dance to its self-reliance as an absolute language of art.... Laban's work, seen in completely objective terms, culminates in two aspects of his nature: he is the ingenious discoverer and, consequently, the great theorist. We all are more indebted to Laban's work than we are aware, involved as we are in our own process. As previous student and assistant to Laban during part of his journey, I feel compelled to thank him for all he did for dance and for dancers. And if I may express a wish, it is that he might be able to realize the ideal that motivated all his

creations and configurations--the creation of the great celebration which unifies participants and audiences in a strongly shared experience.[34]

Kurt Jooss's assessment of Laban, though different from Wigman's, was also adulatory. He saw Laban first of all as a dancer. In his struggle for a twentieth-century aesthetic, Laban had fought the existing ballet because of its frozen formality, but later he recognized the value of the classical principle in its abstract logic:

> Laban's historic contribution is the discovery of a new concept of form within the sphere of Western dance; he is the founder of the modern choreographic principles of harmony (choreographische Harmonielehre), a vast field yet to be fully explored. These principles will be the framework for the new concept of form in the future of dance.[35]

For a moment, the struggle over Modern Dance came to a halt in recognition of Laban's thirty years of work. The heated question of whether Ballet, Modern Dance, or a combination of both should reign on the German theater stage was never answered.

NOTES FOR CHAPTER II

1.   Laqueur, Walter (1974) *Weimar A Cultural History 1918-1933*, p.182. New York: G.P. Putnam's Sons

2.   Ibid., pp. 164, 65

3.   Kandinsky, Wassily (1977) *Concerning the Spiritual in Art*, translated by M.T.H. Sadler, p. 33. New York: Dover Publications

4.   Brandenburg, Hans (1921) *Der Moderne Tanz*, 3rd edn., p. 9. München: Georg Müller Verlag, Translation I. Bergsohn

5.   Laban, Rudolf (1920) Kultische Bildung im Feste. *Die Tat*. June 1920, 161-168

6.   Laban, Rudolf (1922) Festwille und Festkultur. *Die Tat*. **Vol**. 13 1922, 846-848

7.   Laban, Rudolf (1920) *Die Welt des Tänzers*, p. 15. Stuttgart: Walter Seifert Verlag

8.   Wigman, Mary (1921) Rudolf von Laban's Lehre vom Tanz. (Laban's Theory of Dance) *Die neue Schaubühne*, February 1921, pp. 30-35

9.   Bodmer, Sylvia (1987) Interview by Isa Bergsohn, in Manchester, England, Dec. 5

10.   Laban, Rudolf (1926) *Des Kindes Gymnastik und Tanz*, Translated by Vera Maletic, p. 35. Oldenburg: Gerhard Stalling Verlag

11.   Hodgson, John & Preston-Dunlop, Valerie (1990) *Rudolf Laban:An Introduction to his Work & Influence*, p. 19. Plymouth: Northcote House

12.   Hutchinson, Ann (1954) *Labanotation*. A New Directions Book, New York: James Laughlin

13.   Orff, Carl (1976) *The Schulwerk*, p. 8. Tutzing, Germany: Hanns Schneider Verlag

14.   Brandenburg, Hans (1921) *Der Moderne Tanz,* p. 202

15.   Orff, Carl (1976) p. 15

16. Sorell, Walter (1986) *Mary Wigman: Ein Vermächtnis*, p. 56 Wilhelmshaven: Florian Noetzel Verlag

17. Jooss, Kurt (1976) Interview with I. Bergsohn in UC Santa Barbara, Ca. September 20

18. Markard, Anna & Hermann (1985) *Jooss*, p. 29 Köln: Ballet Bühnen Verlag

19. Bartenieff,Irmgard with Lewis Dori (1980) *Body Movement--Coping with the Environment*. London: Gordon and Breach

20. Jooss, Kurt (1976) interview by Tobias, Tobi, Sept. 26, Oral Project, Dance Collection, The New York Library

21. Jooss, Kurt. (1973) Interview by John Hodgson, Kreuth, Bavaria

22. Hodgson, John & Preston-Dunlop, Valerie (1990) p.36

23. Markard, Anna & Hermann (1985) p. 31

24. Ibid., p. 34

25. Ibid., p. 29

26. Maletic, Vera (1987) *Body-Space-Expression*: *The Development of Rudolf Laban's Movement and Dance Concepts*. Berlin. New York. Amsterdam: Mouton de Gruyter

27. Wigman, Mary (1975) *The Mary Wigman Book*, edited and translated by Walter Sorell, p. 115. Middletown, Ct.: Wesleyan University Press

28. Jooss, Kurt (1927) Tanzerziehung in der Folkwang Schule, Translated by Anna Markard. *Essener Zeitung*, Wiesbaden: Jooss Archiv

29. Wigman, Mary (1975) *The Mary Wigman Book,* pp. 107-109

30. Cohen, Selma Jeanne (1958) Laban dies at age 78. Dance Magazine, Aug.,28,& 71

31. Laban, Rudolf (1926) *Choreographie*, 1st **Vol** Jena: Eugen Diederichs

32. Laban, Rudolf (1926) *Gymnastik und Tanz*, (*Gymnastics and Dance*). Oldenburg: Gerhard Stalling Verlag

33. Maletic, Vera (1987) p. 16.

34. Wigman, Mary (1929). Rudolf von Laban. Translated by I. Bergsohn, *Singchor und Tanz*, Heft 24 (in honor of Laban's 50th birthday).

35. Jooss, Kurt (1929) Rudolf von Laban und das Ballett, Translated by Anna Markard. *Singchor und Tanz*, Heft 24

CHAPTER III: FIRST ENCOUNTERS ACROSS THE ATLANTIC.

The twenties saw the gradual formation and definition of the Modern Dance in Europe. A similar process of crystallization in dance occurred in America a decade later, when an even more methodical language of the Modern Dance emerged, making America a leader in the international dance scene. At the same time, in the brief period between the late twenties and the establishment of the School of the Dance at Bennington College in 1934, the leading modern dancers in Europe reached a closeness and affinity in artistic intent with their American colleagues unparalleled either before or since that short span of cross fertilization.

The German dancers brought to America Ausdruckstanz (literally, dance of expression), the European Modern Dance of the twenties, which was shaped by the need to express their inner world in terms of twentieth-century movement. The American modern dancers of the same generation also desired, in Doris Humphrey's words, "to dance from the inside out."[1] Because self-identification was their most urgent concern, their maturation process followed along lines parallel to those of their German counterparts: American modern dancers also started out as solo performers and gradually developed an interest in choreographing group works. Artists on both sides of the ocean felt that Modern Dance as a contemporary form of art should communicate and comment on the twentieth-century world. Between 1930 and 1934, however, American artists created an indigenous American Modern Dance. In contrast, the group works choreographed in Germany during the same period did not show one direction but rather reflected the decisions German artists were forced to make in the face of the crumbling Weimar Republic and the dawn of National Socialism.

For a long time, the American public had considered dance a diversion rather than a form of art. Christian church teachings connected dance with eroticism; stigmatized in this way, dance could not become a part of the realm of art or education. The situation changed in the twenties. Women got the right to vote, started to enjoy their newly gained freedom of movement, and, through recreation and sports originally practiced only by the privileged, developed a greater self-confidence. Indeed, all societal levels gained access to recreation because of the prosperity of American life after victory in World War I. The general social climate in the United States was thus very different from that of Europe in the twenties. At the end of a successful war, the entire country seemed to be actively engaged in sports and recreation. Liberated women appeared in streamlined fashions, their hair bobbed short, their clothes loose with hemlines at the knee and waistlines dropped, showing a good portion of their legs as they danced the Charleston to jazz music. A dance boom captured young and old alike. The entertainment industry flourished; hundreds of shows and revues opened on Broadway, and Hollywood produced the first talking pictures with singing and dancing. The production of records with music from the shows became big business, offering dance music with jazz and Latin rhythms. Arthur Murray promised in an advertising campaign: "A New Way to be Popular Quickly, Learn to Dance in One Evening!"

Education also benefitted in this era of unequaled prosperity. Progressive methods, already under discussion before World War I, were now introduced to the school system.

This progressiveness was taught by teachers who had been students of John Dewey (1859-1952) at Teachers College, Columbia University, New York, and who were educated in his philosophy of the unity of body and mind. They believed in the value of play to further the socialization of the child. The child centered school and the country day school practiced a free approach that led children through movement games designed to expand the child's capacities for non-verbal expression. In 1918, one of John Dewey's students, Gertrude Colby, introduced her first course in dramatic expression with interpretation through characterization in pantomime. This course, which focussed on building an understanding of the artistic aspects of physical education and the relationship of dance to music and literature, replaced some militaristic practices of earlier physical instruction. On the secondary level, various sports and recreational dance forms were now available to every boy and girl. As a result, dance gained a place in physical education in the early twenties in the form of social dance, "aesthetic dance," and interpretive dance. ("Aesthetic dance" used simplified forms of ballet and was relatively easy to learn because it was stereotypical in movement and repetitious in form.) Also, clog and folk dancing became very popular. During the twenties and thirties dance programs flourished in physical education.

Bird Larson along with Gertrude Colby, progressive teachers of physical education in high schools and colleges, developed "natural dance," a form that was influenced by Isadora Duncan's work and closely followed her movement style. "Natural dance" used the body in accordance with its proper anatomical and kinesiological functioning. It also gave the student an immediate movement experience without having to learn any step patterns; it focussed on the individual's expressive needs. While incorporating some of the popular folk dances, it prepared the way for a creative approach to dance. Bird Larson, herself a fine dancer, was especially interested in the spiritual aspects of dance. On this base she built a concert group which performed "Sacred Dance" before the altar of St. Mark's in the Bowery. Though her spiritual approach to dance spanned only a few years, she developed quite a following in the late twenties and during the Depression. Sacred Dance as part of liturgical services was later revived and further developed by Ted Shawn.

While Colby and Larson paved the way for the acceptance of expressive forms of dance in high schools and colleges, it was Margaret H'Doubler who focused on the creative process in movement as a way of integrating the individual emotionally, physically and mentally. Her goal went far beyond body culture, gymnastics and recreation; it was educational and arose out of the spirit of idealism which characterized the philosophy of American liberal arts colleges: "Education should be a building toward the integration of human capacities and powers resulting in well-adjusted, useful, balanced individuals."[2]

Margaret Newell H'Doubler became the leading exponent of Modern Dance as an essential part of physical education in an academic setting. Born 1889 in Beloit, Kansas, she was the daughter of an amateur photographer and artist of Swiss descent. After receiving a B.A. degree with majors in philosophy and biology in 1910 from the University of Wisconsin, Madison, she attended lectures by John Dewey at Columbia University Teachers College and observed how dance was being introduced into elementary education by leading progressive educators of the day. H'Doubler returned to the University of Wisconsin as a faculty member in women's physical education, where she explored dance rhythm as a tool to open new psycho-physical experiences. When H'Doubler formed the first performing group in a liberal arts education program, her students selected the name "Orchesis," which became the prototype of college dancing in America. By 1921, H'Doubler had designed the first comprehensive dance curriculum in American higher education. In 1927 the Bachelor's degree in dance, the first dance major of its kind, was instituted, and one year later, a Master's degree became available.

Margaret H'Doubler's pioneering efforts raised the esteem of dance in higher education all over the United States. Physical educators studying dance with Margaret H'Doubler shared her belief in the link between a healthy body and a healthy mind and her concern for the creative potential in every human being. Social consciousness, in H'Doubler's view, was an essential part of the makeup of the educator as well as the artist.

Margaret H'Doubler initiated the first summer school of dance in an academic setting at the University of Wisconsin in 1931, three years earlier than the famous School of the Dance at Bennington. Since she recognized Harald Kreutzberg as a model of her ideal of physical and spiritual integration, she invited him to teach. H'Doubler thus chose the European approach as a practical model for her movement philosophy and familiarized a whole generation of physical educators with Laban-based, European creative methods of teaching dance. Some of these students later became the founders of dance departments in American colleges and universities: Helen Alkire at the Ohio State University in Columbus, Margaret Erlanger at the University of Illinois, Alma Hawkins at the University of California at Los Angeles, and Elizabeth Hayes at the University of Utah in Salt Lake City. Kreutzberg conveyed to these students the value of creative work as a way to regenerate the individual. This respect for the creative potential of their own students produced educators with a broad approach to movement education. Thanks to H'Doubler's vision, the University of Wisconsin set the example for dance in Liberal Arts colleges and universities from the thirties to the fifties. H'Doubler herself sympathized with the Modern Dance movement, but her place was clearly within the academic world. There was no relation yet between her work and the experiments of the young performers of American Modern Dance who practiced their art within the narrow confines of the private dance studio.[3]

While dance education benefitted from the era of prosperity in America and gained generous support for appropriate facilities and faculty in high schools and colleges as part of health and recreation programs, performers of American Dance did not share in this wealth. Physical education teachers were still wary of anything connected with theater because of the American Puritan tradition, and performers were equally wary of the academic world.

Ted Shawn and Ruth St. Denis were the first to open an institution of dance which had higher aspirations than simply to offer ballet classes to children or vaudeville routines and acrobatics to professional entertainers. Their school, called "Denishawn," became the first place in America to offer young dancers the opportunity to study dance forms from all over the globe. Opened in Los Angeles in 1915, the school, along with its company of the same name (which was started in 1917), is considered the parent organization of American Dance.

St. Denis's exotic femininity was complemented by Ted Shawn, a young man from Kansas City, originally a student of theology. Shawn had recovered from paralysis by doing St. Denis's movement exercises. After his recovery, he gave up theology to become St. Denis's dance partner, husband and fellow teacher at Denishawn. Miss Ruth's efforts centered on teaching the company various ethnic dance forms and giving inspirational lectures, while Ted Shawn instructed students in social dance forms and in a modified version of basic ballet based on the Russian style. He also taught Delsarte's system of expressive gestures, a system brought from Europe to America by Genevieve Stebbins. Stebbins had developed sequences of these expressive gestures, which became quite fashionable as a kind of dramatic gymnastic within the Denishawn offerings. Ted Shawn enriched the program by presenting European teachers of another method, that of Emile Jaques Dalcroze. Ruth St. Denis in particular was very impressed by Dalcroze's popular system. The practice and teaching of both methods at Denishawn added a semi-academic aura to the institution.

Company and school were a commercial success, particularly with the advent of the cinema and Denishawn's participation in such large scale movies as D.W. Griffith's *Intolerance* in the early nineteen-twenties. Gradually, however, the growing obligations to stage dance numbers in Broadway shows and to tour with revues undermined educational and artistic considerations. Miss Ruth, as a theater person, enjoyed all the production aspects, but financial necessity began to becloud her production aspirations. Her initial quality of mysticism faded and was replaced more and more by glamour and spectacle. Denishawn, the school and the company, came to an end in 1931, when Ruth St. Denis and Ted Shawn decided to go their separate ways. Miss Ruth continued as a solo performer on her own, while Ted Shawn, as performer and educator, saw as his mission the fight for the acceptance of the American male on stage. During the thirties his group of physical education teachers performed at his dance farm, Jacob's Pillow in Massachusetts, and also in colleges and universities.

Assessment of the role of Denishawn in the history of American Modern Dance varies considerably. Denishawn did not create what has come to be known as American Modern Dance. The founders of Denishawn had courage and good initial intentions but were naive in their artistic judgment. Receptive to multi-cultural influences, they were open-minded only within the confines of their basic Victorian values. This limitation was probably precisely the reason for the company's public success. Denishawn's productions did not offend society and appealed to broad audiences with their theatricality. Denishawn was, however, the spawning ground for dancers who, after leaving the school and the company, made important contributions of their own to American Modern Dance. Gertrude Shurr, who later became a dedicated performer in Martha Graham's first company, recalled the enthusiasm of her beginning years at the Denishawn School of Dance:

I have a great reverence for Denishawn. It was my first dance home, my first experience with structured dance classes. I was brought up in

Brooklyn where music and musicals were part of growing up, but in my case, I thought of myself as a Duncan dancer, with a bed sheet draped in half over one shoulder, a tie around the middle, and a band around the head in the Greek fashion, barefoot and performing with hop, skip and jumps to the music of Schubert, Brahms, Beethoven, and even Chopin waltzes. I danced at parties and in the movie prologues so fashionable at that time. I was a Duncan dancer in my teens. Then I saw a performance of Denishawn, and I understood why a dancer had to have a dance technique. I enrolled in Denishawn. It was wonderful. It was the only place where one could learn a dance technique, a dance, be given music for the dance, and even photos and descriptions of the dance costume. I made a living in my early twenties because I performed these dances in the New York area. When the Kabuki Company came to this country for the first time, the Japanese teacher thought I was a professional Japanese dancer. I could do this because I learned in Denishawn classes to perform each week in another ethnic style.[4]

The most important personalities of the new American Modern Dance movement of the late twenties, Doris Humphrey, Charles Weidman and Martha Graham, were all originally Denishawn students who later came to resent Denishawn's open commercialism, stylistic vagueness, and societal conformance. They shared a strong socio-cultural concern that dance should be recognized as an art form communicating the rhythm of contemporary life. Trained at Denishawn, where they had to copy a modified form of ballet under Ted Shawn as well as patterns of pseudo-ethnic forms of dance under Ruth St. Denis, these dancers felt that they had to find their own dance movements from their own motivations. They were independent young artists who existed outside of a society they criticized for its conformist tendencies. They felt very isolated in their field, because most people did not even know at that time what the term "Modern Dance" meant. Dance in the public's mind meant either vaudeville, music hall or social recreational dance, and even some artists in related fields of music, drama and visual arts did not consider Modern Dance to be a form of art. Accordingly, performances of Modern Dance were limited to the large cities. Dancers barely made a living by teaching the new art to a few devoted students, and they struggled very hard to find performance spaces. Consequently, modern dancers turned to each other, building small, family-like groups to support each other in the struggle for survival.

In 1923 Martha Graham became the first student dancer to leave Denishawn, along with Louis Horst, the accompanist of the school. Horst spent time in Vienna in 1925, where he observed the newest developments of contemporary art in Europe. He returned from Vienna in 1926, in time to accompany Martha Graham's first independent solo dance concert and subsequently became her closest collaborator and mentor. Graham's first program showed a strong resemblance to Denishawn, both stylistically and in the choice of themes. Soon after, Horst shared with Graham his newly gained insights on twentieth-century art and inspired her to a fresh investigation of movement. In 1928 Graham started to work with a small group of female students in the seclusion of her studio. Four of these dancers, who later became leaders in the American Modern Dance, were with Graham in the studio through this ground-breaking period and performed the works that first signaled Graham's new choreographic language. Martha Hill and Bessie Schönberg together, the same evening, were invited by Martha Graham to join her company in 1929;[5] Gertrude Shurr and Anna Sokolow advanced to company membership in 1930.

Martha Hill was a teacher of ballet and folk dance in the early twenties, and in 1923, she became director of dance at Kansas State Teachers College. As a young ballet dancer, Hill had been searching for something beyond pleasant form. In 1927, Martha Graham's concert changed her life. While she recognized that a great deal of the program was derived from Denishawn, there was enough that was avant-garde and new to inspire her to study with Graham at the John Murray Anderson-Robert Milton School of the Theater on East 58th Street in New York. After several months of classes with Graham, she ran out of money and took a position at the University of Oregon. She kept in contact with Graham, however, and returned after two years, in the summer of 1929, when Graham invited her into her company. Hill danced with Graham's Company from 1929 to 1931. In 1930, she also joined the faculty of New York University School of Education, where she taught from 1930 to 1951. In 1932, she founded the Dance Department at Bennington College in Vermont, and in 1934, in collaboration with Mary Josephine Shelly, who was on the faculty of Teachers College at Columbia University, the School of the Dance at Bennington College became the proving ground of American Modern Dance. The American Dance Festival also was Hill's creation. In 1951, Martha Hill became the founding chairperson of the Dance Division of the Juilliard School, which provided the model for dance education in the United States.

While Hill was teaching at the University of Oregon, she discovered Bessie Schönberg. The daughter of a well known opera singer in Germany, Bessie, in her high school days, studied Dalcroze Eurhythmics. She experienced the Modern Dance revolution of Mary Wigman in Dresden, her home town, as well as dancers like Harald Kreutzberg and Gret Palucca and the unique manifestations of German expressionistic art of the twenties. In 1925, Schönberg came to the United States and studied art at the University of Oregon. She enrolled in one of Hill's dance classes to fulfill a Physical Education requirement; she showed exceptional talent. After joining Martha Hill in New York Schönberg was encouraged by her to apply for a scholarship to study at the Neighborhood Playhouse under Graham. There she continued her dance studies in 1929, and, from 1930 to 1931, she performed in Graham's Company. She also taught at Bennington as assistant to Martha Hill before joining the faculty of the Bennington School of the Dance, in 1934. During the American Dance Festivals at Bennington College, while teaching choreography and a team-taught "Experimental Production" workshop with Martha Hill and Arch Lauterer, Schönberg came in close contact with the leading artists of the American Modern Dance. In 1938, Bessie Schönberg joined the faculty of Sarah Lawrence College, where she brought a broad background in all the visual arts as well as theater to her teaching. As the Director of Theater and Dance between 1956 and 1976, Schönberg transformed the Dance Department into one of the most prestigious institutions in the country. After she retired from Sarah Lawrence College as Professor Emeritus, she entered a new phase of her professional dance life in New York. As a member of the Dance Theatre Workshop she has worked with experienced choreographers for the past twelve years in spring and fall laboratories conducted at The Bessie Schönberg Theatre.

During the summer months she works at Jacob's Pillow Dance Festival in Lee, Massachusetts, in a similar capacity and serves as artistic advisor to the "Yard" at Martha's Vineyard in June and August. An artist who defies all categorization, Bessie Schönberg has guided the careers of innumerable artists in American Dance, through her impartial eye and instinct for quality. In recognition of her own contribution to dance, Bessie Schönberg was honored by being asked to present Alwin Nikolais with the prestigious Samuel Scripps American Dance Festival Award, on June 12, 1985, at Duke University.

Gertrude Shurr was one of Martha Graham's first students when Graham opened her studio in 1928. Between 1925 and 1927 she had given solo performances of early Denishawn dances, but had left Denishawn with Doris Humphrey and Charles Weidman. From 1927 to 1929 she danced as a member of the first Humphrey/Weidman Concert Company. To prove her loyalty to Graham, Shurr was made to wait a year until she could officially join Graham's Dance Group. She was a member of Graham's Company from 1930 to 1938. In later years, together with Rachael Yocom, she wrote a book on Graham's teaching of Modern Dance, *Modern Dance Techniques and Teaching*;[6] the book is still in use in colleges and universities. Shurr's phenomenal recollection of Martha Graham's choreography has helped the company many times in restaging some of the earliest works. As recently as 1991, she acted as a rehearsal coach.

Anna Sokolow, born in 1913, was the youngest of these first members of Martha Graham's group. She grew up in New York, danced with Bird Larson, and then studied with Martha Graham and Louis Horst at the Neighborhood Playhouse. Sokolow joined Graham's company in 1930 and performed in such early Graham works as *Primitive Mysteries* (1931), *Tragic Patterns* (1933), and *American Provincials* (1934). While a member of Graham's Company Sokolow also joined a dancers' collective, which became known as "The New Dance Group"; she considered dance as a medium of political communication. She created works such as *Excerpts of a War Poem*. In 1937, she became a Bennington Fellow. She remained a member of Graham's Company until 1939, when she accepted an invitation from the Mexican government to teach and choreograph in Mexico, where she founded the first Mexican Modern Dance Group. She remained in Mexico until 1943, and has since returned many times, commuting between there and New York.

Sokolow is one of the most prominent dance artists who comment on social issues, creating works for the theater with uncompromising directness. In the fifties, sixties and seventies, she choreographed for her own company, for groups in Mexico and Israel, and for the Juilliard Dance Ensemble. *Lyric Suite* (premiered in 1953), *Rooms* (in 1955), and *Dreams* (in 1961), are considered classics of the American Modern Dance which have never lost their original impact. Very different in personality, these four among the original Graham dancers made a decisive imprint on the American Modern Dance.

The results of Graham's vigorous experimentation were revealed in her first group composition, *Heretic* in 1929, with music arranged by Louis Horst. Martha Hill described this first piece, in which she performed as a member of Graham's group; it especially stood in her memory:

Heretic was probably one of Graham's most provocative early works. In this collaboration, Louis Horst was Graham's mentor; he made her aware of the inner pulse which grew out of her dramatic body tensions and contrasted this strong pulse with an old Breton song of eleven measures played over and over. This use of the music brought out the starkness of her movements. The dramatic theme of *Heretic* was the one against the many. Graham counteracted the group, compelled by a strong inner pulse in high contraction, while in a slight forward lean. The strange, very tensed confrontational walk led to a block-like, sculptural pose, and the group made all the following changes in silence.[7]

This very sophisticated way of using the music accompaniment to intensify the dance movement by contrast was new to America at this time. Horst was perhaps inspired by European modern dancers' experimentation with body rhythm that he had observed while in Vienna. In any case, this new relation between dance and musical accompaniment freed Martha Graham to listen to her own dramatic impulse first and to disengage herself from the music visualization and decorative theatricality of Denishawn.

In 1928, Doris Humphrey and Charles Weidman presented their first independent concert after breaking away from Denishawn. *Color Harmony* and *Water Study* (1928) exemplified Humphrey's abstract, impersonal approach to choreography. She created the image of ebb and flow in *Water Study* by the collective action of fourteen dancers seen in changing energies and shapes. The dance, about momentum and the play of gravity, applied her theory of Fall and Recovery as a source for choreographic invention. In this early period of Modern Dance, as Marcia Siegel has commented, "the Americans were the closest they ever came to expressionistic modern dancers of Europe, and *Water Study* would not have surprised the followers of Wigman."[8] However, Wigman, in a way, had an easier artistic path to follow, because she had only to listen to her inner rhythm. Her dance primarily arose from a tactile source and became visual only in the shaping process, whereas Denishawn-trained dancers like Humphrey had to overcome the pictorial concept of dance established at Denishawn. Nevertheless, by 1928, Humphrey had freed herself from this influence, and had, independently from any European influences as well, discovered her own motivation and articulation of energy changes. Like Wigman, she created dance movement out of the body's rhythm, using weight as a propelling force, but preferring an unadorned shape that emerged out of the natural flow of motion. Both choreographers were inclined to abstract movement. In their dance creations, they preferred not to illustrate, but instead to evoke a particular texture, quality, or image.

American modern dancers first became aware of the striking artistic similarities between themselves and Mary Wigman and her followers through the writings of the first dance critic for the *New York Times*, John Martin. He had experienced the upheaval in Modern Dance while studying abroad, and he took the German Modern Dance movement very seriously. American modern dancers came to have mixed feelings about European modern dancers--a combination of appreciation and envy--because dancers in Europe, by Martin's account, were recognized as artists and even celebrated as creators of contemporary art on a par with leading painters and sculptors. There was a tremendous tension on both sides before the actual first encounter between European and American modern dancers took place on American soil. At least Wigman was very nervous, since she had no clear idea what to expect from American audiences, and it was essential for her to find acclaim in the new world.

AMERICA'S FIRST EXPOSURE TO GERMAN DANCE

Eugen von Grona's first appearance as a German dancer in New York, in 1925, served as a prelude to the encounter between European and American modern dancers. The young man had only briefly studied with Mary Wigman and also with Jutta Klamt. He made his American debut in a solo concert, and two years later at the Roxy Theater staged a dance work, *Spirit of Labor*, which attempted to mirror the functioning of a machine in robot-like motions made by the dancers and supported by realistic sound effects. The press treated this event as novelty: "The Roxy has brought it to America, this number is composed by Eugen von Grona and a company of eight girls who just have arrived from Germany, as the exponents of a new school of dancing based on the abstract. The Germans were the pioneers in motion pictures in the abstract, so why not in dancing, too?" [9]

Harald Kreutzberg was the first German dancer of stature to cross the Atlantic. A solo dancer of the Berlin State Opera, Kreutzberg came to America in 1927 with the ensemble of Berlin's Deutsche Theater. Engaged by the famous director Max Reinhardt during the American tour, he performed as Puck in Reinhardt's production of *A Midsummer Night's Dream*. While in the United States, he also appeared in several dance recitals. At the beginning of his first American tour Kreutzberg described himself:

> I am not a leader nor a creator of any school of dancing, he stated. I dance to express myself. I dance from my heart, blood and imagination. As an actor uses words to tell the story of the drama, as a composer narrates his themes in bars of music, I express my mood, my poesy, my inner feeling with movement, with my body. I do not believe that dancing should tell a story or have a meaning; nor do I feel that a dancer must draw upon his experiences to express fully dances of great joy or great sorrow. I love music very dearly but do not seek to interpret in my dancing the compositions of immortals, Bach, Schubert, Mozart, etc. I create my dances and then begins my search for the ideal music, for the music that will best reveal my mood in movement. [10]

In his now classic *Introduction to the Dance*, John Martin opened his discussion of Kreutzberg with the above statement and adds:

> Self-expression, however, is far from the complete story, for besides that inner exuberance that moves him to action, there is a superb craftsmanship to hold him within bounds. It is compounded of several things in addition to mere bodily technic--a gift for the theatrical and a phenomenal instinct that tells him how things will look to an audience, a highly developed visual sense and an innate talent for design. [10]

Harald Kreutzberg was born in the small Bohemian town of Reichenberg in 1902. His grandfather was a famous circus director, and at age six Harald entertained at the local operetta house. He became a student of the Academy for Applied Art at Dresden and soon made his livelihood as a dress designer in a large fashion store at Dresden during the inflation. He took a few evening classes with Mary Wigman in 1920 and, encouraged by her, changed his vocation to dance. He became a member of her first outstanding class along with Hanya Holm, Gret Palucca, Yvonne Georgi, Margarethe Wallman and Max Terpis. Terpis had come to Wigman with a solid background in ballet and was the most mature artist in this student group. When Terpis accepted the position of ballet master in Hannover in 1923, he offered Kreutzberg a contract. In the following year, Kreutzberg followed Max Terpis to the State Opera Berlin as soloist.

It is hard to say what influenced Kreutzberg more: his three years of intensive studies under Mary Wigman, or his experiences as solo dancer in the theater under Terpis, who knew how to accentuate Kreutzberg's particular talent. In any event, he was sufficiently talented and well trained to catch the eye of Max Reinhardt, who spotted Kreutzberg performing as a court jester in Terpis's *Don Morte*, to music by Friedrich Wilkens. The ballet was inspired by Edgar Allen Poe, and Kreutzberg had shaved his head to fill this bizarre part. Impressed with Kreutzberg's pantomimic dance talent, Reinhardt offered him the role of the Master of Ceremonies in his Salzburg Festival production of Gozzi's *Turandot* in the summer of 1926.

Work with Reinhardt in Berlin opened new doors for Kreutzberg during the following season. In 1927, Reinhardt entrusted Kreutzberg with the role of Puck in *Midsummer Night's Dream*, which required refined delivery of text in addition to dance movement. Kreutzberg started to explore connections between the spoken word and his world of gestural dance. Reinhardt also put him in charge of directing the ensemble's stage movements in *Midsummer Night's Dream*. In 1928 Reinhardt took this Salzburg production on tour to America, and Kreutzberg entered the United States as a member of Reinhardt's ensemble. His interpretation of Puck won him the enthusiastic acclaim of the New York audience. In addition to his work with Reinhardt, he performed his first American dance recital at the Cosmopolitan Theater in New York City with Tilly Loesch, a sylph-like actress/mime, expertly accompanied by pianist Louis Horst. According to his own writing, "the theater was completely filled, he was enthusiastically received and also invited to return in the coming year."[11] His phenomenal technical facility, his craftsmanship in designing his own costumes, and his effectiveness in cleverly manipulating his props dazzled and delighted American audiences, who, expecting a dark soul of German dance, were entertained instead by an exquisite magician.

Kreutzberg's appeal to American audiences is succinctly captured by Martha Hill, an eye witness to his first appearances: "Kreutzberg added a theatricality that we did not have at this time."[12] Gertrude Shurr recalled "his dramatic quality and terrific intensity" as her strongest impression; "on stage, he appeared seven foot tall, and he had a demanding spaciousness utilizing the whole stage."[13]

Kreutzberg apparently spoke his very own, individualistic movement language, which he had developed during his studies with Mary Wigman. To his glass-clear gestures which showed the polish of a classical solo dancer, he added a theatrical element gleaned from his theater experience under Max Terpis. To his dances he was able to apply with taste and sophistication theatrical performance techniques gained while working in the Reinhardt ensemble. This combination of styles made him irresistible to the American audiences.

Kreutzberg left Reinhardt after his great American success and, with Yvonne Georgi, worked on a new program in Hannover, Germany, for his second American tour. Georgi had replaced Max Terpis as ballet mistress. She was able to hold the stage dancing next to Kreutzberg, and both, originally trained by Wigman, preferred the theater to the recital stage. They exquisitely performed Kreutzberg's dance creations of characters and dream figures. Kreutzberg was a master of the small form; he worked best alone or with a partner like Yvonne Georgi. Clean in details, witty and full of surprises, Kreutzberg was a great craftsman who knew well how to present himself and his partner. In 1929, he spent a full year on tour in America, performing with Georgi, and once again both were enthusiastically received. As John Martin observed, they helped dispel the common stereotype of German Dance as ugly and grotesque:

> The revolutionary element in the German dance lies deeper than the post-war hysteria which has swept through all branches of the German theater. It is a complete restatement of physical technique going back to nature and away from art for its experimentation. It also lays great stress on expressionism. But in this it can scarcely be credited with anything very radical; for expressionism is merely another phase of that seemingly unrelated research Delsarte made long ago for gesture that expresses something.[14]

THE THIRD DANCERS' CONGRESS

Many American dance lovers were motivated to cross the Atlantic by Kreutzberg and Georgi's performances in order to experience this new German Dance on its native soil. The expectations ran high, particularly when, in 1930, the Third Dancers' Congress sent invitations to American modern dance groups to appear at this first international Modern Dance Congress. Eleanor King, a member of the original Humphrey-Weidman Company, described how disappointed she and the other company members felt when Doris Humphrey was unable to accept this invitation because of funding problems.[15] The Third Dance Congress promised to have a larger scope than the two previous ones; a new festival hall was built at Munich, and 1400 participants enrolled, among them many guests from abroad. Elizabeth Selden wrote a detailed prospectus of the planned congress in the *New York Evening Post* of May 31, 1930, titled "Masters of the New Mode Gather at Munich."

It must be pointed out that the Third Dance Congress in Munich is to be devoted not to ballroom dancing but to the interests of the modern art dance. To judge from the important preparations which are being made, it promises to become an event of great artistic and cultural significance. The whole program of lectures, discussions and dance productions aims at presenting a comprehensive view of the art dance at the present moment. It will show how the modern dance is inextricably bound up with the whole artistic, social and intellectual structure of the present, being a potent factor in the cultural life of the age.[16]

The focus of the Congress was the relation between professional dance and group dance as communal expression, the tasks of the dancer in drama and opera, and the social function of the dancer in the current theater. However, in actuality, the guests from abroad witnessed heated debates which reflected the disarray of German cultural life in 1930. This was a year of economic and political crisis in Germany. Extremist factions from the right and the left started to undermine the Weimar Republic, which had supported modernism in all of the arts. The crash of the stock market in Germany created an atmosphere of economic insecurity. The great hope of finding a new basis for twentieth-century life had turned into an illusion; unemployment reigned, and the future looked dim. The atmosphere of political and economic crisis also impaired the German modern dancers. Under the title "A Futile Congress," John Martin expressed his disappointment in an article in the *New York Times* in the summer of 1930. He described how," the chief opposing camps are headed, respectively, by Mary Wigman and Rudolf Laban, as well as innumerable lesser divisions and alliances. In fact, there is apparently a great game of politics being played which is at least as absorbing as the business of making and performing dances."[17] The political nature of the Third Dancers' Congress involved more than the old rivalries between representatives of Classical Dance and adherents of the New Modern Dance. The form and themes of some of the dances, at least in retrospect, had ideological implications. Laban, for one, recognized this when he pointed out, in his lecture to the Congress, the inherent danger of the misuse of the movement choir as a form of mass celebration in the hands of religious, ideological or political agitators. His warning was prophetic, because only a few years later, National Socialism utilized the movement choir concept as a vehicle for mass celebrations of the Aryan race.

Wigman's *Totenmal* (*Call of the Dead*) also turned out to have political implications that were highly controversial. One of the major productions staged at the Congress, it was planned as a memorial for the World War I dead. Performed by fifty men who were not trained professional dancers, *Totenmal* challenged Wigman to go beyond Laban's movement choir practices by integrating a group of amateur male dancers into a block-like unity. Wigman demanded more than the amateur group was able to give: to function like a Greek chorus, and to bear witness to the tragic fate of World War I Germany.

Wigman had actually forced herself to embark on this large scale, experimental work, which she set to a script of Swiss poet Albert Talhoff. It was his idea to use a speaking choir instead of music as the auditory accompaniment for her choreography. Although Wigman had dealt with the theme of death before, this was the first time she had combined speech and dance on such a large scale. It was a bold undertaking, especially since Wigman's creativity was not flowing at this time. Moreover, she was working with amateurs, having dissolved her well-trained female dance group in 1928 owing to economic pressures. Her effort to contribute to the Third Dancers' Congress a model of a dance ritual on such a grandiose scale was surely daring; her reliance solely on sound effects, light changes, and spoken words added to the experimental nature of the work.

Totenmal was a controversial event both as art and as politics. Louise Kloepper, an eighteen-year-old American who danced in the other major production, Orpheus Dionysos by Margarethe Wallman, was in the audience when Totenmal was performed. She remembered how the production "made a strong impression on me. It was not so much the movement, but what was very haunting was the fact that this hall was especially built for the Totenmal production, and the voices of the dead soldiers spoke and came from all over the room. The whole place was surrounded by these voices which recited letters of fallen soldiers. What they said was very stirring."[18] Wigman herself confessed later that she had felt swept away by Talhoff's intensity and enthusiasm. Her choreography and Talhoff's script aimed for universality; they intended to create a "Gesamt Kunstwerk" (a Total Work of Art), in Talhoff's words "a choreic vision in light, dance and speech!"[19]

From a late twentieth-century perspective, however, Talhoff's poetry seems more like a reversion to the excesses of early twentieth-century expressionism, and Wigman's simple, stark group movements, in their pounding directness, appear dated even for their own time. There were choreographic incongruities too. All the dancers wore masks; however, while a group of women were individualized characters in their movement, masks and costumes, all the male performers wore the same, stereotyped mask and appeared in stylized uniform-like cloaks. Wigman, alone, as the central figure, danced without a mask; she was the only human being on stage confronting these large, disguised, abstract group formations that magnified her dramatic impact. Louise Kloepper remembered how Totenmal ended: "Mary Wigman went in a very slow motion backbend. It took forever; it was the epitome of dying, leaving the audience in nearly unbearable tension while the spotlight closed in on her head finally touching the floor. That hit me."[20] There were practical difficulties as well. The new Festival Hall was still not completely built, so rehearsals on stage were not possible until the last minute. Meanwhile, the dancers had to rehearse on the building site. Talhoff changed his text several times, causing a reworking of the choreography. Desperate, Wigman finally sent the unflappable Hanya Holm to Munich to take over the preparations, while Wigman spent her last weeks before the Congress travelling between Dresden and Munich. The production was performed as work in progress, and it never was completely finished.

Opinions about Totenmal varied greatly in 1930 and still do today. The dance writer Walter Sorell, biographer, admirer and close friend of Mary Wigman since the nineteen-fifties, revealed some of Wigman's thoughts as well as his own views of Totenmal in his book on Mary Wigman: Ein Vermächtnis (A Legacy). According to her own testimony, Wigman believed in the strength of Talhoff's work and the necessity of presenting it even after it met with a controversial response. Sorell, after discussing various aspects and problems of combining dance with the spoken word, took the position of a mediator in his conclusion that Wigman in her "visionary enthusiasm" tried to "give a dream reality" which because of unfavorable circumstances "remained a dream."[21]

Dance historian Susan Manning came to a very different conclusion in her discussion of *Totenmal* in her article "Ideology and Performance, Between Weimar and the Third Reich: The Case of Totenmal." In her words: "The production also anticipated Wigman's and Talhoff's accommodations with Fascism."[22] In this author's view, Wigman was not guilty of anticipating fascistic production tactics. If there is a "case" for incrimination, it would be not for any pure political reason, but for the escape into a foggy Universalism, which somehow was based on the belief that dance could save the future of man.

Similar ideological beliefs had infiltrated Laban's enthusiastic youth choirs at Monte Verita in 1917, where Mary Wigman had danced the leading part in his pacifistic manifestation, *The Song to the Sun*. Wigman had adopted Laban's concepts of reviving ritual in twentieth-century terms. Her mistaken artistic judgment led her to try to resume mass choir practices, which had worked effectively within a close community of enthusiasts thirteen years ago, but which, when enlarged and dramatized in 1930, were no longer in a communal context. Moreover, Wigman combined these naive ritual forms with an ideological message: "Don't forget the Fallen of World War I." Whom did she address with this message? The young generation did not want to dwell in grief any longer; the message served only her own need to create a monument of gigantic size, a further manifestation of the "Gesamtkunstwerk" (Total Work of Art) in expressionistic starkness. It is questionable whether that was fascism, or simply misguided patriotism.

Wigman had experienced World War I on a highly emotional level. She was old enough to share the post-World War I resentment against the Treaty of Versailles, and for years she had the desire to formulate these feelings of grief in dance. *Totenmal* grew out of a specific German mentality of hurt; by the 1930s, however, it was regressive and served no clear political purpose. It had no relation to the political reality of the time, a reality that Wigman did not clearly perceive. This was not Wigman's failing alone, however, but was representative in general of the German middle class, which tried to maintain a neutral position between radical forces of the right and of the left in Germany in 1930.

The second example of Choreic Theater was free of any political implications. Margarethe Wallman, a previous student of Wigman, the director of the Berlin Wigman School from 1927 to 1928 and the first teacher of Wigman's technique in the U.S. (beginning in 1928), created *Orpheus Dionysos* using the classical opera score of Christoph Willibald Gluck. American guests were delighted to see Ted Shawn in the leading role of Orpheus, the first American male dancer performing in a Modern Dance work in Germany. Ted Shawn was at his best; he brought to the part serenity and elegance in his beautifully erect posture, which Wallmann contrasted with the flowing movements of her own thoroughly trained group of female dancers. In addition to Ted Shawn, another young American danced in this work, Louise Kloepper. In 1929, she went to Europe to study the new German Dance at a Wigman School. She entered the Wigman School Berlin, which was under Wallmann's direction, since her parents felt that Berlin was a little closer to Tacoma, Washington, than Dresden! Kloepper described Margarethe Wallmann as a very strong woman; she also commented on Ted Shawn's performance in the role of Orpheus. Apparently, Shawn adapted very well to Wallmann's style. It was a combination of elements of classical ballet, which she had acquired studying with Eduardowa at the Vienna Opera before joining Wigman, and the specific quality of fluently swinging group motion in Wigman's style. Also, the way she utilized space incorporating an impressive sequence of stairs showed the influence of Wigman. A photo from the original production, graciously given to the author by Louise Kloepper, shows a symmetrical structure in the overall form of a ballet and very expressionistic, ecstatic gestures in the handling of the chorus. There was nothing provocatively radical in her production except possibly her use of percussion instruments simultaneously with Baroque music, which most of the critics found objectionable. Her choreographic use of the dance group, however, was classical and formal in concept; in accordance with three hundred years of European Opera tradition, she created beautiful visual images in the counterbalance between Orpheus and the dancing chorus. She received a warm audience response for this work.

WIGMAN TOURS AMERICA

The Third Dancers' Congress showed the growing fragmentation among the German leaders of Modern Dance, but it had one very positive effect: it intensified the cross-Atlantic exchanges which Kreutzberg and Georgi had started in 1927. The Congress at Munich in 1930 was the first German dance event to gain international attention, and quite a number of American dancers attended.

At the time, the young American Modern Dance movement was still searching for its identity. Although Martha Graham, Doris Humphrey, and Charles Weidman differed in personality and artistic temperament, they shared the goal of freeing themselves from the view of dance as patterned movement, the way it was taught to them in their years of study at Denishawn. They knew from their Denishawn exposure that movement borrowed from another culture could not serve as their own way of self-expression; dance must begin with feeling the movement within themselves. For this very reason, their earliest efforts took the form of solo performances. Thus, American and European modern dancers were alike in their search for the source of movement within themselves. Though their resulting movement may not have been the same, their primary motivation was. It was only natural, then, that the American Modern Dance community, open to experimentation and striving to forge a new dance vocabulary, would be curious to learn what European Modern Dance was all about.

Because of the cultural revolution which had taken place in Germany in the early twenties, European artists had started their search for a new basis for the arts about five years earlier than their American counterparts. From 1920 on, while the "New Dance" in America was still in its infancy, Laban gave European Modern Dance its strong theoretical foundation. John Martin went to Europe and returned to prepare American audiences for the exposure to this New German Dance, which he introduced in his 1930 article, "The Dance: Mary Wigman's Art."

> What is its purpose? Why has it succeeded in fastening its tentacles on every city and hamlet of the Reich, and even in reaching out beyond the borders in all directions except the west, where France alone has erected a stubborn barrier? The answer is not to be found in any of these multifarious manifestations but in Mary Wigman herself. Just as Isadora Duncan included in herself the modern dance of a quarter of a century ago, Mary Wigman is the embodiment of the dance movement of present-day Germany. Before her, there was no German dance, though she cannot be said to have invented anything in the strict sense of term. The members of the old Imperial Ballet will tell you with entire truthfulness that long before Isadora was ever heard of in Moscow and St. Petersburg, there were agitations for a more liberated dance. Similarly there are those who will point out forerunners of Wigman, and it would be folly to attempt to deny that there were such. Wigman, like Duncan, was merely the instrumentality for the expression of a new idea which so generally underlay the thought and the desire of the era that, when it found a receptive channel, it came pouring forth with an impetus that could not be resisted. In the quaint translation of a phrase used about her by a Norwegian critic,"she breaks the frame of our conception of dance."[23]

John Martin had started his crusade for the acceptance of modernism in the American modern contemporary arts even before Wigman appeared at the Chanin Theatre. Both he and Louis Horst, after his European stay, informed American modern dancers quite thoroughly about the German developments in dance. In addition, a number of young Americans had studied at various Wigman schools in Germany in the late twenties.

Wigman herself, however, before embarking on her first American tour, had mixed feelings about the United States. She admired the spontaneous energy and abundant vitality of her American students, whom she saw as a reflection of the land of great promise. Her image of America was colored by Hollywood. She loved jazz music, and she thought of Americans as the great car makers and builders of high-rise edifices. She had no clear idea what to expect from the Modern Dance movement in America. She knew about the stock market crash of 1929, but she was not aware how strongly this economic crisis affected the young American modern dancers, who were desperately looking for chances to perform and barely survived with the little money they made by teaching dance classes.

Sol Hurok, the dance and theatrical impresario, presented Mary Wigman to the American audience in grand style. When the ship, Bremen, arrived in New York on December 22, 1930, journalists and photographers were already waiting at the dock. Sol Hurok obviously planned Wigman's first appearance as a big publicity event. The senior leaders of the American Modern Dance, Ruth St. Denis and Ted Shawn, welcomed Mary Wigman with a splendid reception organized by the Concert Dancers' League on December 26, 1930, at the Plaza Hotel.[24] Wigman was greeted also by Harald Kreutzberg and Yvonne Georgi, who had both just returned to New York from their American tour. Graham, Humphrey and Charles Weidman represented the younger generation of American modern dancers.

Wigman's first concert on American shores was a great success. She appeared to a packed houses at Chanin 46th Street Theatre, on December 28, 1930. New York's professional dance audience and followers of the various modern dancers as well as critics and theatergoers filled the theatre for eleven debut performances that had an extremely strong impact on the New York dance world. Doris Humphrey wrote her parents the next morning: "Mary Wigman was a thrill, about the only dancer outside of Kreutzberg who can do that to me. She will be hard on audiences who are still in the graceful stage though. But a magnificent artist, you absolutely must see her. She backs every other female dancer off the map."[25]

Martha Hill described to me her impressions of Mary Wigman's first concert in New York, on December 28, 1930:

It was a Sunday performance we went to, and it was the American debut in Chanin 46th Street Theatre of Mary Wigman. I was sitting in the Mezzanine. We had heard about Wigman and the German dance, and we were very tense at seeing how she would compare with Martha Graham, who was the director of our company, and with other American dance groups, and what her concert would be like. The house was sold out; there was a tremendously large crowd. When the curtain opened we all stood up to greet her. She was standing still upstage right for her opening dance called *Invocation*, and she was held in place by the tremendous applause of the audience. You could see her almost quiver with the excitement of the occasion. We were told afterward that Mary had been lying down for one hour before going on stage. She was staying quietly, every muscle, every nerve, and every fiber was moving as she stood upright.

I particularly remember *Face of the Night* (Gesicht der Nacht). Her first crossing from stage left to right was very compelling and moving. My reaction was that this was a foreign language, and I felt that I was in the presence of some great artist. The dance was accompanied by a single piano and some percussion instruments similar to our sparse American dance accompaniment. What was foreign was the visual look of the costume, with bare midriff and little decorations, such as a medallion hanging from the brassiere, showing her belly button, which seemed to us in our, what Martha called "long wollen period," somehow outré, extreme, and different. The subject matter seemed to be universal, but we had to get used to its type of universality, because Wigman did dances into death, and dances of death. I was fascinated, I was impressed, and I viewed it with respect, but it was foreign to me. We were in a state of flux afterward so that the whole group of us in Martha's company went out on Broadway still talking and discussing Wigman's concert. We were not feeling like going home, we were not in the habit of going to a cafe, but when we saw a notice of Emil Jannings' *Blue Angel*, we all went to the midnight show in order to let off steam.

After that first strong experience, I went directly from the rehearsal with Martha and the company class to Wigman's performances, whenever I could. I thought that I must see what that was all about, and by the end of the season it was no longer foreign to me. I had entirely embraced all of it, and I still remember many dances, such as the beautiful *Summer's Dance*, which she performed in a yellow velvet-like dress. I was familiar with the form of her dances because they were derived from music (as taught by Louis Horst). There would be an A section, a B section, and maybe a return to the A section. She was very meticulous about form which was very clear and ordered. She performed *Witch Dance* with a mask and that was much caricatured. Very funny things were done with it in caricature in the American press. Somebody in New York wrote a skit about it saying that he ran home immediately after the performance and tried the turns sitting on the floor, but it did not work for him, he only got a terrible shine on the seat of his pant from turning around on the floor.

I also remember some folk dances derived from Italian and Spanish folk tunes, and particularly, I still see turning dances. She came on stage and turned in one spot, faster, slower, with her body bending forward, rotating and spiraling somehow similar to Martha's contraction and release. I saw her turn so fast that her hair was flowing across her face, and the dance would end in a gradual fall; immediately she rose and was perfectly on balance to take those beautiful bows. Wigman's turning dances were completely mesmerizing. Early on, I was not able to analyze it, but it was her sense of space which made it so different. Our dance in America is a dance centered in the dancer himself. Wigman brought in the idea of space being very effective in shaping the movement in dance; space pressing on you, space as an active partner. The relationship between the dancer and space became very important in my own teaching. I had been aware of space unconsciously; for instance, a narrow room affects you in a different way than a broad expanse. You immediately respond to the space surrounding you. A monograph of Rudolph von Delius' *Mary Wigman*, which one of my graduate students translated for me, captured beautifully Mary Wigman's very personal relation to space. Wigman's heightened awareness of space was one of the biggest contributions to the American modern dance, because this was something which was not in our consciousness before. I felt that Wigman was kin to Martha Graham in her intensity and in the passion of feelings, and the dedication to the moment of what she was doing, although Wigman and Martha were physically not alike. Wigman talked about earth dancers, middle dancers and air dancers (as it was part of the Laban tradition), and she certainly was an earth dancer with a very active use of weight, whereas Martha was in general dancing in all ranges of space. Martha had more a painter's look at the dancer's body in space.[26]

It is a tribute to Wigman's impact that Miss Hill recalled this debut performance of Mary Wigman in such a vivid and detailed way after sixty years of a very active life in dance.

Press reviews of Wigman's debut in the United States ranged from perplexity to enthusiasm. As an example, Sarah Chotzinoff wrote in *The New York World* on December 30, 1930: "It was all very exciting and quite 'stark' to quote a modernist platitude, and we thought of trapped bats and perodactyls and other unpleasantries of the night. Miss Wigman is an extraordinary person, as subsequent events proved. Various adjectives crowd upon the mind attempting to describe her. Vital, arresting, intense--none of them quite filled the bill. Perhaps the word 'incredible' comes nearest to the truth. The style of all her creations rests upon the principle of ebb and flow."[27]

In contrast to these vague generalizations, John Martin analyzed Wigman's debut performance in detail. He admitted that some of Wigman's costumes did not help the audience to a better understanding and appreciation of her artistic intentions, but he put her personal power as performer in focus in his review titled "Triumph in Dance by Mary Wigman:"

> Mary Wigman achieved an unequivocal triumph in her American debut last night at Chanin's Forty-sixth Street Theatre, and achieved it against odds which probably no other dancer had to face within memory. Already a tradition before we had ever seen her, hailed as the liberator of the dance from the aridity of ages, the symbol of modernity in the minds of the dance world, hers was a fame which it seemed impossible for her to live up to when she should finally come face to face with her first American audience.... It is Mary Wigman, the artist, who was revealed to us last night with all the freshness of an unknown; her method, her theory, her philosophy, meant nothing except in so far as they served her own ends and permitted us thereby to glimpse the fine spirit of a great artist. Her personal powers cannot be dimmed even by much telling....The art of Mary Wigman is heroic in stature. Though her dances treat common human impulses, they have thrown off all that is petty and unessential, until they stand forth free, simple, warm, transcendent, like great sculptures of antiquity suddenly breathed into movement. Indeed, on the beautiful stage of the Chanin Theatre, with the sound of primitive music rising as a background, she struck the keynote of the ancient Greek theater so vividly, without any apparent intention of so doing, that she made the many conscious efforts of others to recreate the Greek dance pale into the merest insignificance.... As a choreographer Mary Wigman is gifted among the select few. The elements of her designs are of amazing originality; she rarely employs a movement that does not seem peculiar to her own uses. These she arranges in patterns of equal distinction, and both movement and pattern seem to grow before our eyes out of the requirements of the moment. Her employment of dynamism in various shades of control makes her crescendos things of breath-taking power.[28]

After eleven sold out performances, Wigman left New York to tour the country. She was fascinated with the efficiency, speed and comfort of the American train system in 1931, travelling at night from coast to coast. America appeared to her a tremendous, fascinating dreamland. Those hours on the train by herself were precious to her, since she usually was surrounded by journalists as soon as she arrived at her next destination. People talked too fast for her to understand or they asked her to explain the meaning of her dances. She was amazed to find the wildest interpretations of her choreography in the press, particularly of her dance *Turning Monotony*. Her sole intention was to give her visions expression through dance. Her standard answer was, "If I would be a poet, I would say it in words, but as a dancer, I have to speak through movement!"[29] Most of the time people wanted fast answers; at those times, confronted with a culture so different from her own, she experienced bouts of loneliness.

Wigman's performance schedule was, unfortunately, so tight that she was unable to observe American Modern Dance creations. She had met Graham, Humphrey and Weidman very briefly at the first reception before her New York performance, but a further direct contact did not occur during her first American tour. Physically exhausted but spiritually lifted, Wigman completed this engagement on March 13, 1931, with a farewell performance at Carnegie Hall.

The tremendous success of her first American tour came at just the right moment in Mary's life; it acted as an affirmation of her strength. At the age of forty-four she had proven to herself that she was still at the climax of her career. American audiences confirmed her as the "Great German Ausdruckstänzerin," and this acclaim counterbalanced the controversial reception of *Totenmal* in 1930. Wigman returned to Europe in the Spring of 1931 to perform at the Theatre des Champs Elysee in Paris and, in May 1931, even gave a lecture in French at the Sorbonne.

John Martin was fully aware of the importance of Wigman's tour for the American Modern Dance. In "The Dance: Vital Issues," he discussed how Wigman had provided a great stimulus to the American dance scene:

> It was not until Wigman arrived upon the scene that the newest elements of modernism were presented by an acknowledged master, one who had become the symbol of movement. The response was instantaneous and electrical. It is no longer possible to speak of the local dance field as lethargic; it is aroused to an unprecedented activity sometimes compelled to arise in defense of its belief, justifying it with something more than words.... The debt which we owe to Mary Wigman for thus arousing the field to action must be acknowledged both by her friends and by those who believe themselves to be her foes. Such an awakening has not been felt since Pavlova and Mordkin stepped on the stage of the Metropolitan Opera House some twenty years ago and turned the ballet in America once more into a living art. [30]

John Martin's prediction was absolutely correct. Mary Wigman's concerts either deeply impressed her American audiences or repelled them with their "ugliness"; the range of responses was wide and quite emotional. Ironically, however, the controversy about Wigman raised public awareness of Modern Dance, and afterward the "New Dance" in America gradually gained the status of an art form instead of being treated simply as a diversion. Sol Hurok was sufficiently satisfied with the response to Wigman's debut to arrange a second tour from November 1931 to April 1932. Moreover, after visiting Wigman in her Dresden school, according to Wigman's notes, Hurok was so impressed with her teaching methods that he decided to establish a branch of the school in New York. Hanya Holm was the logical choice to direct it.

In 1931, the same year that Wigman was on tour, American modern dancers created significant choreographic ensemble works and addressed a larger public in unmistakably genuine American terms.

DANCE REPERTORY THEATRE

The American modern dancers' creativity reached a high point, even while their financial situation continued to deteriorate. Graham and Humphrey-Weidman had already turned away from theatrical commercialism in revolt against Denishawn. As a result, they had struggled very hard to present concerts during the late twenties, since their only base of financial support was the income from the studios. By 1931, they were recognized as innovators and known as the leaders of the "New Dance," which gave them a joint identity in spite of their artistic differences.

At this critical juncture, Helen Tamiris suggested that she, Graham, and Humphrey-Weidman share production and costs. Helen Tamiris had never had the Denishawn experience; she was an outsider to the recognized innovators of the "New Dance." A daughter of a Russian immigrant family, she had grown up with a great respect for the classical tradition in dance, having studied ballet with Michel Fokine. She also had briefly studied Duncan's approach. Tamiris loved theater. She was a striking dancer in musicals and night clubs, but she also felt compelled to choreograph her own dances.

In 1927, Tamiris had appeared with her first program of a variety of jazz movements to Gershwin's *Rhapsody in Blue*, but it was not until her return from a successful tour to Europe in 1929 that she was able to dance her *Negro Spirituals*, at New York's Martin Beck Theatre with Louis Horst at the piano, as a benefit for the New School for Social Research. Tamiris's heightened awareness of social injustices found a fresh and original expression in these short vignettes designed with amazing clarity in form and compositional distinction. Christina Schlundt's fine monograph on Tamiris points out that Tamiris lacked the motivation to create a new technique, but that "she had a drive to do what the time requires."[31] Tamiris came up with ideas about dance that touched on problems of her time and on societal aspirations, but she had developed her solo repertory very individually, outside the group of the "New Dance." Nevertheless, in 1930 when she approached Martha Graham, Doris Humphrey and Charles Weidman with the idea of giving a series of concerts each season, sharing the production staff and one common theatre, Graham, Humphrey and Weidman agreed. Dance Repertory Theatre was established with Louis Horst as musical director.

The proposal for a common Modern Dance theater arose out of the desperate financial situation. It certainly was not an artistic liaison; there was little agreement among the participants, whose opinions soon clashed. But in spite of the need for very different artistic temperaments to deal with one another in the two years of its existence (1930 and 1931), the Dance Repertory Theatre helped to strengthen the young modern dancers and brought them closer to constituting a movement with some identifying characteristics.

There was, first of all, a clear focus on American themes. Martha Graham, assisted by her dance group, presented *Primitive Mysteries*: "Hymn to the Virgin," "Crucifixes" and "Hosanna," to music by Louis Horst, at the Craig Theatre, on February 6, 1931. Graham had received a Guggenheim Fellowship which enabled her, together with Louis Horst, to visit several American Indian reservations in the Southwest and in Mexico during the summer of 1930. "They both came back fired with the idea for a work based on American Indian themes," Martha Hill recalled. "Louis Horst wrote the music incorporating some authentic American Indian melodies. *Primitive Mysteries* was very stark in its form and realization. Graham was concerned with what she was saying, not how she was saying it. What concerned her was to get into dance form her appreciation and her understanding of what she experienced in her travels in Mexico and the American Southwest."[32] *Primitive Mysteries* broke new ground in the history of dance in America, as stated in Martha Siegel's analysis.

> The movement language of *Primitive Mysteries* is untranslatable in the terms that had served theater dance audiences up to that time.It wasn't narrative. It wasn't a codified system of abstract steps that could be appreciated for their aesthetic value. It had none of the joyful abandon associated with folk or ethnic forms. Nor was it expressionistic in seeming to come directly out of the emotions of the dancers. It was austere, formal, controlled. The dancer's body line was never allowed to soften; the face was blank, not to betray the message of the body.[33]

While Graham projected her vision of an American Indian-based dance ritual with the abstracting eye of a contemporary painter, Doris Humphrey and her Concert Group performed *Shakers* as a dramatic structure with accumulating rhythms building to the intensity of a religious purification ritual. Presented at the Craig Theatre, on February 1, 1931, this group work featured Doris Humphrey as the Eldress. Eleanor King, who performed *Shakers*, called this work

> the most infectious of all Doris's compositions, because the simple rhythms to drumbeats were so well built. These decorous Shakers controlled within fine boundaries the tension inherent in their lives.... It was good Americana, good religious ritual, excellent theatre, and just long enough to establish the mood, make its point and build to an exciting climax."[34]

Thus, both Graham and Humphrey returned to ritual, finding in the American heritage the roots for an indigenous American Modern Dance. A return to ritual frequently occurs in times of crisis and re-evaluation, when artists search for an existential basis. A sense of crisis also motivated artists in Germany in the late twenties, when a similar "digging their way back to the roots" took place.[35] Although German and American artists articulated their choreographic works in very different ways, there was a similarity of purpose: they wanted to communicate directly and forcefully. Their movement language was unadorned, and they danced very consciously about rituals. Thus, on both sides of the Atlantic ritual was re-invoked to convey a very individual way of feeling connected with the cosmos. In the rise of Modern Dance this rare moment of similar search and discovery might be seen as a confluence, a remarkable consonance that facilitated later crosscurrents and influences.

MARY WIGMAN'S SECOND AND THIRD AMERICAN TOURS

When Mary Wigman returned to New York on November 31,1931, audiences greeted her warmly: they now knew what to expect. Wigman in turn was less nervous than at her debut and gave herself chances to communicate. She thanked the New York audience on the radio for their wonderful response to her debut the previous year, and she also explained her views on dance. The sense of rhythm, as she put it, was a special characteristic of the times. (Humphrey could have said this.) Man revealed himself in dance; he was the eternal theme. The form of dance had to change, since each epoch had to find its own formal language. The art of Modern Dance deserved the interest of everyone influenced by the time in which they were living.

On her second tour Wigman presented dances which were new to the American audience, but which represented a summation of her mature work. The major portion of her solo program consisted of a cycle of six dances, entitled *Opfer (Sacrifice)*. John Martin compared the effect of this cycle to the impact of Greek drama. "It is a magnificent achievement, heroic in vein, composed with the utmost simplicity, and building with that perfection of form which is such an unfailing attribute of a Wigman work."[36]

Wigman reached the climax of her popularity in America with this fine example of the "New German Dance." She crossed Canada and the middle west in over seventy performances on her second tour, renewing contacts with American friends as she travelled from coast to coast. She also met with Louise Kloepper, her first American student, who had received a teaching certification at her school in Dresden in 1931, and she asked her to join Hanya Holm as assistant in the newly-established Mary Wigman School at New York. Kloepper agreed and thus started a very close collaboration with Hanya Holm, her previous teacher, who became a decisive influence on her as choreographer and teacher of modern dance throughout the thirties. Personally and artistically, the second American tour was, for Wigman, the most rewarding of her American stays; she returned to Germany feeling much closer to America.

It was a different Germany to which she returned. The economic crisis was now very evident. Many of her students were out of work and could no longer afford to take classes, and some of her Jewish students had left the country. The coming political events threw shadows upon Wigman's further work. In July 1932, when Sol Hurok came to negotiate an additional South American tour, Wigman proposed to form a new group of advanced students and bring them to the U.S. Wigman made this suggestion not for artistic reasons, but in the hopes of keeping some of her better students. By September 1932, Wigman had started rehearsals, desperately trying to bring these young students to a performance level. This second "Wigman-Tanzgruppe" (Dance Group) performed her new work, *Der Weg* (*The Journey*), in Dresden and in Berlin in December 1932, as a tryout for the coming American tour. It was based on an Everyman theme which presented Wigman as pilgrim, with her dancers simultaneously moving and playing flute and percussion instruments. The audience response was cool; some of the critics found the piece not up to Wigman's previous artistic standards. Nevertheless, Wigman and her twelve dancers embarked for the United States on December 13, 1932, for their first performance in New York.

John Martin, usually Wigman's strongest supporter, was also disappointed:

It must be admitted that Wigman with a group is not to be compared with Wigman as a solo dancer. Her composition for the group is extremely objective: she moves the dancers through surprisingly set figurations, while she herself scarcely enters the design at all. Her singular power as an artist lies in her ability to project her highly personal inner experience through movement of sometimes breath-taking originality. When she gives these movements to other dancers, she runs the risk of making them appear manufactured and unconvincing.[37]

As in *Totenmal*, Wigman had overextended herself. She also had misjudged the growing sophistication of the American audience, which expected any group that Wigman presented to be up to professional standards. To end on a good note, she herself gave a slashing farewell solo performance that was a great success: it was not until she gave a farewell speech that the last curtain, after more than twelve calls, finally fell.

This was not just the final curtain's closing on Wigman's third American tour; it was the last time that an American audience saw Mary Wigman in performance in America, and it finalized for them the direct personal contact with this radiant artist. "After three tours in the early 1930s," Marcia Siegel noted, Wigman "was swept from us on a tidal wave of politics and war; she never performed again."[38]

While Wigman gave this memorable solo performance in New York on March 5, 1933, elections in Germany made the NSDAP (National Socialist German Workers Party) the strongest party in Germany. Wigman had just returned when, on April 1, 1933, the boycott against Jewish store owners gave a first taste of Nazi brutality. She buried herself in her work, dissolved her group, and tried to bring her school through the difficult economic crisis.

Reading through Wigman's diary entries for this period reveals that she did not feel compelled to record any general observations of the political situation; indeed, an incident described in her diary in 1934 proves quite clearly how little attention she paid to politics. A Gestapo (Secret Service) officer entered her studio insisting that he had to conduct a search since one of her students was allegedly distributing communist propaganda. His three hour search failed to turn up any incriminating evidence. Wigman was not upset about the unwarranted search, but complained that this distraction had cost her three hours of valuable rehearsal time! Perhaps because Wigman's closest friend held quite an influential position in German industry, she initially sympathized with the new regime. The days of her American success seemed far away, and Wigman resigned herself to making the best out of the ambiguous situation in Germany, which was still her home land.

Her priority was, as always, to maintain her position as Germany's first dancer. Initially, the Ministry of Propaganda treated her with respect as long as she produced dances that conformed with the Nazi ideology. But, by 1936, it became apparent that Wigman was not willing to compromise in questions of her art; as a consequence, thereafter her dances were labeled "degenerate art." (see Chapter V).

On the occasion of Wigman's eightieth birthday, on November 13, 1966, Clive Barnes assessed Wigman's overall influence in the light of Germany's political experience of the 1930s and 1940s:

> Today Wigman is part of the lost and currently discredited European modern dance movement. In places such as Holland and Germany, where once modern or expressionist dance found much favor, it is now rejected, largely on the false but powerful emotional reason that this style of dance is thought "Teutonic" and, by implication Hitlerian.... [39]

But perspectives on German culture have changed since Clive Barnes made this assessment twenty-five years ago. Prewar and wartime stereotypes of "Teutonic" art need to be thoroughly re-examined, which will hopefully shed some new light on Wigman and the European Modern Dance. Barnes, however, correctly assessed Wigman's situation and that of the expressionistic school of Modern Dance in Germany from the perspective of the sixties. At that time, when American Modern Dance artists brought their contemporary dance to Germany, they stimulated German dancers and audiences who, ironically, no longer remembered their own Modern Dance traditions.

The first encounter in the United States between Wigman and American audiences, therefore, is especially important, since it showed Wigman just before National Socialism obscured the view. Now, more than half a century later, it would seem appropriate that Wigman be re-evaluated in the light of the influence she has exerted on the American Modern Dance, free from emotional prejudgment.

NOTES FOR CHAPTER III

1.   Cohen, Selma Jeanne (1972) *Doris Humphrey: An Artist First,* p. 83. Middletown, CT.: Wesleyan University Press

2.   H'Doubler, Margaret N.(1957) *Dance a Creative Art Experience.* p. 60. Madison: University of Wisconsin Press

3.   Wilson John M. (1990) Interview by I. Bergsohn, Tucson, Arizona, June 6

4.   Shurr, Gertrude (1990) Interview by I. Bergsohn, Tucson, Arizona, May 27

5.   Schönberg, Bessie (1992) in a letter to the author, March 18

6.   Shurr, Gertrude & Yocom, Rachael Dunovan (1980). *Modern Dance Techniques and Teaching*, 2nd edn. New York: Dance Horizons, (1st edn, New York: Ronald Press, 1949)

7.   Hill, Martha (1989) Interview by I Bergsohn, Brooklyn, July 20

8.   Siegel, Marcia (1979) *The Shapes of Change*, p.28. Boston: Hougton Mifflin Co.

9.   *The World*, May 16, 1928

10.   Martin, John (1965) *Introduction to the Dance.* pp.282-283 Brooklyn: Dance Horizons, Inc. Republication of the original edn.(1939)

11.   Kreutzberg, Harald (1939 *Über mich Selbst (About Myself)*. Detmold, Germany: E. Hammann Verlag

12.   Hill, Martha (1989) Interview, I. Bergsohn, Brooklyn, New York July 20

13.   Shurr, Gertrude (1990) Interview by I Bergsohn, Tucson, Arizona May 27

14.   Martin, John (1929) The Macaber in Germany's Dance. *New York Times*, February 16

15.   King, Eleanor (1978) *Transformations,* p. 66. Brooklyn: Dance Horizons

16.   Selden, Elizabeth (1930) Masters of the New Mode Gather at Munich. *New York Evening Post*, May 31

17.   Martin, John (1930) A Futile Congress. *New York Times*, July 20

18.   Kloepper, Louise (1990) Interview, by I. Bergsohn, Madison, Wisconsin, March 18

19.   Sorell, Walter (1986) *Mary Wigman: Ein Vermächtnis*, p. 110. Wilhelmshaven: Florian Noetzel Verlag

20.   Kloepper, Louise (1990) Interview, by I Bergsohn, Madison, Wisconsin, March 18

21.   Sorell, Walter (1986) *Mary Wigman: Ein Vermächtnis,* p.116

22.   Manning, Susan (1989) Ideology and Performance Between Weimar and The Third Reich: The Case of Totenmal, p. 222. *Theatre Journal,* May

23.   Martin, John (1930) The Dance: Mary Wigman's Art. *New York Times*, Aug. 3

24.   Cohen, Selma Jeanne (1972) *Doris Humphrey: An Artist First.* p. 92. Middletown, CT.: Wesleyan University Press. Cohen gives details on the Concert Dancers' League

25.   King, Eleanor (1978) *Transformations,* p. 66.

26.   Hill, Martha (1989) Interview by I Bergsohn, Brooklyn, July 18

27.   Chotzinoff, Sarah (1930) Other Music. *New York World,* Dec. 29

28.   Martin, John (1930) Triumph in Dance by Mary Wigman. *The New York Times*, Dec 29

29.   Sorell, Walter (1986) *Mary Wigman: Ein Vermächtnis,* p. 147

30   Martin, John (1931) The Dance: Vital Issues. *The New York Times*, March 8

31.   Schlundt, Christina (1989) Studies in Dance History. Fall. *Society of Dance History Scholars.* **Vol** I, Number I

32.   Hill, Martha (1989) Interview by I Bergsohn, Brooklyn, July 18

33.   Siegel, Marcia (1979) *The Shapes of Change*, p.57

34.   King, Eleanor (1978) *Transformations,* p. 74

35.   Siegel, Marcia (1979) *The Shapes of Change,* p. 49

36. Martin, John (1931) Cordial Reception for Mary Wigman. *New York Times,* Dec. 11

37. Martin, John (1932) Festival of Dance opened by Wigman. *New York Times,* Dec. 26

38. Siegel, Marcia (1973) Mary Wigman 1886-1973: A Tribute, *Dance Magazine,* Nov. 80

39. Barnes, Clive (1966) Wigman at 80: Still an Influence. *New York Times,* sec.2, November 13

CHAPTER 1V: DANCE IN THE TIDE OF POLITICS: THE THIRTIES.

The first encounter of American audiences with German dance artists resulted from Sol Hurok's initiative; he knew that a personality like Mary Wigman would be attractive to American audiences. Her individualism, her degree of independence as a woman, and her close ties to expressionist European artists were fascinating to American dance enthusiasts even if the bold look of her dances at first shocked them. This fascination with Wigman's personality did not fade during her three American tours in the United States between 1930 and 1933. Her solo performances were so unique, as John Martin wrote, that no other dancer could equal her power of communication.

It was Hanya Holm, however, who planted the seeds of a more enduring Laban-Wigman legacy. Holm arrived in the fall of 1931 to direct the New York Wigman School. As a person in many ways different from Mary Wigman, Holm's first priority was not to make a personal impact as a performer, though she was a fine dancer, but to establish the Laban-Wigman tradition in the New World. Whereas she knew Laban only from dance congresses and indirectly through Mary Wigman's teaching, she had collaborated with Mary Wigman very closely during Wigman's most productive period, from 1920 to 1930. Not surprisingly, Holm's teaching was strongly based on Wigman's philosophy.

Hanya Holm had left Dresden just before the economic crisis reached its peak. In Germany, the depression caused by the American stock market crash had a damaging psychological effect, because it followed so closely the catastrophic inflation of the early twenties. Holm, having more political instinct than Wigman, foresaw the serious dangers posed by the National Socialist party. Compared to the state of political and cultural collapse she had left behind in Germany, Holm immediately sensed an atmosphere of vitality in the American scene. In America, the Great Depression had added urgency to the process of defining cultural identity, and Holm recognized that American modern dancers were perfectly in tune with the trend of re-evaluation and searching for new form and content.

There was a sense of solidity and weight particularly in those works of Martha Graham and Doris Humphrey that were derived from ritual. Their companies were firmly established and they trained young dancers in their particular styles. American Modern Dance, was, however, far from homogeneous. It was extremely diversified and, moreover, it was in the midst of a transitional period. Interpretive dancers still continued in Duncan style; Ted Shawn had started to work with physical educators, creating dances for men, and Graham, Humphrey and Weidman were emerging as recognized leaders. After the failure of the Dance Repertory experiment, Tamiris continued to make choreographic statements with her group; social protest was the undercurrent of her dance creations, seen most vividly in her *Cycle of Unrest*. Coming from a Russian-Jewish immigrant background like Tamiris, Anna Sokolow also involved herself choreographing works of intense social consciousness, such as *Slaughter of the Innocents*. Other artists emerged who felt that they had to raise contemporary issues in direct response to the time of crisis; however, their names have been largely forgotten. Since there was no school or company to carry on or represent their point of view, they became America's lost generation.

Holm observed the diverse field of entertainment with amazement. In addition to these modern experimenters, professional dancers were employed in minstrel shows, vaudeville and musical comedies. Holm recognized hitherto unused possibilities for dance in the commercial theater, which seemed to offer so much more color than the municipal theaters in Germany. There were no clear borderlines yet established between commercial and modern dance, as the opening of the Roxy attested. The director, Samuel L. Rothafel, who once had hired the young Martha Graham for a vaudeville act during her Denishawn days, envisioned the combination of Martha Graham's work side by side with guest artist Harald Kreutzberg as a safe guarantee for filling the huge elaborately equipped 6,000 seat-house. The opening night, on December 27, 1932, was, even for New York, an extraordinary spectacle. It became a most memorable event for young performers like Gertrude Shurr who were dancing in Martha Graham's *Choreic Dance for an Antique Greek Tragedy*, and were observing Harald Kreutzberg's entrance while warming up in the wings. "We all watched Kreutzberg when he came down the stairs swinging his cape in the *Dance of Death*. He dominated the whole stage. Martha just adored him. He was a tremendous success. I thought that he was a great theater person."[1] The fact that Martha Graham was willing to appear on the same program with Kreutzberg shows the transitional state of affairs in dance as well as the desperate shortage of performance spaces for modern dancers during the Depression. Following this event, in 1932, Kreutzberg entered into an artistic partnership with the American ballet dancer Ruth Page. She had performed with Anna Pavlova's company in South America in 1918, had briefly danced in Diaghilev's last company, and was prima ballerina of the Chicago Summer Opera from 1929 to 1933. Page, a very dynamic personality, matched Kreutzberg in virtuosity, alertness, and sense of humor. In this collaboration Kreutzberg emphasized his light side, and he and Page, two exponents of operatic theater, forged a very successful partnership on two well reviewed tours in 1932 and 1934. Page, quite well known in Scandinavia and Paris, choreographed *Frank and Johnny* for the Chicago Federal Theater in 1938 and, thereafter, as choreographer of the Chicago Lyric Opera, pioneered a dynamic American ballet with social content.

Holm spent her first four years in the United States as a teacher and keen observer of this dynamic American Modern Dance scene. She realized that Wigman's unconventional dances and costumes had alienated many Americans. Since she was of a very different temperament from Wigman, her goals were to listen to and learn the language, to study the different ways people communicated in the new environment, and to observe how modern dancers expressed their point of view. Holm kept a low profile, adapting Wigman's pedagogic approach to the needs of American students. She later remarked that she learned just as much as she taught. In her unthreatening way, Holm gradually became an important member of the evolving American Modern Dance scene.

HANYA HOLM

Hanya Holm was born in 1893, only seven years after Wigman. The daughter of a German middle-class family, she attended a convent called "Convent of the English Ladies"[2] and believed in the value of a good education. Although she had studied music and completed her teaching diploma at the Dalcroze institute at Hellerau, when she saw Mary Wigman dance, she decided it was not music but dance that she wanted to pursue as her lifetime goal. She separated from her husband, having already a small son, and joined the Wigman School in Dresden in 1921, starting her dance studies with characteristic determination. Thanks to her solid musical background, her sharp movement observational skills, and her analytical mind, she became one of several outstanding students who were part of Wigman's first dance ensemble. She also became Wigman's closest collaborator. During the ten years of her collaboration with Wigman in Germany from 1921 to 1931, she had more than once demonstrated her unflappable personality. For example, she took over the rehearsal direction for the performance of *Totenmal* during the last frustrating month of preparation, and she acted in this difficult role as a stabilizing force. Again, while Wigman was on her first American tour, the direction of the Wigman School at Dresden was placed in Holm's capable hands. Thus, there was no question in Wigman's mind that the only person who was qualified to direct a Wigman School in New York was Hanya Holm.

The new Mary Wigman School under Hanya Holm's direction was the first dance school in the United States offering a well-rounded dance education rather than solely training in one particular performance style. Very different in outlook from the existing modern dance studios, the curriculum that Hanya Holm designed in 1931 followed the example of the Wigman School at Dresden. Holm, however, adapted the original offerings to the new environment, gradually demystifying Wigman's movement material. Wigman's hypnotic turns, for instance, became a study of meticulously analyzed footsteps, and the students developed a heightened spatial awareness through her methodical explanations of Laban's spatial theory. (Wigman herself had emphasized the initiation of the movement more than its visible form in her teaching.)

One of Holm's former students from the Dresden school, Louise Kloepper, the first American to earn the teaching diploma in Dresden, in 1931, became Holm's assistant in 1932 in the New York Wigman School. Kloepper recalled the examination she took with Wigman and Holm. She had to perform two pieces of her own choreography and take a written test. The examination pertained to concepts of space (Raumlehre), investigating the three planes of motion, as well as levels, directions and pathways, and concepts of time (rhythm, meter, tempo, and unmeasured time). Concepts of force dealt with smoothness and sharpness of the movement and the varying amounts of energy used, following Laban's movement theories without using his specific terminology. Classes in anatomy and use of percussion instruments supplemented the curriculum.[3] Hanya Holm maintained these original concepts in her new Mary Wigman School in New York; however, she de-emphasized movement choir practices, and instead cultivated ensemble dance instructions. She offered a well-rounded dance education for aspiring professional dancers as well as dance for amateurs and children.

Students came to Holm to learn the New Thought, as Wigman's approach was called. Some came for the love of movement, and others came as physical education teachers who felt that they could gain from Holm's methodical teaching. Some also went to the Wigman School to learn to express themselves through movement, with the goal of voicing their feelings of social injustice. The New Dance Group, which began in 1932, provided a vehicle for this expression. The School offered classes to young amateur dancers with the aim of performing dances based on contemporary issues, in union halls and other political gatherings. Holm taught them all, listening to and absorbing the new cultural environment. While some of the younger members of Graham's group helped the New Dance Group with their choreographic projects, Holm did not involve herself actively in the New York performance scene, but began to choreograph in her studio.

The only times Holm appeared in public during the four years between 1931 and 1935 was to present Wigman's approach to dance in an expanded lecture-demonstration. Her trained students showed curves, diagonals and spirals, bringing Laban and Wigman's theories of space, time and energy to life. They served as living illustrations of John Martin's introductory lectures on Modern Dance at the New School of Social Research at New York City. Walter Sorell, in his diary notes published in *Looking Back in Wonder*, described Holm's particular movement quality: "Her group lecture-demonstrations, which explored the concepts of space and tension as the base of her teaching, were almost dreamlike in their lyric molding of space and mood. The distinctive movement quality of the best of Hanya Holm-trained students is as hard to describe as a swoop of a wing, the flight of a bird--it belongs to the space about it."[4]
The clarity and dynamic versatility of Holm's well- trained dancers had a strong appeal to the New York dance audience. She proved that she was able to turn out beautiful dancers for the stage, and this brought her in league with the leaders of American Modern Dance, who were also striving to articulate their own language of movement.

If American modern dancers were not at all a homogeneous group, they were unanimous in their rejection of ballet. American ballet companies did not yet exist (American Ballet Theatre was established in 1940) and only a few people could remember the 1916 performances of Diaghilev's company at the Metropolitan Opera. Generally, Anna Pavlova's image exemplified classical ballet for an entire generation till the middle of the nineteen-thirties. Leonide Massine's staging of the first American performance of Stravinsky's *Sacre du Printemps* was still considered experimental in 1930, and there was a great gulf between Massine's theatricality and use of mime and Kurt Jooss's unadorned directness in dance drama.

THE GREEN TABLE

As the tremors of National Socialism began to shake the feeble foundation of the Weimar Republic, Jooss, sensitive to those signals of destruction, had conceived his masterpiece, *The Green Table*. In November 1931, the president of the Archives Internationales, Rolf de Maré, had invited Jooss, the new director of the Essen Opera dance ensemble, to participate in the upcoming international choreography competition. At first Jooss refused, but in January 1932 he decided to accept, and began rehearsals for the new work. *The Green Table*, patterned after the "Dance of Death" of the Middle Ages, showed the experience of death in different ways. In the opening scene, masked diplomats, clad in black, gesticulate grotesquely around a green conference table, while their frustrating discussions produce war. Death appears as a skeleton-like figure, powerfully in command. In the next six scenes, Death gradually leads various archetypal characters to their destruction, felling soldiers in battle, seducing a young girl as a dance partner, and receiving an old mother with gentleness. In the final scene, Death alone reigns while the gentlemen in black continue their grotesque gesticulations around the conference table.

With this work, Jooss, at age thirty-one, won the first prize at the "Concours de Choreographie" in Paris, on July 3, 1932. *La Table Verte*, according to the original program, was a "Dance macabre." The two piano score was played by the composer Frederic Cohen himself and by Will Goetze, who had accompanied Wigman until 1929. Costumes were the creations of Hein Heckroth, and the work was performed by members of the Folkwangbühne of the City of Essen.

Jooss, new to the international dance scene, became known relatively overnight. His dance drama *The Green Table* had emerged from the anti-war spirit of the twenties in Europe. In the eyes of the National Socialists, *The Green Table* was pacifist and therefore unacceptable. The work did not glorify the "Frontkämpfer" (the front-line fighter) and the men and women who had to meet death in the interest of the fatherland. Instead, it appealed to "international intellectualism," one of Hitler's famous slogans. Of course another important reason to reject this work was that its music was written by Frederic Cohen, Jooss's close collaborator, who was Jewish. Any one of these reasons alone would have been enough to arouse the suspicions of the National Socialist regime.

As early as the fall of 1932, Jooss, sensing political complications, had decided to separate his company from the Essen Opera and to establish a private enterprise, the Ballets Jooss. The company successfully toured Holland, Belgium, Paris, and London. In August 1933, four months after the seizure of power by the National Socialists, Jooss was warned to leave Essen immediately; within forty-eight hours the entire ensemble had secretly crossed the border into Holland.[5]

Homeless and in exile, Jooss had agreed to a six week run in New York at the Forest Theatre. He did not have the chance to prepare the American audience gradually for his choreographic language, and some misinterpretations of his work were unavoidable. The title "Ballets Jooss" was misleading in America, since it created immediate associations with the old country's Imperial Court, that is, with pomp, stardom and etiquette. Perhaps for this reason, the debut performance of Ballets Jooss in New York, in November 1933, had an impact that is hard to imagine today. The company's overwhelming success is reflected in one of the earliest revues in the *New York Herald Tribune:*

> *The Green Table,* has won for Mr. Jooss and his associates prominence unequaled in the dance world since the days of Diaghilev. Jooss has evolved a technique wherewith, by a dexterous blending of theater and dance, a new form is achieved, based on classic tradition, developed with modern media. The result is at the same time both aesthetically valuable and amusing. The projection of sardonic commentaries reflecting the turbulent times in which we live is one of Mr. Jooss's objectives....[6]

Eleanor King recalled in her memoirs, *Transformations:*

Now came the Kurt Jooss company from Germany by way of England,

Now came the Kurt Jooss company from Germany by way of England, with their international artists and their eclecticism. They blended modern dance with a classical base, then a daring and risky idea, today the commonplace aim of most companies. For ballet people it wasn't balletic enough to use soft shoes and eliminate pointe; for the moderns, any concession to ballet at all was still unforgivable.[7]

Kurt Jooss, fifteen years younger then Wigman, came to America as a choreographer seeking to develop contemporary dance drama in the theater, and he put his energy into his choreographic compositions, relying for impact on his well-trained dance ensemble. Jooss had early distanced himself from the expressionism that Wigman epitomized: "The creative adventures of expressionism lie behind us, also the convulsive cries of early jazz, the primeval tones of expressionist poetry, and the free-in-its-way-barbaric-Ausdruckstanz. We are living in an age which is rediscovering artistic form."[8]

John Martin must be credited for his perceptive insights into the nature of Jooss's special artistic contributions. His article "The Dance Art: of Jooss," in the *New York Times* of November 5, 1933, introduced Jooss "as one of the most vital forces in the development of the contemporary dance. The title "Ballets Jooss," is in itself misleading," he warned, because " his dancing is a development of the modern dance .... and it is distinctly of German origin, stemming directly from Rudolf von Laban.[9]" Martin explained how Jooss's work was similar to American Modern Dance in the thirties in certain ways, but different in others. Like some of the leading American modern choreographers, "Jooss built his ballets entirely from within.... He was deeply aware of the life about him and of the men and women who are living it."[9] Martin saw Jooss as a realist and recognized his intention "to lead Modern Dance out of the recital field and into the theater."[9] Martin was less astute in the evaluation of *The Green Table,* which he described as "eloquent propaganda for intelligent international leadership, but it is also a tender and moving work of art. As is perhaps generally known by now, it deals with the stupidity of a diplomatic conference which results in war."[10]

Kurt Jooss would not have agreed with this last statement. He argued more than once that *The Green Table* was not a political piece. "I am firmly convinced that art should not attempt to change people's opinion, nor do I intend to change behavior."[11] What John Martin's review failed to grasp was that in Jooss's work content and form had found a balance; this relation between meaning and form was of crucial importance in Jooss's view. The diplomats, for instance, were not just caricatures of contemporary parliamentarians, but were used clearly as metaphors, realized in rhythmically composed movement. Jooss paid scrupulous attention to rhythmic articulation and created characterization in this manner. His obsession with clearly articulated movement forms set him apart from passionate exaggerations of German Ausdruckstanz, as well as from the American modern dancers' realism of the thirties. Jooss himself, in regard to The *Green Table,* used to say that "every movement is based on an intense study of the relation of inner movement and muscular movement. Our movements became very eloquent; this is one of the secrets of the work."

The eloquence of Jooss's movements resulted from his intense investigations of movement qualities. He had experimented with Laban's analysis of expressive dynamics for five years in order to train his company to produce dramatic action on stage. Through Laban's Eukinetics (theory and practice of expressive movement), Jooss could precisely define the intended expressive aspect. "Much more than anything else I have done," Jooss reflected in regard to this work, "the choreography of *The Green Table* had been done at a point of achievement in Eukinetics. It is full of interesting and rather clear applications of Eukinetics."[12] Jooss went out of his way to state that he was a pupil of Laban. He liked to say that he stood on Laban's shoulders.

In contrast to Wigman, Jooss left very little original writing. However, he did write an article on "The Language of Dance Theater" in the mid thirties, which revealed the same characteristics in his verbal expression that were seen in his choreographic work: directness, clarity and brevity, as the following excerpts demonstrate:

> In drama therefore if one side of human expression, the language of words, is eliminated, the other side--gesture--must be so elaborated and stylized that it becomes a new, independent and generally intelligible language.... Dance is the art form in which this general language speaks. The Dance?-- yes--but a kind of dance that can meet every demand of the theatre, a kind of dance capable of fully expressing all phases of drama.[13]

With these statements, Jooss acknowledged his respect for and love of theater traditions as well as the need for creating a new language capable of fully expressing twentieth-century life. As the youngest of the German Modern Dance leaders of the twenties, he was the least radical; his synthesis of classical elements with concepts of the new dance simply expanded Laban's ideas. Still, in 1933, Jooss was half a century ahead of his time and therefore created controversy among his contemporaries. In spite of the tremendous audience response, American Modern Dance choreographers were not immediately influenced by Jooss's example. Although American modern dancers admired Jooss's finely tuned ensemble work, at first view his movement language seemed theatrical to them. Ironically, Jooss's work arose from the same spirit of "community of men" they tried to express in their own works, but because Jooss's dancers were trained to articulate their movements, they looked too technically polished to the American modern dancers of the early thirties, and too closely identified with European ballet. In 1933, at the time of Ballets Jooss's American debut, American modern dancers were still largely involved in defining their own style. Wrapped up in their own process of freeing themselves from the bondage of an imported nineteenth-century ballet, they were unable to accept Jooss's idea of synthesizing modern dance with balletic elements. In Suzanne Shelton's words, they unanimously rejected "the aristocratic implications of classical ballet."[14] In tune with the Great Depression, when cultural concerns gradually shifted from self-expression to societal issues, the American modern dancers had come together in working alliances and shared a growing sense of community; they had developed a workman-like attitude. This was typified by Dance Repertory Theatre even though it existed for two seasons only. The themes of the dances presented dealt with social revolt, brotherhood and daily life occurrences. "We are going to dance man and woman in American society," said Charles Weidman in the well-known film *Festival of the Dance*.

There was a pervasive sense of democracy underlying American Modern Dance, and a growing pride of this genuinely American art form. Jooss thus attracted a different audience than Wigman in America. His emphasis on dance theater appealed more to general theatergoers than to the American modern dancers.

After six successful weeks in America, Ballets Jooss departed for London for a 1933 Christmas season there and then went on tour in Western and Eastern Europe, England, and then for a second visit to America. While in England, Jooss, his family, his school and his company lived in Dartington Hall, Devonshire, on the estate of Leonard and Dorothy Elmhirst. From its new homebase, Ballets Jooss gained a unique international reputation and undertook world tours annually between 1935 and 1938, performing in South America and the United States.

The example of Ballets Jooss encouraged further experimentation in England, Holland, and Scandinavia. Ballet in Britain, though young, followed mainly traditional lines. Marie Rambert, however, who had studied and taught at the Dalcroze Institute at Hellerau, presented some experimental works by new choreographers such as Antony Tudor, in the early thirties. Tudor choreographed psychologically motivated ballets for Ballet Rambert that explored in detail, in explicit gestures, relations and situations expressing the inner feelings, but using a movement vocabulary based on the classical syllabus. Dance and drama were no longer separate media. In this respect Tudor and Jooss pursued parallel goals.

Ballets Jooss returned to the United States in 1936 and 1937, and, with each tour, became more familiar to the American audiences. While most American critics commented on the exemplary ensemble spirit of the dancers and on Jooss's gift for satire, Walter Terry in the *Boston Herald*, focused on the controversy between balletomanes and modern dancers. As a critic moving freely between ballet and modern performances, Terry understood Jooss's intentions of combining classical precision with the imagination and aesthetic of a twentieth-century art. So did Agnes de Mille, who had studied with Marie Rambert in London. De Mille left Rambert's Ballet Club in 1937 to create dramatic ballets based on the American heritage. Tudor was intrigued by the individual's societal conflicts. When they became leading choreographers for American Ballet Theatre in 1940, both De Mille and Tudor continued to work with characterization similar to that of Jooss.

Coincidentally, the year the Ballets Jooss performed in the United States, the School of American Ballet was conceived by George Balanchine and Lincoln Kirstein and plans for the Bennington School of the Dance were made. The debut of the first truly American ballet company, Ballet Caravan, owed much to the initiative of Lincoln Kirstein, who, in 1936, assembled a small group of students from the School of American Ballet and formed this company. The group was invited by Martha Hill to perform works choreographed by Eugene Loring and Lew Christensen at Bennington College in 1936 and 1937. This was the first rapprochement between the classical and the modern camp in American Dance. These young choreographers wanted to create a freer, more realistic form of ballet, colored by the American spirit that captured American dancing in both ballet and modern forms. As the center of Modern Dance, the School of the Dance at Bennington gave them their first chance to be seen.

THE BENNINGTON SCHOOL OF THE DANCE

The next logical step in providing exposure for the New Dance was initiated by Mary Jo Shelly, who was on the faculty of Teachers College, Columbia University, from 1929 to 1932, and Martha Hill, a member of Martha Graham's first group and concurrently dance instructor at New York University and at Bennington College. The two came up with the idea of a center for studying Modern Dance in an intensive summer school program at Bennington College. Robert Leigh, the first president of Bennington College, recognized the value of this program for reaching a new population, thereby broadening the college's prestige during a financially depressed period. Thus, he lent his strong support.

The summer school opened its doors in 1934. Martha Hill invited Hanya Holm, Martha Graham, Doris Humphrey and Charles Weidman as the unquestioned leaders of the American Modern Dance, to serve on the faculty. Though Holm was the only one who did not have a company, Hill recognized her methodical mind and the contribution she could make toward the goal of bringing American Modern Dance out of the studio and into America's colleges and universities. She also knew that Holm would act as a neutralizing force between the two rivals Graham and Humphrey, both strong personalities. It speaks highly for Martha Hill's generous perspective that she made a place for a foreign contribution. Suzanne Shelton later summarized Hanya Holm's impact:

> The German influence of Mary Wigman through Hanya Holm was central to the formation of American Modern Dance. The German School emphasized a stripped-down modernist aesthetic, a percussive thrust, and a burning expressionism that sharpened American edges and helped to propel its dance on a modernist course.[15]

Hanya Holm joined the project wholeheartedly and thus completed the second phase of her mission, to make Wigman's approach available to physical educators and a much more diverse circle of people than she usually reached in her New York studio. Like her American colleagues, she started to create exercise sequences appropriate to the needs of American teachers of physical education. Since the American educators were not at all accustomed to improvisation, Holm did not stress Wigman's focus on the creative process in dance education and on individual development during the summers at Bennington. But when Hanya later introduced Wigman's approach into American physical education departments and universities, educators learned to value improvisation as an essential tool of the creative process. The influence of Wigman's concepts reached a whole generation of dancers and educators through Holm's methodical teaching.

In 1936, Holm had gained Wigman's approval for changing the name of the New York School to Hanya Holm School of Dance; it was politically the right thing to do, and Wigman agreed. Simultaneously Holm established her own dance group which she had carefully built through her lecture-demonstrations, and took them on transcontinental tours. (With a good sense of humor, Kloepper described to me some of the groups's less glamorous experiences. For instance, in Nebraska, in order to get to the stage, the dancers had to go outside, cross over through the snow and come down via a fire escape.) Holm's lecture-demonstrations helped to set standards for dance in colleges and schools. John Dewey, the famous educator, was very impressed by the clear structure and educational value of Holm's work, which attracted teachers from all over the country to her school in New York and also to the Bennington School of the Dance. There, these pedagogic notions became integrated into the texture of the American Modern Dance, not as a separate vocabulary of dance movement, but as a structural way of thinking about movement. Holm avoided expressionistic exaggerations, and her more rational approach changed the color of Wigman's Ausdruckstanz, blending it with the American Modern Dance of this period. This approach to teaching dance was summed up in the official announcement of the Bennington College Bulletin:

> The Bennington School presents contrasting approaches to technique and composition and, by giving a large place to the related aspects of the dance, such as music, undertakes an integrated analysis of the whole structure of the art. Under this plan, the student of the dance has access to the experiences necessary to the formation of a well-rounded point of view.[16]

The Bennington program pursued two aims: the first was instruction in modern dance, teaching materials, methods of learning, and practice. This focus dominated the first trial year under the guidance of the permanent instructors of Bennington College. The visiting artists, in addition, gave exposure to their particular movement language; Louis Horst taught dance composition through pre-classic dance forms, and John Martin introduced a contemporary perspective into his course of history and critical theory of Modern Dance. The second goal was performance, which was added in 1935 with the creation of the Bennington Festival, to show dance compositions produced by one or several of the major guest artists. The school became a laboratory for choreographers, musicians, composers, scenic designers, and dancers. Each visiting artist had his own company in residence to prepare a major work within six weeks, augmenting his group with Bennington students when appropriate. This opportunity to produce a large-scale composition, with student dancers and production help provided, was unique in times of political, social and cultural turmoil.

The Bennington Summer Festivals, initiated in 1935, served, in Marcia Siegel's words, "as a center for the development of American Dance ideas. A strong patriotism prevailed there in the years before the war."[17] In the first year of the festival, Doris Humphrey daringly choreographed the large-scale group work *New Dance*. This forty-five minute piece, performed by an even number of male and female dancers, conveyed in abstract symphonic form her vision of the ideal relation of man to man. John Martin referred to *New Dance* as the first work by an American choreographer to make the transition from dance as a recital art to dance as a theater art. "There are few works in the history of the dance that mark so definitely the beginning of a new era. Henceforth the recital form, consisting of a succession of unrelated little compositions without theatre dimensions, was cast aside, and composers turned their attention to large forms dramatizing the conflict between the individual and his universe.... The dance had become a theatre form."[18]

Also in the festival's first year, Martha Graham created her first full length work, *Panorama*, with thirty-six dancers. Norman Lloyd composed the music, Arch Lauterer designed a multi-level stage, and Alexander Calder contributed mobiles. It was Graham's first experience working with so many collaborators and dancers, and it changed her relationship to the theater; she started to enjoy the additional possibilities of production.

In 1936, Humphrey, continuing in the direction of dance drama, performed as the powerful matriarch confronting her dance ensemble of forty-five in *With My Red Fires,* and at the Bennington Summer Festival in 1937, Holm, now acclaimed as a great teacher, presented her first major work, the eagerly anticipated *Trend*: A Dance in Two Sections, choreographed for thirty-three female dancers. Holm surpassed the expectations of the American dance community with this piece. The complex theme focussed on the process of man's survival. Holm proved to be an excellent craftsman, particularly in her articulation of group movements. Louise Kloepper, her first soloist and most authentic interpreter of her choreography, recalled: "It was very satisfying to dance under Hanya; actually she was more skillful with large groups first, but she became a very versed choreographer with *Trend*.[19] She worked out the main movement themes with great clarity and structured them architectonically. She was not only a fine choreographer, but her imagination worked simultaneously with the element of theater, music, stage design and lighting to produce a unified statement through movement." Holm herself remarked: "The theme issued from life itself, rather than being built up as an intellectual construction."[20]

Holm's objective, distanced description of her own creative process cannot be explained by her association with Wigman. Already in Dresden she had shown this cooler and more abstract approach to dance. The way she applied concepts of design in music and visual arts to the teaching of choreography revealed her debt to Dalcroze's training, and her early exposure to Appia's functional stage was perhaps just as formative as her kinetic experiences with Wigman. The attraction of Holm's composition was ultimately largely based on her abstract, methodical and visually-oriented composition. John Martin praised *Trend* because it had:

> all the dynamic quality that is characteristic of the American dance, but it
> retained, also, the more subjective qualities of the German dance--its sense
> of space, its fluency, its unbroken relationship of movement to emotion,
> and at least its attitude to music, if not a full realization of it in practice.
> All these elements....brought the dance to a new realization of its theater
> possibilities.[21]

Holm worked very carefully on the different aspects of the multi-layered production. A light plan by Arch Lauterer and his settings showed three dimensional spacial effects; for the first time Modern Dance could be viewed on a stage especially designed for dynamic group movement flow. The essential purpose of design for the dance, said Lauterer, was "to show movement."[22] Different musical scores were combined, and a forty minute original score was written by Wallingford Rieger; a recording of *Ionisation* (1931) by Edgar Varese required special playback equipment, and for the New York production, Holm added a final movement, with Varese's *Octandre*. After its New York premiere, John Martin concluded: "Miss Holm brings to the business of composing a point of view totally different from that of any other major choreographers, and opened up a new vista for the production of great dance dramas."[23] In retrospect it appears that Holm was closer in spirit to Jooss than to her American colleagues; both thought in European terms creating dance works for the theater. They proved that dance can be innovative while using all the production tools of the twentieth -century theater.

The fifth session of the Bennington School of the Dance culminated in a week-long festival showing all four leading artists with their concert groups. Humphrey presented her most significant work, *Passacaglia in C Minor,* to music of Bach. The 1938 Bennington Dance Festival closed appropriately with *American Document,* Martha Graham's amplification of the theme of *Panorama.* A highly experimental work, this piece found Graham using a male dancer, Eric Hawkins, for the first time. Hawkins trained at the School of American Ballet, and was one of the choreographers and dancers from Ballet Caravan. In *American Document* he partnered Graham. To contrast the male dancer, Graham articulated spinal movement as a fresh element of her dance language. Ray Green, the composer, adapted his musical score to the demands of spoken words used in this work.

In retrospect, the Bennington Summer Festivals had accomplished even more than Martha Hill and Mary Joe Shelly had consciously planned, and German dancers had played an important part in this development. Thanks to the Bennington Dance Festivals, in the years from 1934 to 1938, American Modern Dance progressed from dance as a recital art to dance as a theater art. Simultaneously American audiences became more sophisticated and demanding, and a gradual rapprochement between modern and classical dance opened a wider, newly gained perspective.

The photographer Barbara Morgan superbly captured the spirit of the American dance artists of this period in images that documented their artistry. As official photographer for the Bennington Dance Festival during the summers of 1936 to 1938, Morgan, who considered her work at Bennington "exploratory and experimental, like that of the dancers," (as she mentioned in the introduction to her book *Martha Graham, Sixteen Dances in Photographs),*[24] took more than one hundred photos of rehearsals. She achieved her authentic images by lengthy manipulations of lights in the set-up of her studio. For two weeks she familiarized herself with the moments of the dance that she wanted to condense in her photographic image. Morgan sympathized with the leaders of the Modern Dance movement in their struggle for acceptance, because photography, commonly seen as documentation of news items, was not considered a form of art. Morgan, who had been a painter for more than a decade before turning to photography as a more appropriate medium for expressing her socio-cultural concerns, recognized that Modern Dance, more than any other art form, needed documentation that captured its artistry. In an article entitled "Dance Photography" she wrote about her own process: "I demand from myself a combination of expressive emotional projection and a good abstract design.."[25]

The earliest work in Morgan's series of famous dance photographs of Martha Graham is *Lamentation,* choreographed in 1930. This uncompromising dance destroyed the conventional idea of a dancer. Morgan's photographic image added light to the movement dramatizing the background and creating a dramatic dynamic of space and a superhuman dimension.

Satyric Festival (1935) emphasized the freedom of motion that Graham had gained in the Bennington years, captured by Morgan in Graham's free-flowing hair.*Every Soul is a Circus* showed Graham framed by her flying costume, exemplifying Morgan's manipulations to catch Graham in the air. Examples of her composed photographic images include: the drama of Charles Weidman in *Lynchtown*, and particularly, the superimposed images of "Rehearsal Nightmare", showing a tense and frustrated Humphrey with her group. Louise Kloepper, who was particularly noticed in reviews for her powerful solo in "Statement of Dissent," is caught in an ecstatic gesture. Morgan's lighting was particularly sensitive in portraying Jose Limon's colorful and forceful personality.

Barbara Morgan's photographic images of the dancers at the Bennington Dance Festivals had a powerful impact on the tradition of the American Modern Dance; her images are still strong today and speak with directness and force of the generation who believed in modernism and shaped the American Modern Dance. More than mere documentation, these widely viewed photographs contributed to a change in attitude, helping American Modern Dance gain acceptance as an art form. What is more, within these pictures is captured the spirit of the age. As Morgan explained, "Two fundamental things are always a source of wonder and delight to the photographer: the dancer's imagination and the latent powers of light by which beauty and meaning can be expressed.... Light has a real parallel with dance, being itself a dance of frequencies."[26]

Thanks to the Bennington Festivals, by 1938, Hanya Holm was an accepted member of the American Modern Dance scene and a respected choreographer and teacher. By the end of this decade, American Modern Dance itself had discovered the tools of theatrical production, and the Spartan look of early American Modern Dance had changed gradually to a smoother, less rebellious art form. With growing sophistication, the Modern Dance gradually shifted audience awareness to the choreographer. By the late thirties, Kurt Jooss was recognized in the dance world of the United States and Europe as both a dramatist and a great craftsman of choreography. He was not a German Ausdruckstänzer or a British ballet master, yet his internationally known Ballets Jooss had encouraged younger classically and modern dance trained choreographers to find their contemporary language of Dance Theater. Hanya Holm and Kurt Jooss, each in his and her own way, combined a flair for experimentation with a solid knowledge of European theater; they exemplified the usefulness of Laban's concepts in the United States. Their example encouraged the younger generation of choreographers such as Alwin Nicolais and Glen Tetley to a freer use of their craft.

THE DILEMMA OF THE GERMAN DANCERS.

While American modern dancers experienced a period of unrivalled growth during the thirties that raised the expectations of American audiences, the development of Germany's dance stagnated because of stifling regulations imposed by the Nazi regime. In 1935, the first indication of this change was apparent to John Martin's critical eyes, when Harald Kreutzberg returned to the U.S. after an interval of two years. "The dance was developing at a phenomenal speed in America," as Martin noticed in the *New York Times* of March 22,1935, and Kreutzberg's seven or eight year old dances seemed "thin and trivial." Martin missed "a participation in emotional experience which one is entitled to expect from a first class artist." Kreutzberg had not lost his technical proficiency; it was only that, in the nineteen-thirties, while American dancers enjoyed the freedom to develop, some of the German dancers, in order to continue to perform, had adjusted to the restrictions of fascist ideology. Art had to be accessible to the masses. Thus, they had modified their art in order to be accepted as entertainers.

It took Adolf Hitler and his Nazi regime two years to implement their ideology. Hitler pursued his aims very systematically. His first moves were to eliminate the Social Democratic party, the Catholic Center party, and the existing German Nationalist party. By September 15th, 1935, the Nürnberg Laws denied German citizenship to people of Jewish blood, and marriages between Jewish and Aryan people were prohibited. Since currency regulations impeded immigration, many Jewish people delayed leaving until it was too late. New, stringent regulations began a policy of terror embodied in an organization called the Gestapo (the Secret State Police), which had its headquarters in Berlin and reigned over all of Germany. Hitler's "final solution" of his anti-Semitic policy was the total annihilation of Jews in Germany in order to breed a pure, superior, German race." This goal colored the tactics of cultural politics. The burning of unapproved books in 1933 gave an early indication of Hitler's barbaric methods. The Ministry of Education made sure that Nazi ideology infiltrated teaching in public schools and universities. Press and publishing houses were controlled by the Ministry of Propaganda, which also was in charge of giving direction to the visual arts. The "Reichtheaterkammer" (Ministry of Theater), established in May 1934, governed the theater; it had a special dance division, called "Fachschaft Tanz." Radio, the press, the visual arts and the theater were strictly controlled, whereas opera, music and dance seemed to be treated less rigidly, perhaps because Adolph Hitler loved opera, particularly Wagnerian operas.

When Hitler assumed power in Germany, the director of movement and dance at the State Opera Berlin, Rudolf Laban, also the choreographer of the Bayreuth Festival *Tannhäuser Bacchanal*, was in a highly influential position. Laban recalled later in his memoirs, *A Life for Dance,* his fine collaboration with the director Sigfried Wagner, the son of Richard Wagner: "I was cured of my excessive rejection of representational scene theater by the magnificence offered there." Laban saw in Richard Wagner a "decisive influence on the art of movement."[27]

Hitler personally considered himself an artist; he had studied painting in his youth. Therefore he was particularly keen to change the arts in Germany. He believed that art should give an exact image of reality and therefore condemned expressionism as "degenerate art." Instead he propagated "German Art," as documented in the first German Art Exhibition, in Munich, in July 1937. The subject matter of German Art was to show the German worker attached to "Blood and Soil", one of Hitler's favored standard phrases; the German woman should reflect the spirit of "Faith and Beauty", or should be seen as mother of at least four children. The architecture of the Third Reich embodied most clearly the aesthetic ambitions of Hitler to recreate Roman monumental buildings. Vast halls were built with no other true function than to eternalize the spirit of Hitler's

Third Reich.

Laban apparently enjoyed his position of power and recognition as director of ballet and movement at the State Opera Berlin, which he held until July 1934. Hitler even attended the farewell matinee given in Laban's honor. His contract, however, was not renewed, since Laban did not have German citizenship. Nevertheless, Laban had hopes that his life's dream, to bring dance into a position of high esteem in society, might find realization under the new regime, particularly since he was offered the directorship of the "Neue Tanzbühne," a dance association of the twenties which was to reappear as a creation of the Ministry of Propaganda. Laban accepted; he had taken so many chances in his unstable life. Perhaps he thought that he could use the aspirations of the Nazis not only to revitalize dance in the theater, but, according to official Nazi guidelines, to show dance as an expression of "healthy folk energies." As Laban gradually discovered, the Nazis intended to use Laban's movement choir concept as a tool to strengthen body awareness and simultaneously to develop the feeling of racial superiority. Laban's original movement choirs, such as his large pageant signifying many-sided craftsmen's guilds, referred to medieval times and expressed a communal experience within a cultural context, in an atmosphere of brotherhood. The Nazis very consciously strove for an expression of the race in mass celebrations in which community was defined in purely biological terms.

In Laban's zeal to maintain his leading role in Modern Dance in Germany by establishing amateur dancing as part of theater in the Neue Tanzbühne, he failed to notice the ideological goals of the regime. He met with severe competition from Dr. Rudolf Bode, a leader in body culture (Körperkultur) and gymnastics, and a member of the party since 1922. Bode's work truly illustrated the slogan "Truth and Beauty"; he created movement sequences which were taught in all the public schools in Berlin to thousands of blond Aryan teenage girls. Laban, however, held his ground, organizing summer meetings for his amateur groups at Rangsdorf, a summer camp 20 miles outside of Berlin. In contrast to Bode's work, which exclusively addressed young girls, Laban's amateur dancers in his movement choir were predominantly males.

The first performance of the German Dance Festival, organized by Laban in November 1934, showed his dilemma quite clearly. Some fascist reviewers complained that the "dominant direction" of the dancers still demonstrated an "overemphasized individualism reminiscent of expressionism." One year later, in 1935, the week-long German Dance Festival drew complimentary reviews from German reviewers, who now acclaimed Laban for inclusion of his movement choirs into the festival and praised their lively, spirited performance. The program progressed to showings of Palucca, Kreutzberg, the Günther School of Munich, and the Mary Wigman Group in the performance of *Tanz Gesänge* (*Dance Songs*), a group work which showed how far Mary Wigman had also been willing to bend to the demands of the new regime. A commentary on this event by Virginia Stewart appeared in Louis Horst's *Dance Observer* in October 1935. It charged that Laban, as leader of the "Neue Tanzbühne," was subordinate to Dr. Goebbel's Reichstheaterkammer and that all German dancers followed Laban's lead. The next issue of *Dance Observer*, besides printing an article by Hanya Holm on Wigman's life, also published a letter of concern regarding Wigman's participation in this event, which was "under the direct control of Dr. Goebbels."[28] Indeed, all public performances in Germany were controlled by the Reichstheaterkammer, and Wigman's participation in the Annual German Dance Festival in 1935 was not more politically disturbing than any other dancer's public performance. As Wigman said of the first dance, "Lobgesang" (Song of Praise), "No more I and you, only we all."[29]

In the 1930s Wigman adjusted her work to fit the demands for simplicity, "Germanness," and "true womanhood," thereby proving herself just as "German" as Dr. Bode with his displays of body culture. Her choreography, widely successful, helped to support her group financially. Wigman was mostly concerned about keeping her group; she wanted to ignore the ideological implications of her work, because it was important to her to represent German Modern Dance even at this price. Similarly, Wigman compromised herself in some of the statements she made in her first book, *Deutsche Tanzkunst*, written in 1935. Wigman used language which revealed her early entanglement with National Socialist ideology, as, for example, in her introduction, when she referred to "the call of the blood." She also discussed in length "the question of true Germanness in regard to the arts."[30]

These words offended politically active American modern dancers in New York, and the anti-German feelings intensified particularly when, in March 1936, Hitler occupied the Rhineland, an action which clearly violated the Treaty of Versailles. In July of the same year, the Spanish Civil War broke out, and France and Russia became involved helping to strengthen the republican side, while the Spanish military received aeroplanes from Italy and Germany. Men from all over the globe volunteered to fight for the Spanish Republic against the fascism of Hitler and Mussolini.

Meanwhile, the Nazis prepared for the Olympic Games of 1936 in Berlin hoping to draw international attention to Hitler's accomplishments. Laban, a master at arranging mass scenes in choral dancing, was commissioned to direct the triumphal celebration of German Dance at the Dietrich Eckart Freilichtbühne (Outdoor Theater) and to organize a great International Dance Competition in July 1936. Martha Graham and company were invited, but Graham declined the invitation, as she mentioned in her autobiography *Blood Memory*.[31] Laban planned a gigantic event, *Vom Tauwind und der Neuen Freude* (*Spring Wind and the New Joy*), with a thousand dancers divided into twenty-two movement choirs, all trained by him. The music, composed by Hans-Klaus Langer, was played by the Berlin Radio Orchestra and Choir. The play was based on words of Nietzsche's *Zarathustra*, divided into four sections: Fight, Contemplation, Joy, and Initiation. The program explained that the dances did not illustrate the words of the poet, but were inspired by the atmosphere the words created. On June 20th the final dress rehearsal of this work took place before an invited audience at the Dietrich Eckart Theater. Goebbels attended and wrote the following remark in his diary:

> Rehearsal of dance work: freely based on Nietzsche, a bad, contrived and affected piece. I disliked it intensely. It is also intellectual. I do not like it. That is because it is dressed up in our clothes and has nothing whatever to do with us.[32]

The greatest evil according to Nazi ideology, was to be intellectual. Goebbels saw through Laban's intentions to use the Nazis for his own goals, and he reacted with outrage, prohibiting the performance of Laban's piece. Consequently, only a few programs are left from this huge project. Lola Rogge's *Amazones*, seen as more in tune with the spirit of the Third Reich, replaced Laban's *Spring Wind* and the New Joy.

The opening night of the 1936 Olympiad in Berlin featured a festive play, *Olympic Youth*, produced by Niedecken-Gebhard, an old friend of Mary Wigman, and performed in the Olympic Stadium. The event was thoroughly prepared by the organizer of the 1936 Olympic Games, Dr. Carl Diem. Dorothea Günther collaborated with the composer Carl Orff, who specially mixed natural sounds of recorders, viols, guitars with percussion instruments, xylophones and glockenspiels, and sent a magic sound over the huge stadium. I still recall the sound of a glass bell, struck closely to the microphone, opening the first event, *Child's Play*, in which 2500 girls and 900 boys between eleven and twelve years of age performed. The second part presented 2300 blond, club-swinging girls between fourteen and sixteen, under the title *Grace of Youth*, moving to Schubert's Moments Musicales. The intermezzo that followed featured a waltz choreographed by Gret Palucca, framed by the girls' circle. The fourth part offered as contrast a weapon dance, choreographed by Kreutzberg, with sixty male dancers. *Lament for the Dead* was choreographed by Mary Wigman and danced by her in the center of the stadium, surrounded by an additional eighty female dancers. This piece led into Beethoven's *Ninth Symphony* and the *Olympic Hymns*. With bells ringing and fires lit, light projectors in accordance with Nazi aesthetic and ideology created the effect of a dome-like structure arching the Olympic Stadium. This grandiose spectacle was supposed to give the international visitors an example of the Nazi's mass celebrations as a new form of twentieth-century ritual.

Wigman and Laban, old rivals, were the two leaders of German Modern Dance who tried to work under the National Socialist regime, determined to save the German Modern Dance they had created. Wigman still wanted to show that she represented serious Modern Dance in Germany and resented the fact that Laban and not herself had been chosen as administrator of the German Masterstudios in Spring 1936.[33] While these old rivalries endured, ominous political developments threatened to overtake both Wigman and Laban.

Following the fatal dress rehearsal Laban was thoroughly investigated and became a political case overnight. The Nazis found that he was once a member of the Freemasons with the rank of master, and he was taken into custody and held under house arrest in the Schloss Bantz cloister. Laban eventually escaped and made his way to Paris in November 1937.[34] It was Kurt Jooss who found him there, in very poor health. He arranged for Laban to follow him to Dartington Hall, England, where he gradually recovered both mentally and physically.

Despite her feud with Laban, Wigman was deeply shocked by his disappearance and personal ordeal. The realization that her early teacher and mentor had fallen into disgrace forced her to confront political reality. Disillusioned by the Nazis, Wigman, in her fiftieth year, was now alone in her fight for the German Dance. The Nazis had been more interested in ballet from the beginning, but since she had an international reputation, they presented her at the Olympic Games once more as Germany's greatest dancer. As soon as the Olympic Games were over, however, Wigman recognized that the Nazis no longer had any use for her. This fact became apparent when they asked her to contribute a dance in honor of Hitler for the Day of German Art; Wigman hesitated to accept since she knew that she would have to compromise her art even further. Her delaying tactics made it obvious that she was not interested in cooperating, and the Nazis' reaction was prompt: the support for her school was terminated. Once considered Germany's first dancer, she was now placed in the category of the "unwanted." From then on, her dance was labeled "degenerate art," like the work of her artist friends Nolde, Heckel and Kandinsky. She was told to keep her artistic production on a small scale. The temporary excitement created by the international event of the Olympic Games in Berlin gave way to a growing sense of cultural isolation very difficult for Mary Wigman. By 1936 many of Wigman's Jewish friends had quietly left Germany; to those who remained, she appeared too successful under the new regime. Internal political struggles with her closest collaborators poisoned the atmosphere in her school in Dresden. She escaped into her work and created *Herbstliche Tänze (Autumnal Dances)*, restoring herself as an artist. The cycle *Autumnal Dances* did not betray any of the problems she was experiencing. Still, Wigman's fall out of favor with the regime, while less abrupt than that of Laban, was no less devastating. In the eyes of the Nazis, she was now seen as an expressionist and intellectual and was treated accordingly. Wigman finally ignored Nazi ideologies, and danced as the American audiences still remembered her. In *Autumnal Dances* she returned to some of the best of her works. Unfortunately, American audiences experienced *Autumnal Dances* only on film and never saw her *Niobe*, a dance about the mother who, because of her pride, was punished by the gods with the loss of her children. This dance was Wigman's response to the humiliations she suffered when she finally confronted the political reality under the Nazi regime. Ironically, in summer 1939, a proposal for another American tour of solo dances reached Wigman and temporarily raised her hopes again; but the proposal did not materialize because of the outbreak of World War II. Her diary of September 4,1939 reads: "The unthinkable has become reality; we have war."[35]

NOTES FOR CHAPTER IV

1. Shurr, Gertrude (1990) Interview, by I. Bergsohn Tucson, May 27

2. Sorell, Walter (1986) *Looking Back in Wonder*, p. 28. New York: Columbia University Press

3. Kloepper, Louise (1990) Interview, by I Bergsohn, Madison, March 18

4. Sorell, Walter (1986) *Looking Back in Wonder,* p. 29.

5. Markard, Anna & Hermann (1985) *Jooss*, p. 53. Köln: Ballett Bühnen Verlag

6. Jooss Ballet to Make Debut at Forrest Theatre, (1933) *New York Herald Tribune*, Oct 29

7. King, Eleanor (1978) *Transformations*, p. 120. Brooklyn: Dance Horizons

8. Markard, Anna & Herman (1985) *Jooss*, p. 15,

9. Martin, John (1933) The Dance: Art of Jooss. *New York Times*, November 5

10. Ibid.

11. Jooss, Kurt (1976) Audio tapes from Choreographic Workshop UC Santa Barbara, September 14

12. Ibid. All quotes from Jooss on p. 139,140 taken from the same audio tape.

13. Jooss, Kurt (1935) The Language of Dance Theater. *Ballett 1986,* Edited by Regitz Hartmut, P.17 Translated by Anna Markard

14. Shelton, Suzanne (1984) *American Dance Festival Brochure*. Duke University, Durham, N.C.

15. Ibid.

16. Kriegsman, Sali Ann (1981) *Modern Dance in America: The Bennington Years*,p. 11. Boston: G. K. Hall

17. Siegel, Marcia (1979) *The Shapes of Change*, p. 22. Boston: Houghton Mifflin Co.

18.   Martin, John (1940) Dance Since Isadora. *Theatre Arts*, 24 , 645

19.   Kloepper, Louise (1991) Interview, by I. Bergsohn, Madison, March 18

20.   Kriegsman, Sali Ann (1981)

21.   Martin, John (1965) *Introduction to the Dance*, pp. 267-268. Brooklyn: Dance Horizons

22.   Lauterer, Arch (1937) Design for Dance. *Magazine of the Art*, **3**, 137

23.   Martin, John (1937) New York Debut for Hanya Holm. *New York Times*, Dec. 29

24.   Morgan, Barbara (1941) *Martha Graham, Sixteen Dances in Photographs*. New York: Duell, Sloan and Pearce

25.   Morgan, Barbara (1942) Dance Photography. *The Complete Photographer*, March 10

26.   Morgan, Barbara (1941) *Martha Graham, Sixteen Dances in Photographs*, p.150. New York: Duell, Sloan and Pearce

27.   Laban, Rudolph (1975) *A Life for Dance*, p. 173. London: MacDonald & Evans

28.   Sorell, Walter (1986) *Mary Wigman: Ein Vermächtnis*, p. 182-183,Wilhelmshaven: Florian Noetzel Verlag

29.   Müller, Hedwig (1986) *Mary Wigman*, p. 236. Berlin: Quadriga Verlag

30.   Sorell, Walter (1986) p. 184

31.   Graham, Martha (1991) *Blood Memory*, p. 151. New York: Doubleday

32.   Preston-Dunlop, Valerie (1988). Laban and the Nazis. London: *Dance Theatre Journal*, 6, 2, 4-7

33. The German Masterstudios established under Goebbels were the partial realization of attempts to create a German Dance Academy, under discussion since the Dancers' Congress in Essen in 1928

34. Preston-Dunlop, Valerie (1988) 6,2, 4-7

35. Müller, Hedwig (1986) *Mary Wigman*, p. 252. Berlin: Quadriga

Figure 1. Pastel drawing of Isadora Duncan by Gordon Craig, ca. 1904. (Courtesy George Chaffee Collection).

Figure 2. Scene from Impressions of Modern Russia, "Labor". Choreography Isadora Duncan. Performed by the Isadora Duncan Studio, touring the United States between December 1928 and January 1930. Dance Collection, The New York Public Library for the Performing Arts.

Figure 3. Mary Wigman, Abenliche Tänze (Three Elegies) Dresden, 1924.
Photograph: Ursula Richter, The Mary Wigman Archiv, Akademie de Künste, Berlin.

TUESDAY MATINEE, DECEMBER 30, AT 3:30
(AUSPICES OF THE WALDEN SCHOOL)

S. HUROK

PRESENTS

MARY WIGMAN

PROGRAM

AUS DEM TANZCYKLUS "SCHWINGENDE LANDSCHAFT"
(From the Dance Cycle, "Shifting Landscape")

1. Anruf (Invocation)
2. Gesicht der Nacht (Face of the Night)
3. Pastorale (Pastorale)
4. Festlicher Rhythmus (Festive Rhythm)
5. Sommerlicher Tanz (Summer's Dance)
6. Sturmlied (Storm Song)

INTERMISSION—FIFTEEN MINUTES

AUS DEN "VISIONEN"
(From "Visions")

7. Hexentanz (Witch Dance)

AUS DER "FEIER"
(From "Celebration")

8. Monotonie (Drehtanz), (Monotony Whirl Dance)

INTERMISSION—FIVE MINUTES

AUS DEM TANZCYKLUS "SCHWINGENDE LANDSCHAFT"
(From the Dance Cycle, "Shifting Landscape")

9. {Zigeunerweisen (2 Tanzlieder)
  {(Gypsy Moods—Two Dance Songs)

Piano and Primitive Instruments . . . HANNS HASTING and META MENZ

Costumes by Elis Griebel, Dresden

Baldwin Piano Used.

BEAUTIFUL AND INFORMATIVE SOUVENIR BOOKLETS OF
MARY WIGMAN MAY BE PURCHASED IN THEATRE LOBBY.
ENVELOPES FOR MAILING BOOKLETS SUPPLIED

MARY WIGMAN-SCHULE, ZENTRALINSTITUT, DRESDEN
Artistic Direction, Mary Wigman
Paedagogical Direction, Elisabeth Wigman, Hanya Holm
Professional Classes for Stage Dancing and Dancing Teachers
Dresden — N6, Bautzner Strasse 107, Germany.

MISS WIGMAN'S

Coming New York Appearances:

CHANIN THEATRE, FRIDAY (MATINEE), JAN. 2nd, AT 3:00.
CHANIN THEATRE, SUNDAY (EVENING), JAN. 4th, AT 8:45.
JOLSON'S THEATRE, SUNDAY (EVENING), JAN. 11th, AT 8:45.
Seats for All Above Performances Now, at Box Offices

ISA KREMER

Celebrated Singer of Ballads and Folk-songs.
First New York Recital in Three Years, Following a
Triumphant Tour of Europe.
CHANIN THEATRE, SUNDAY (EVENING), FEB. 1st, AT 8:45.
Prices $1 to $3. Now on Sale at the Box Office.

ANTON DOUNIS

"The Kreisler of the Mandolin"
BIJOU THEATRE (West 45th St.), SUNDAY (EVENING), JAN. 25th, AT 8:45.
Seats $1 to $3. Now on Sale at Box Office.

EXCLUSIVE MANAGEMENT, HUROK MUSICAL BUREAU, INC.,

No. 1560 BROADWAY, NEW YORK

Figure 4. Program of the First Concert of Mary Wigman at Decmber 30th, 1930 at the
Chanin Theatre, New York City. Courtesy of Martha Hill.

Figure 5. Mary Wigman. (From her Dance Cycle Visions 1928).
Photograph: Carlotte Rudolph, The Mary Wigman Archiv, Akademie de Künste, Berlin.

Figure 6. Kaschemme (Tavern), choreography of Kurt Jooss, Municipal Theater
Münster, in 1926. Photo courtesy of Anna Markard.

Figure 7. Martha Graham, Désir. Performed at the Klaw Theatre, New York City, November 1926. Photographed by Soichi Sunami.

Figure 8. Martha Graham, Ekstasis. Performed at the Guild Theater, New York City, 1933. Photograph by Soichi Sunami.

Figure 9. Martha Hill, Dance study. School of the Dance at Bennington, 1934. Courtesy Martha Hill.

Figure 10. L-R Rosalia Chladek (Austria), Hans Züllig (rear, Swiss), Harald Kreutzberg & Kurt Jooss (German) at the International Summer School at Magglingen, Switzerland 1950. Photo courtesy of Jooss-Archiv.

Figure 11. Le Sacre du Printemps, choreography by Mary Wigman, premiered in the West German Opera House for Berlin Festival 1957. L-R Majid Kashef and Dore Hoyer. Photograph: Siegfried.

Figure 12. Hanya Holm in rehearsal with Labanotation score for the revival of Kiss Me, Kate, 1965. Photograph: Hal Bergsohn.

Figure 13. Kurt Jooss checking the Labanotation score in rehearsal, Essen 1952. Photograph: Robert D'Hooghe.

Figure 14. Patricio Bunster and Alfonso Unanue in Weg im Nebel (Journey in the Fog), choreography by Kurt Jooss, premiered in 1952 in Essen Opera House. Photograph: Robert D'Hooghe.

Figure 15. L-R Robert Joffrey with Kurt Jooss. Rehearsal for the Joffrey's Ballet performance of the Green Table in New York City, March 1967. Photograph Hal Bergsohn.

Figure 16. Pina Bausch in Choreographic Study, Folkwang Schule Essen, 1959. Photograph: Hal Bergsohn.

CHAPTER V: DANCE IN THE SHADOW OF WORLD WAR II.

In the middle of the nineteen-thirties the Spanish Civil War, a struggle that involved not only Europeans but also some American volunteers who fought in Spain, had helped raise international awareness of the impending threat of fascism. Still, even after Hitler annexed Czechoslovakia in the Spring of 1939 and then marched his troops into Poland on September 3, launching the Second World War, hostilities appeared to be limited to Europe. Although the reality of the war was brought home to European families in letters from the army announcing the death of their brothers and sons, for Americans, the war raged on a distant continent. Their cultural life proceeded relatively undisturbed, at least until America, too, was dragged into battle.

THE RESPONSE OF AMERICAN CHOREOGRAPHERS TO THE SPANISH WAR

While Europe was bowed under by fascist dictatorships and war, dance flourished in America. Wigman's influence, suppressed in Germany, continued through Holm and Holm-trained dancers, although significant changes occurred in style, movement quality and themes. The European conflict inspired American dancers of the Bennington generation to articulate their response to political turmoil in choreographic works, thereby challenging their artistic scope and achieving a new dramatic depth. Meanwhile, in Europe the ideological restrictions of fascism reduced the choice of approved themes to a very superficial level and gradually paralyzed what still existed of the German Modern Dance.

At the Bennington Dance Festival in the summer of 1937, Martha Graham, reacting to the outbreak of the Spanish Civil War, created *Immediate Tragedy--Dance of Dedication*, a solo that celebrated the fearless spirit of Spanish women. Henry Cowell's music, consisting of two basic phrases similar to a saraband, played by oboe and clarinet, blended beautifully with Graham's sparse and somber dance, which did not refer to any particular event, but presented her response to the events in Spain in a strongly emotional, abstract, universal statement.

In the same year, the Bennington Dance Festival also focussed on the Spanish Civil War with José Limón's *Danza de la Morte (Dance of Death)*, a suite of dances that opened with a group ritual honoring the dead. On the same program, Anna Sokolow, a young choreographer, who together with Limón and Esther Junger had received Festival Fellowships, showed a satiric comment on the theme of Mussolini; *Facade-Esposizione Italiana* was "something I had thought about a lot but never had a chance to do." Sokolow explained:

> In that period I was finding my way to express what I felt about life. And what I felt about life had a very deep relation to the social times. It came out of the fact that I was born with a feeling that I would never forget my roots. Never. And the marvelous thing was that I was encouraged. At Bennington I was never told you can't do this or that. I was told you could do anything you want. Nobody censored you there.... [1]

Coming from a Russian-Jewish immigrant family, Sokolow was particularly sensitive to any political oppression. In this piece, she danced the role of a citizen who witnessed dictators' phoney exhibitions of self-aggrandizement. Placing herself in confrontation with her group, she made a powerful figure of protest. According to John Martin, it was a role she played magnificently.

One other recipient of the choreographic fellowship for 1938 was Eleanor King, a former member of the Humphrey-Weidman group. King danced *Ode to Freedom* in a revolutionary spirit. But the most momentous response to German fascism was probably Holm's *Tragic Exodus*. Following Holm's suggestions, Vivian Fine composed a musical score of Hebrew coloring that in a sensitive, but unsentimental manner, addressed the ordeal of Jewish people persecuted by fascism. In July 1939 Holm received the Dance Magazine Annual Award for this work, which was praised for its "uniform excellence as a dance," its "great emotional appeal" and its "topical significance." Reviewing *Tragic Exodus* in the New York Times, John Martin wrote:

> It proved to be a brief, but tremendously moving piece of choreography, inspired apparently by the plight of the German Jews. If it falls technically into the category of "Social comment," it is completely devoid of any doctrinaire approach, but stems manifestly from a depth of feeling, part indignation, part compassion. It is a powerful bit of dramatic dancing, and Vivian Fine's music provides a relentless and eloquent background.[2]

This strong commitment to political issues diminished when the Bennington School of the Dance moved to Mills College on the West Coast for the 1939 summer session. At the closing of the 1938 session, Martha Hill had announced a temporary move of the summer school to allow for internal administrative changes at Bennington College. At Mills, twenty-six Bennington faculty and staff persons from the East Coast taught equal numbers of students from both coasts, unlike at Bennington, where the student body had been mostly Easterners. This move also brought about a slight shift in emphasis from performance to teaching, which increasingly became the responsibility of the younger generation of modern dancers trained by the Big Four (Graham, Humphrey, Wideman, and Holm).

The move to Mills was facilitated by Rosalind Cassedy, director of the Mills College Physical Education Department. Inspired by her visit to Bennington in 1934, Cassedy attempted to build a Center for Modern Dance in California. In 1934, she appointed Tina Flade as Head of the Dance Department. To many West Coast dancers, Flade provided their first exposure to European Modern Dance. One of the youngest of the original Wigman students in Dresden in 1922, Flade had studied with Wigman for eight months. She was the youngest member of the Mary Wigman Concert Group, which performed in Berlin, Dresden, Austria and Switzerland. She returned to the Wigman School to be trained as a teacher, and then prepared a solo program she showed in New York in November, 1932. Flade received a favorable review from John Martin for her first concert; later, in July 1935, she also performed at the Bennington College Theater. A review in the *San Francisco Chronicle* from May, 1935, found Miss Flade to be:

one of those curious human beings seen only on the dance stage: so slight
in limbs and chest that one wonders where the breath and strength are to
come from for the vibrant exertions of the dance, yet tiring not at all and
demonstrating herself at the end as a veritable symbol of wispish beauty
and dynamic and supple grace.... [3]

Tina Flade's dances reflected Wigman's early expressionistic style; she had after
all, during the early twenties, in Dresden, been trained in improvisation rather than in any
formal technique. John Martin reviewed her concert in the New York Times, July 21,
1935, as "not only a superb performance from the standpoint of technique and theatrical
presentation, but also genuinely big creative talent." As a teacher, she was a good
example of Wigman's emphasis on individual creativity, as opposed to Holm, who
appeared to be at the other end of the pedagogical spectrum in her very structured, more
American manner of teaching. Holm was well aware of the many facets of Wigman's
personality; she once mentioned to me that Wigman changed her approach to teaching
almost daily, and that it was Holm's decision to stress the structured aspects of Wigman's
work in her own teaching in America. The comparison between Flade and Holm
illustrated clearly how Holm had adapted to the more systematic teaching methods of her
American colleagues, while Flade continued to focus on individual movement experience
and expressivity.

Although the move to Mills College signaled for some dancers a "welcome
exchange of ideas," as dance writer Margaret Lloyd put it,[4] not all the West Coast dancers
embraced the new techniques. Recalling a residency with Lester Horton's Group in 1938,
Horton-trained dancer and choreographer Bella Lewitzky described her impressions of
Mills College to me:

> It was my first exposure to Graham technique (taught by Bonnie Bird), and
> Graham and Horton seemed to be on different ends of the world. Tina
> Flade taught Wigman's approach in 1938, and Hanya Holm came for a
> sequence of workshops. Flade's work felt like home to me since it was
> open and spatial, like Lester Horton's technique. The German school was
> apparently closer to what Lester had developed and where my sensibilities
> were. Flade had an unearthly quality. I did not take from her a body of
> information. The difference between Hanya Holm and Tina Flade was that
> Hanya was totally conceptual. She had a basic idea from which she
> moved; she was orderly and understood clearly what she asked you to do.
> You went through a sequence of things with Hanya. I did not really study
> with her, but my perception of her was that she was highly structured.[5]

In Lewitzky's perspective, which was formed by her work with Lester Horton, the
German school, due to its focus on space, was more accessible to West Coast dancers
than the Modern Dance approach of the East Coast. Her recollections show clearly how
dance developed along different lines on the East and West Coasts.

Similarly, the East coast faculty found the California atmosphere very different from Vermont. Although Margaret Lloyd had hoped that the "somewhat egocentric Eastern seaboard would profit by a generous closeup view of work of other active dance centers,"[6] Bennington teachers were in fact disappointed; they missed the highly charged atmosphere of the Bennington summers. In retrospect, however, that summer of 1939 at Mills might appear in a different light. To be sure, the level of political awareness was not as high as it was at the Bennington festivals of 1937 and 1938. On the other hand, the highly capable teaching associates represented the methods of the Big Four so well that the choreographers were freed to pursue their own artistic goals. Among the teaching associates, Ethel Butler taught Graham technique, Louise Kloepper taught for Hanya Holm, Katherine Manning represented Doris Humphrey, and José Limón taught for Charles Weidman. Martha Hill and Bessie Schönberg directed the program in Dance Composition. The atmosphere at Mills was also less competitive than at Bennington, and East and West coast dance students shared the same studio, an experience that later led to an appreciation of the diverse approaches to Modern Dance in America. Moreover, experimental events, such as a workshop which focused on the use of the spoken word in poetry and prose, and a concert of percussion music under the direction of John Cage, added a new component to the summer offerings. At the joint program staged by teaching associates at the end of the session, José Limón's choreography *Danzas Mexicanas*, which related directly to his Mexican heritage, stood out for its "beautiful staging, tense emotion, and dramatic quality."[7] The great discovery of this summer at Mills was a student from the Cornish School in Seattle who took Ethel Butler's technique class: Merce Cunningham.

In 1940, the first session of the newly established Bennington School of the Arts: Dance Division altered the format of the summer festival considerably. Now only one of the Big Four, Martha Graham, produced a major work, while Hanya Holm taught master classes for advanced students. Thanks to this new arrangement, Martha Graham, choreographer-in-residence (1940 to 1943), had the opportunity to create two new works, *El Penitente* and *Letters to the World*. The expanded arts curriculum of the Dance Division added courses in ballet and Labanotation, and focussed on closer collaborations with actors, musicians and scenic designers. After 1941, only Martha Graham produced major works as artist-in-residence with her company at the Bennington School of the Arts. The School of the Dance held its last summer session in 1942. The War had grown from a European conflict to a global war and made it impossible to hold a Festival of Dance.

Hanya Holm later summed up what the Bennington years had meant to her:

Bennington brought together for the first time four people who were pioneers in their field and who were trying to develop the modern trend beyond a fad. It gave the whole modern dance movement a concentrated push. This was the beginning and everything was embryonic. Now the dance has roots; then we had just about slithering feet. Bennington gave the dance a body.[8]

AMERICAN MODERN DANCE DURING WORLD WAR II

"The War swallowed up most of the ambitions of my generation. From 1942 on, it was a matter of keeping the wolf from the door."[9] Nona Shurman, a member of the Humphrey-Weidman Group, wrote these words, which vividly bring back the feelings of many modern dancers who had their first enthusiastic dance experiences at Bennington in the late thirties. By the time they finished their dance studies, America was at war and they had no chance to perform. In Germany, there was a similar lost generation of aspiring dancers, born between 1916 and 1925, who never reached the stage.

After America entered World War II, in December of 1941, modern dancers had to face the question of survival in a country whose list of priorities would most certainly slight the arts. Some male modern dancers such as Alwin Nikolais and José Limón were drafted, and since men were always in the minority in Modern Dance groups, the companies that still existed were badly hurt. Bennington College, however, continued its support of dance even though the formal dance festival was suspended. Merce Cunningham and Jean Erdman appeared in a joint concert at Bennington College in 1942, and John Cage's music was heard there for the first time. Martha Graham and Company continued as artists-in-residence for the next college spring and summer sessions, enabling Graham, with Louis Horst and Erick Hawkins, to complete *Deaths and Entrances* in the summer of 1943.

With *Deaths and Entrances*, Graham reached the first height of her large scale choreographic productions of the early forties. The piece was inspired by the relationships of the three Bronte sisters, who lived with their memories of the past. Graham danced one of the three sisters, Cunningham was the Poetic Beloved, and Hawkins the Dark Beloved. Graham and Arch Lauterer presented the piece as workshop performance with limited props and costumes. It had a surrealist form; events followed in psychological sequence, not in a narrative order. This choreographic device reflected Graham's involvement with Carl Jung's theories, and she increasingly used his psychological approach in the choreographic treatments of Greek heroines.

While the residency in the college's summer session enabled Graham to keep her company functioning during the summer months, even for her it became increasingly difficult to line up performances for the fall season. Some of her company members went on tour, others found work in Broadway shows and musicals. But in spite of the war and its difficulties, Graham produced *Herodiade* and *Appalachian Spring*. These works were shown at the Library of Congress in Washington, D.C., on December 30, 1944. Although World War II halted the development of dance in Europe and also impeded young dancers in America and Europe, it did not stop Martha Graham's choreographic productivity and the further development of the Contemporary Dance in the United States. However, the War did slow down the unparalleled progress that dance had made during the thirties, and moreover, in the forties, the dancers' earlier preoccupation with social issues, a reflection of the Great Depression, gradually changed to focus on different subject matter. Martha Graham was quite sensitive to this change of interests in her audiences. The analytical exploration of man's psyche gained public interest particularly in the years of war and insecurity. Graham's focus turned to outstanding woman figures in Greek literature and mythology as individuals exploring their lives in psychological depth. This was particularly true of works such as *Cave of the Heart* (1946), *Errand into the Maze* and *Night Journey (*both 1947). She identified herself with these archetypal models, making visible, in her words, the "inner landscape."

Doris Humphrey and Charles Weidman continued their company work in frequent studio performances, but under great financial and physical stress, and without new directions in their choreographic approach. Humphrey started to be seriously affected by the first signs of arthritis, which forced her, after her last appearance as a dancer in *Inquest* (1944), to give up her performing career. By the end of World War II, she had given up the Humphrey-Weidman school and company, but she continued to choreograph. When José Limón returned from the war, he made her artistic director of his newly established company. There she reached a new level of choreographic maturity, creating the serene works of her last decade of productivity.

In 1936, Holm had officially changed the name of the New York Wigman School to the Hanya Holm School. She also struggled to maintain the group she had established in 1936. She added men to the group in 1939 to make her work more theatrical, but soon they were drafted. Louise Kloepper, Hanya Holm's closest associate, left Holm in 1942 after ten years of association. She decided to pursue a college degree in dance offered by the University of Wisconsin's Physical Education Department under Margaret H'Doubler, while simultaneously teaching Modern Dance in the Wigman-Holm tradition in the Physical Education Department. With Kloepper's departure Holm lost not only a fine teaching associate but her first female soloist and the most authentic interpreter of her choreography. The relationship that had grown between Kloepper and Holm was similar to Holm's relationship with Wigman between the years between 1921 and 1931.

At Wisconsin, Kloepper became familiar with methods of academic research. She gained a deeper knowledge of the human body's functioning and gradually recognized similarities in concepts between the European approach to dance and Margaret H'Doubler's philosophy of movement, which had crystallized since H'Doubler had established the dance program in Madison in 1927. Both were thinking in terms of space, time and force. "Marge went deeper into single elements, and in careful analysis based on anatomy, physiology and psychology, she found out how they are interrelated."[10]

H'Doubler recognized in Kloepper an ideally trained model, personifying her theories of motion. Her goal, however, was not to train performers for the stage, but to further the individual growth of each student. Since Louise Kloepper had absorbed H'Doubler's philosophy of the function of movement experience in education, she was able to integrate into her classes H'Doubler's methodical analyses, which were based on the foundation of the Wigman-Holm approach. Kloepper also showed a deep concern for developing the individual's creative potential as well as physical skills.

In 1946, as soon as Kloepper had completed her Bachelor's degree, she became assistant professor in dance, teaching Modern Dance technique, composition, improvisation and percussion for dancers. She also advised Orchesis, the student dance group, helping the students create their own choreography. By 1957, Kloepper had become chairperson of the Wisconsin Dance Program. Not only did Holm's teaching influence the dancers she trained, but thanks to Louise Kloepper's fine example, also influenced the Wisconsin model. Subsequently, this model was widely followed by dance departments in American colleges and universities across the country. During the forties, American Modern Dance progressed mainly in the colleges and universities. These educational institutions integrated dance into their liberal arts programs and built a broader audience for dance in America. In this process of integration, the Laban-Wigman concepts were objectified and gradually detached from Wigman's personality, still remembered by those who had experienced her radiant performance.

HOLM'S PUPILS

In the summer of 1941, Hanya Holm became director of the dance summer sessions at Colorado College. While teaching there occasionally in past summers, Holm became enraptured with the clear mountain air and the peaceful surroundings. In 1941, she designed a six-week summer dance program. In Colorado, she became a different person, recharging her energies.[11] Without her American professional colleagues around, she could let loose and express herself freely. For over twenty-five years she returned to her summer institute, which came to be a second home to her. The curriculum consisted of technique, theory, composition, music for dance, Labanotation, and dance pedagogy. Whenever possible, instruction was given outdoors, and informal meetings took place on the lawn, where Holm talked about her philosophy of dance and composition. Students became close to each other in this restful atmosphere, and friendships grew there that lasted for life. Some of these students became leading artists and choreographers in the forties and fifties.

Holm conceived some of her pieces in these summer sessions, and as long as she had her company, her dancers performed in these new works, as well as in revivals such as *Dance of Introduction* and *Metropolitan Daily*. Among the experiments with dance and the spoken word, *From This Earth*, with music by Roy Harris and scenario by Arch Lauterer, brought to life characters of a Western small town. After 1945, Holm had to disband her company for financial reasons. She concentrated her creative endeavors within the Colorado summer school, where she invited former students such as Valerie Bettis, Ray Harrison, Molly Lynn, Alwin Nikolais, Don Redlich and Glen Tetley to teach and choreograph in the final productions. As one Colorado dance critic commented:

> Miss Holm brought us, as usual, her consummate artistry and craftsmanship, her sincere conviction in her art, both in its light and profound veins.

> *The Walt Whitman Suite*, a Holm-Harris collaboration, which opened the program, must surely stand as one of the most exciting events of the past week. The music, based on great texts and calling for the use of chorus, was strong and individual, speaking of space and intense feeling.... As fine contrast to this, stood the closing dance *The Garden of Eden*, a rare compound of satire and high comedy, of primitive and contemporary frippery, executed to Milhaud's music, which was shockingly close to American jive, in spite of its French origin.... It was

interesting to observe in Saturday night's performance the development of Hanya Holm away from the abstract and toward the pictorial and legitimately theatrical, a tendency which, wisely handled, should bring the contemporary dance closer to a wider public.[12]

The reviewer Elizabeth H. Hylborn recognized that Holm's personality had gradually objectified Wigman's movement and had unconsciously changed the coloring, from earthy to transparent, from mystical to rational, from dramatic to satiric. This gradual evolution was reflected in the diverse approaches to choreography seen in the works of her former students.

Valerie Bettis exemplified Holm's approach in the thirties. Born in 1920 and ten years younger then Kloepper, she had her early training with Tina Flade on the West Coast, and became a member of Holm's group in 1938. She performed in *Trend* at Bennington when she was seventeen. She also participated in experiments with the use of text at Bennington, and many of her later works were based on the spoken word. Her highly dramatic solo dance *The Desperate Heart*, choreographed in 1943, was based on a poem by Malcolm Brinin and showed a resemblance to Wigman's unadorned directness. As a powerful, dramatic artist, she is particularly remembered for her 1948 solo piece *As I Lay Dying*, after William Faulkner's novel with music by Bernado Segall. Bettis continued to work in Holm's style during the middle thirties, as did Nancy Hauser, another Holm alumni, who pursued Holm's lyric approach as a modern dancer and teacher in her own dance theater and school in Minneapolis.

The students who studied with Holm during and after the war, in contrast, seemed further removed from the Wigman roots. Their focus was on theatrical dance, as, for example, in Glen Tetley's works. Born in 1926, Tetley started studying dance with Holm in the middle forties and danced in her production of *Kiss Me, Kate*. He also studied with Antony Tudor and Margaret Craske. He danced in Tudor's *Pillar of Fire* and replaced Lucas Hoving when Hoving stopped dancing with the Limón Company. Glen Tetley choreographed for the Joffrey Ballet from 1956 to 1957, and for American Ballet Theatre in 1960. He was co-director of the Netherlands Dance Theater from 1962 to 1970, and he is well known in both Israel and England, having choreographed for the Batsheva Dance Company as well as for the Ballet Rambert and the Royal Ballet. In Germany, he worked at all the great opera houses: Stuttgart, Munich, and Hamburg. His *Pierrot Lunaire* (1962) is in the repertory of many middle-sized German opera house dance ensembles, as is *Embrace Tiger and Return to Mountain* (1968), based on Tai Chi. Tetley has bridged the gap between classical and modern dance, and works toward a fusion of both styles. He also has continued in the direction of Holm's work of the forties; his choreography shows Holm's sense of theater in the way he uses production tools and works with dramatic structure, which pleases the European taste.
His choreography is widely accepted in Europe.

Don Redlich's choreographic sensibility is perhaps closer to that of Hanya Holm than any of her other pupils. Redlich, born in 1933, was a student of H'Doubler and Kloepper at the University of Wisconsin before he joined Holm's company. He established his own group and started choreographing in the late fifties. Redlich is able to create a particular situation with a few sparse gestures, as in his outdoor piece *She Often Goes for a Walk just after Sunset,* which was performed on a summer evening on the lawn of Connecticut College at the American Dance Festival, New London, in the early seventies. The way he utilizes the outdoor environment for his choreographic intentions characterizes him as a Holm pupil, but he also shares with his teacher both a choreographic wit and a light touch. An excellent teacher of composition, he combines the Wigman-Holm tradition with material from his Wisconsin upbringing. Redlich choreographed theater works such as *Age of Anxiety* in 1960 and *Woyzeck* in 1970. His work is articulate and sophisticated, not purely abstract, and cleverly incorporates the concern of choreographers of the sixties for unconventional performing spaces.

In the summer of 1965, six former Holm students returned to celebrate a quarter of a century of their teacher's association with Colorado College. They brought their companies and presented their works to thank her with a summer session that turned into a "Hanya Holm Dance Festival."[13] The three day event proved, as Walter Sorell observed, "that Hanya Holm's approach to teaching is based on an intensive, but generally valid discipline imposing no definite style on the individual."[14]

Appropriately, Alwin Nikolais' work closed the celebration, since it was Nikolais who took Holm's abstract approach to motion to its extreme in his theater of movement, sound, color, and light. Marcia Siegel defined Nikolais' debt to Wigman and Holm in the following way:

> In this country, however, Wigman's style lost its personal quality. During the war, all the German arts and artists lost ground here, and though Wigman's line was carried on by Hanya Holm, who excelled as a teacher, without Wigman's own genius-presence it took on a more abstract character. When Holm's most famous pupil, Alwin Nikolais, began to emerge as a choreographer, he rejected the psychological approach completely in favor of exploring design and pure motion.[15]

Nikolais was born in 1910, the same year as Louise Kloepper, and grew up in New England. When Kloepper went to Germany to study dance at the Wigman School in Berlin, Nikolais was an accompanist playing piano in a silent movie theater. In his late teens, he saw one of Wigman's performances, and was fascinated by her use of percussion instruments. He did not really consider becoming a dancer, but the performance inspired him to take some dance classes with Trude Kaschman, Wigman's pupil, and he accompanied her to the Bennington festival in 1937. Nikolais participated in the full curriculum, taking a course with John Martin in history and criticism, as well as well as Louis Horst's course Fundamental Choreography. The experimental production workshop taught by Martha Hill and Arch Lauterer made the strongest impression on him. Besides working as an accompanist he also had experimented with puppetry and was fascinated by aspects of mechanically produced motion. He returned to the summer session in 1938, but was drafted into the military shortly thereafter.

When he returned from military service, Nikolais decided to study dance seriously with Hanya Holm. He became Holm's production assistant in Colorado Springs for the summer of 1947. Holm's method suited him because it seemed to be clearly based on movement concepts; she was the least psychologically inclined of all the dance teachers Nikolais had experienced.

Nikolais' vision of dance theater incorporated all the production aspects, such as light, electronically mixed sound, and projected images, with the dance movement. In 1948, Nikolais put his ideas of multi-media theater into practice, when he started to teach in the Henry Street Settlement on New York City's Lower East Side. He transformed an old movie house to serve as studio and performing space. His teaching method consisted of suggesting movement possibilities to his dancers while simultaneously mixing light and electronically produced sound, conducting the class from the light board or directing the group with his big drum. Murray Louis, Phyllis Lamhut, and Gladys Bailin received their early training with Nikolais at the Henry Street Playhouse, and many others came to his improvisation classes. Nikolais was fascinated with two-dimensional shapes, as in his group dance *Sanctum*. Ideas already tested by the painter Oskar Schlemmer in his experimental Bauhaus piece of the nineteen-twenties, *Triadic Ballet* (see Chapter I), now found full realization in Nikolais' Theater of motion, color, sound and light. Nikolais evoked Wigman's idea of the dancer confronting the universe, an idea that had motivated her so strongly. In Nikolais' vision the dancer no longer appeared as an individual; rather, the dancer was a small particle in a twentieth-century science fiction world. Because of his lighting, the audience was able to catch only a fragmented view. "Nikolais' detached view of the dancing person," Marcia Siegel observed, "seems very much in keeping with our times. In his hands, a dance can be a visual "trip," but it is usually one without emotional content, except on the primal levels of laughter, surprise, awe, and exitement."[16]

Disillusioned by the world of the fifties and fascinated by high technology, Nikolais choreographed works reflecting a definite sense of detachment, a quality shared by surrealist painters of his generation. The Laban-Wigman holistic view of the universe as a harmonious organism becomes for him a "total universal mechanism."[17] Marcia Siegel raised the key question: did Wigman's style still make sense without her personal quality? Wigman herself admirably balanced personal motivation and form in dance, summed up in the slogan "Without ecstasy no dance, without form no dance."[18] The idea that dancers could dance without a personal commitment did not enter her mind. At the same time she stressed the necessity for dancers to use more than mere feeling and to create "absolute dance," which to her meant abstracted motion. Holm adopted Wigman's philosophy and particularly stressed objectivity of form in her teaching, an approach consonent with her own preference for clarity of shapes. Being younger than Wigman, she was stylistically closer to the "new objectivity" (die Neue Sachlichkeit) of the late twenties than to the expressionism of the early twenties.

Political upheaval and World War II distanced Holm even further from her expressionistic beginnings under Wigman, with its Neo-romantic influences. In the forties, what Holm transmitted in her teaching of German Modern Dance to students such as Nikolais was an awareness of spatial relationships and an analytical approach to the body's abilities for motion -- Laban-Wigman aspects of abstract form. The ecstatic side of Wigman was apparently tied to her personality and was not transferred to American postwar students, who as a generation were by nature skeptical and opposed to any display of emotion. At a paneldiscussion on Wigman in honor of what would have been her one-hundredth birthday, Nikolais was asked what in his opinion was the most fundamental difference between the Laban-Wigman approach and the American Modern Dance. Nikolais said that "what was particular to Laban and Wigman was that they did not work with a vocabulary and that they were not interested in creating one."[19]

Nikolais used Wigman's methods of exploring space in his teaching and in his choreography, and he followed Wigman in his use of improvisation as catalyst for creative invention. He also adopted Wigman's philosophy, that the student should find what is true for himself, a belief that explained his opposition to all kinds of vocabulary in contemporary dance. Although his personal and artistic values may differ from Wigman, he is still a descendent of Wigman-Holm in his exploration of motion and in his reliance on the individual creative resources of his dancers and students.

HANYA HOLM AND THE MUSICAL.

For twenty years, Hanya Holm had represented Mary Wigman's approach to teaching and choreographing in America. In 1948, on short notice, Holm was asked to choreograph a musical, an area Wigman had never experienced. She was asked to choreograph one of the productions for Ballet Ballades, *The Eccentricities of Davey Crockett*. Holm loved choreographing her fantastic visions of Davey Crockett's adventures, which Davey described in his songs. This story is similar to the German folk tales of Baron Münchhausen, a well known European eccentric adventurer. Critics raved about Holm's unpretentious folk manner and imaginative choreography. Obviously, Holm enjoyed having theatrical machinery at her disposal to support her choreographic fantasies. She came up with a truly entertaining and humorous American piece.

Due to *Davey's* success, she was asked, a few months later, to choreograph a Cole Porter Broadway musical, *Kiss Me, Kate*, based on the theme of Shakespeare's *The Taming of the Shrew*. Again, Holm showed her sense of theater and instinct for characterization through movement. The show, which opened on December 30, 1948, became a breakthrough in the development of the American musical because of the way Holm integrated ballet, modern dance, and social and folk dance to support the dramatic action. As John Martin observed, Holm's distinctive movement style was missing:

> The choreography is at all times completely of the texture of the show.
> Nowhere, from the rise of the first curtain to the fall of the last, is there
> a characteristic Holm movement; she has apparently not been tempted in
> the least to superimpose herself upon the production, but has given her
> attention wholly to bring out and pointing up what is inherent in it.[20]

Holm did not use her "distinctive movement style" on purpose; for the first time, she felt free to follow her choreographic instinct, and she won over the American public with her musical charm, her wit, and her light-footed choreography. Already in 1937 Margarethe Lloyd recognized in Holm's work "a new tempo, a new rhythm, and a new resonance."[21]

Kiss Me, Kate was a milestone in the history of dance for another reason as well. It was notated in Labanotation by Ann Hutchinson, who completed the documentation shortly after the opening night. As the first completed notation score for copyright in America, it placed Labanotation on a par with music notation, and it gave future generations the chance to reconstruct this major work. Holm herself revived it several times, using the notated score and the help of dance notator Els Grelinger.

In 1956, Holm was asked to choreograph *My Fair Lady*. She had enough time to prepare the choreography for this musical, and she enjoyed researching each detail. She even flew to London to familiarize herself with the people of Covent Garden Market. *My Fair Lady* became an international success, popular in the USSR as well as in London and in the United States. Holm also staged several operas, such as Gluck's *Orpheus and Eurydice*. In 1963, Holm created dances for a White House performance hosted by President John F. Kennedy and shown on public television.

Holm was always willing to experiment in finding choreographic solutions for her diverse productions. She occasionally took on the double role of choreographer and stage director in operas. However, she reached her widest audiences in America with her musicals, which succeeded in bringing the two disciplines of classical ballet and modern dance closer together. The financial situation led many dancers to seek employment on Broadway in musicals, which flourished under Agnes de Mille, Helen Tamiris, Hanya Holm and Jerome Robbins. Contemporary issues as subject matter also now appeared on the musical stage, as seen, for example, in the collaboration of Leonard Bernstein and Jerome Robbins on the phenomenally successful musical *West Side Story*.

The combination of American Modern Dance, the American Musical, and a Contemporary Ballet Repertory created by George Balanchine enabled America to enter the postwar era as an international leader in dance. Hanya Holm had played a large role in helping to shape the American Dance tradition from the thirties through the sixties. As an educator and choreographer at the Bennington dance festivals and as a director in musicals and operas, Holm became a vital force adapting the Wigman heritage to the rhythm of contemporary American life. In recognition of her life-long and manifold contributions to the American Dance, Hanya Holm, in 1984, received the Samuel Scripps Award of the American Dance Festival.

DANCE IN NAZI GERMANY.

Following the 1936 Berlin Olympic Games, Germany's cultural life lapsed into provincial isolation. Historically Germany had always been a recipient, rather than an originator, of new ideas in ballet. Italy, France, and, in the twentieth century, England had set examples and the German stages had followed. There were perhaps more dancers employed in Germany's numerous court and municipal theaters than in the rest of Europe, but ballets were mostly imported and copied from France. Through the nineteenth century and up to the nineteen-twenties, corps de ballets were the most conventional, least artistic, and least respected members of German opera house ensembles. Very little creativity had been asked for in the production of ballets, which preserved the stereotypes of an outdated society, the ballet serving as a diversion rather than as a creative art form.

Since the Nazi ideology was opposed to "international cultural Bolshevism," the German opera houses were cut off from the French and English models which had served as examples in the nineteenth century. Under Nazism, they fell far behind the international dance scene. Since they were supported by the fascist government, the programs of the municipal opera houses had to serve mass audiences, who filled the houses under the motto "Vigor through Joy" (Kraft durch Freude), one of the slogans coined personally by Hitler. Ballet became even more limited during the thirties than it had been before, with one surprising exception: Berlin.

Victor Gsovsky, internationally known as a Russian classical dancer, choreographer and teacher, came to Berlin after the Russian Revolution. There he served as ballet master at the State Opera from 1925 to 1928. In 1928, Gsovsky together with his wife Tatjana established a professional school of classical dance. The Gsovskys also worked as choreographers in commercial theater and films. They both exerted a decisive influence on the Berlin ballet scene even during Laban's term as ballet master at the State Opera, from 1930 to 1934. During the thirties, Victor Gsovsky went to London to teach. He established an internationally known school in Paris as well.

Tatjana Gsovsky, born in 1901 in Moscow, had studied under Isadora Duncan and also at the Dalcroze School at Hellerau. She had an understanding of twentieth-century music, but performed first in highly theatrical variety acts. She opposed Modern Dance for years. In spite of Hitler's dislike of Russians, Tatjana had no difficulties with the Ministry of Propaganda and worked as an occasional guest in Leipzig, Dresden and Munich. Tatjana Gsovsky became the first choreographer in post-World War II Germany, from 1945-1952, she built a strong dance ensemble at the State Opera in East Berlin. Later, from 1954 to 1966, she directed the dance ensemble of the Municipal Opera House in West Berlin, as the senior force within the postwar renaissance of ballet in Germany.

Lizzie Maudrick, a pupil of Michel Fokine, took over Laban's position at the State Opera in 1934 and remained as ballet mistress until the end of the Nazi regime, in 1945. Experienced in her work (she had held leading positions in Hamburg, Lübeck and Wiesbaden), she saw to it that the company kept its technical and professional level. During the Nazi regime, the careers of many modern dancers in Germany were tragically altered by political events. Laban and Jooss, who had fought for a regeneration of the German theater dance, left the country taking refuge in England. Jean Weid, a deeply committed socialist of the same generation as Kurt Jooss, made a similar choice. Weid, born in 1904, started dancing in Hamburg, performing the *Dance of the Red Flag* and choreographing for nonprofessional, working men's groups. In 1930, Margarethe Wallman asked him to dance the leader of the "Dark Forces" in her *Orpheus* production at the Dancer's Congress at Munich. There he met Ted Shawn. After this memorable event, Weid choreographed several quite provocative pieces with his "Red Dancers" in Berlin until the Nazis arrested him in February, 1933. He was released a few weeks later and spent the years during the Nazi regime in exile in France. He continued choreographing expressionistic group compositions until he was interned again, this time in France in 1939. He fought as a volunteer in the British Army and finally returned to Berlin in 1948 to become the director of the newly established "Dramatic Ballet" of the Volksbühne in East Berlin.

Once National Socialism had taken over the country, only a few solo performers, who in the late twenties had already established their international reputations as Ausdruckstänzer, could leave the country for tours of solo recitals. In this category were Harald Kreutzberg and his partner Yvonne Georgi (1903-1975), both previous Wigman pupils who had successfully toured the U.S. since 1928. At this point, he was the only modern dancer who managed to keep good relations with the Ministry of Propaganda. Harald Kreutzberg understood that he was expected to perform as a humorous entertainer, without touching on ideological issues.

In contrast, Gret Palucca and Mary Wigman, who considered themselves to be the leaders of the German Modern Dance movement, were determined to save the German Modern Dance as they conceived it, that is, as absolute dance, independent of the conventional municipal theater. Kreutzberg, Palucca and Wigman performed and choreographed for the Olympic Games in 1936, presenting large group arrangements for the outdoor performance on a newly built outdoor stage (see Chapter IV). Wigman's version of a death dance (*Totentanz*), however, displeased the Nazis. As soon as the Olympic Games were over, the Ministry of Propaganda placed both Wigman and Palucca into the category of "degenerated artists," along with the artists of the Weimar era to whom they were closely related. Dr. Goebbels had quite a good eye and observed that Wigman's dances, particularly when she dealt with death, were expressionistic in a style that contradicted the ideology of the Third Reich. Since Wigman was internationally well known, she was dropped gradually; she could still perform in Germany, but not abroad.

In 1942, at age fifty-five, Mary Wigman concluded her performing career with a solo program which presented three new works, *The Dance of Brunhilde*, *The Dance of Niobe*, and *Farewell and Thanksgiving*. These compositions grew out of improvisatory sessions during which both Wigman and her composer, Aleida Montijn, developed the thematic material for the dances. Wigman made a point of working closely with her composers. Will Goetze had been the associate of her early work, Hanns Hastings followed in the thirties, and Wigman seemed to have found a particularly attuned collaborator in the young Dutch student of composition, Aleida Montijn.

Wigman revealed very different aspects of herself in the three dances of her farewell performance. *The Dance of Brunhilde* portrayed a passionate, heroic figure of the Germanic sagas, a queen who has been defeated by fraud, giving in to compromise. Costumed in a court dance style, the theme of the dance appeared remote to me when I saw it in Berlin as a young girl, in 1942; I found it difficult to relate to Germanic legends. In contrast, *The Dance of Niobe* moved me deeply. It had nothing of the pathos and literalness of the first dance, but abstractly condensed desperation in the figure of Niobe, the overly proud mother of Greek myth who was punished by the gods with the loss of her children. It was the restrained dramatic gestures of this dance which motivated me to become a student of Wigman. I did not understand her last dance, *Abschied und Dank* (*Farewell and Thanksgiving*). It seemed that Wigman bowed with lightness and even had a soft smile in this concluding dance. I did not know then the pressures she was experiencing at that time.

In 1942, Wigman was officially ordered to refrain from publicly performing. Simultaneously, political pressures forced her to give up her Wigman School in Dresden. The year 1942 was the darkest in Wigman's professional as well as personal life; her closest friend since 1929 and through the thirties, Hans Benkert, turned away from her, while she seemed to come to the end of her professional career. At this moment, her longtime friend Niedecken-Gebhard, head of the Department of Dramatic Art of the Music Academy in Leipzig, made it possible for her to join his faculty as a guest teacher. Mary Wigman moved to Leipzig to the Mozart Strasse 17, where she lived through the end of World War II and the even more difficult postwar years under Russian occupation.

MARY WIGMAN AT LEIPZIG'S MUSIC ACADEMY.

In fall 1943, Wigman was one of the dance teachers in the Department of Dramatic Art, teaching modern dance, group forms and composition, when I became her student. The word "technique" was not in our vocabulary in those days; it was the very end of the era of solo dance. Wigman defined three categories of dance to us: the solo dance, the group dance, and the choral dance. Wigman herself was the fascinating examplar of the great Dance Soloist to us students. There were many young girls who unconsciously modelled themselves after her. Nobody was thinking of a career in practical terms in those days. Nobody had a clear idea of how to prepare for a career in dance. We studied while total war was the reality.

I will never forget my audition day. Trained in Berlin by a pupil of Max Terpis, I had a combination of classical training with some freer modern movements. I entered the studio in leotard and tights, but everybody was in long skirts, with their hair down. I had short hair and I felt absolutely exposed. Running into the dressing room, I found a friendly soul who lent me an appropriate outfit. Back in the dance room I thought I would do a few pliés. There was no barre, but a beautiful wooden floor, and beside the piano some gongs and other percussion instruments. The room was not a typical dance studio; it had on one side an oval-shaped window with a view of the nearby park, which was clothed in fall colors.

Then Mary Wigman entered. She was actually much smaller than I expected her to be after seeing her perform *The Dance of Niobe*. To me, barely twenty, she seemed ageless, but she was in her late fifties then. She wore a chestnut-colored wide dance skirt, which harmonized with her hair. She faced each of the candidates silently with great directness. Most striking were her eyes, green-blue and crystalline; I also noticed her very expressive hands. With her deep and resonant voice, she dispersed our nervousness at once.

The audition consisted of a few locomotor sequences and some improvisation. Since I liked to improvise, I was accepted and placed into the advanced class although I had really very little previous training. I joined the class in "Tanzübung" (dance practice), which Wigman taught three times a week for the advancd group, as well as the composition class with Wigman twice a week. In addition, I had to take a ballet class as mandated by the Chamber of Theater.

Wigman normally taught a two-hour class, without stopping. To her, class was a performing experience. She was still a beautiful dancer and needed those two hours to feel alive herself. She was a passionate mover who built her classes from a single movement theme, which she expanded, and varied, but which never lost touch with the initial focal point in the body. She would step in front of us, a group of about twelve students, and lift up her spine until her chest faced the ceiling. She actually changed her size as soon as she started to move. The hands were held in front of the chest while we went through a sequence of slight, elastic knee bends which gradually incorporated movements of the whole body. Shifts of weight led in uninterrupted movement flow to weight transfers and level changes. Once in a while you felt Wigman's hand on a tensed shoulder.

Wigman moved around while teaching and gave most corrections through her hands; she seldom interrupted the class for corrections. Movement had to be experienced in its totality. The process of moving was more important to her than the precise execution. She was very clear in analyzing the underlying movement principles, but there were no preset patterns to be repeated and perfected. Each class was built around a specific theme that led to some free movement exploration towards the end of the class.

Wigman's pedagogic method was to address the unconscious in the student. There was no attempt to bring us to one version of executing a given movement. Wigman always supported individuality; she believed that the student has first to discover his own range of movement before conforming to a given movement form. She referred to Nietzsche and Spengler occasionally, but her explanations during class were brief. She usually ended the class with a clear summation, and then she was a wonderful speaker.

Wigman's approach to teaching composition differed from the diverse approaches to composition I witnessed in American college teaching. Wigman did not start from any visual or musical form concepts, but stressed the tactile nature of dance. To intensify our sensation of touch she gave us gongs and tambourines to incorporate into our dance studies; these objects led to different stylizations. Wigman spoke with clarity and sparseness. The formulation of her ideas about composition had the unerring simplicity of a Chinese proverb.

One of Wigman's first assignments was to find a motif of greeting. She described it as "an arch conquering space." This was in contrast to her motif of "oath," which, in her words, "stays in space as a mark of metallic contour." We worked to words, to sounds, and in silence. The dance in silence was the consequence of her early work with Laban. But she did not mention Laban or Dalcroze; whatever she had absorbed in her younger years was completely integrated in her teaching, and she was not even aware of how some of those influences had affected her work.

By the time I came to study with her, Wigman had found the roots of her dance in the ritual theater of the East. One afternoon, Wigman showed us the mask from her second version of *Witchdance*. She explained: "I chose this mask to overcome the individual sphere in order to connect to the archetype." Wigman had found the essential in Eastern art. She asked us to strive for a similar sparseness in dance composition.

Wigman had stated very early that "only when dance got rid of the dictatorship of music was it free to assume fresh stages."[22]

Wigman had a very thorough knowledge of music because of her work with Dalcroze. She applied structural terms of music theory, such as polyphony and monophony, to our dance studies and made us experiment with ways of coordinating movements that did not follow necessarily an organic weight flow. In this process of exploring compositional methods she experimented on ground which Merce Cunningham further explored. Both Wigman and Cunningham developed new ways of dealing with movement out of their contact with Eastern thought.

CARMINA BURANA

One day in fall 1943, Wigman introduced the composer Carl Orff to our composition class. She said that "this man will give us an idea of a new, exciting piece, *Carmina Burana*, and that he would "dance at the piano." He certainly did; he used the piano from all sides, producing unusual sound effects, simultaneously stamping and marking polyrhythms with hands and feet, at a time when the word "prepared piano" certainly was not yet in use in the German language. Orff's explanations, in their rhythmic vividness and diversity of sound sources, were unforgettable to me. Niedecken-Gebhard planned to produce *Carmina Burana* to Carl Orff's music at the the Leipzig Opera House. It had already been successfully performed in Frankfurt, Germany. He invited Wigman to choreograph it. She sketched out some of the dances with us before starting rehearsals with the Opera ensemble to give her students an idea of her rehearsal process. The work was presented together with Orff's *Catulli Carmina*, choreographed by Tatjana Gsovsky, at the Leipzig Opera House. The two great ladies of the German dance who had fought to set new standards for Germany's theater dance at several dance congresses, arguing in favor of a pure modern or pure classical dance, now appeared in a joint production in a municipal opera house. At the end, Tatjana Gsovsky, the famous Russian ballerina, stood next to Mary Wigman, bowing to the applauding Leipzig audience. This memorable event was made possible under the protection of Dr. Niedecken-Gebhard, now a Nazi Party member. For the students, these two productions were unique examples of how dance and music can collaborate without dominance of one over the other; Wigman approached *Carmina Burana* from its rhythmical base, while Tatjana Gsovsky was inspired by the text of *Catulli Carmina* to choreograph in late Roman style.

TOTAL WAR.

Heavy Allied bombardments destroyed the dance building of the Music Academy in February 1944. Wigman saw the building of the Academy going up in flames, and she watched the devastating burning of Leipzig's book trade from the roof in the Mozart Strasse. Leipzig was the main center of German publishing houses. As Wigman confessed in her diary, she was shocked by her reaction: that this elemental power of the giant fire thrilled her in spite of the grandiose destruction all around her. Because the Department of Dramatic Art was completely destroyed, Wigman could no longer teach there. However, she did not give up; she had to dance. Emptying out the furniture from the living room of her appartment in the Mozart Strasse, she continued to teach five students, including myself. We returned to work with her in Leipzig in the spring of 1944 despite the harsh living conditions. We had no electricity, no heat, and the glass in the windows was broken; but Wigman continued to teach, even after nights spent in the cellar during bombardments. Indeed, the total breakdown of civil order during the last year of the war seemed to have an invigorating effect on Wigman. She felt a strong responsibility to give her students whatever she could. This was her way of coping with the reality of a war that finally reduced life to the level of pure survival.

In these desperate times, Wigman concentrated all her energies on her daily hours of teaching. She was a strong performer and taught through example; the "class" was a way for her to prove that she was still alive in the one thing most important to her: dance. This gave her a powerful endurance and even a certain radiance; she held out while war was going on and five young people danced with her in her cold living room. Wigman danced in front of her small group of students, often accompanying herself on Indian drums, talking very little while she moved, keeping a demanding pace without stopping for explanations. She loved the intensity that filled the small room. In her diaries she noted that she considered these weeks in the middle of 1944 the most fulfilling in her teaching career, before the Nazi declaration of Total War forced the last students to work for the war effort. Her hardest time came when the high tension of the war was over. She found herself both physically and mentally isolated and exhausted, living under very deprived conditions in the East zone in Leipzig, which most of her old friends had left.

NOTES FOR CHAPTER V

1. Sokolow, Anna (1981) Biographical statement. *Modern Dance in America: The Bennington Years*,Kriegsman, Sali Ann. p. 264. Boston: G.K. Hall

2. Martin, John (1939) Tragic Exodus. *New York Times*, Feb. 20

3. Flade, Tina (1935). Press Voices from Germany and America 1925-1938. Unpublished print Dance Tina Flade, p. 22. *San Francisco Chronicle*

4. Lloyd, Margaret (1939) *Christian Science Monitor*, June 10

5. Lewitzky, Bella (1990) Interview by I. Bergsohn.Tucson, April 20. Bella Lewitzky had studied dance with Lester Horton (1906-1953) in Los Angeles. His work in theater was first based on language until he staged "Salome." Then he moved away from the written word to evolve a dance theater strongly based on theatrical concepts. He worked with platforms, as had Gordon Craig, and he used masks to abstract a character. He also was fascinated with ethnic cultures. According to Lewitzky, Horton never performed ethnic dances per se, but he gave ethnic based stories as dance assignments, and he was deeply interested in the rituals of the Southwest while always maintaining his sense of theatricality.

6. Lloyd, Margaret (1939) *Christian Science Monitor*, June 10

7. Goode, Elizabeth (1939) Review of Danzas Mexicanas (José Limon) *Dance Observer*, 203

8. Kriegsman, Sali Ann (1981) *Modern Dance in America: The Bennington Years*, p. 263. Boston, G.K. Hall Company

9. Ibid., p. 117

10. Kloepper, Louise (1990) Interview by I Bergsohn, Madison, March 18

11. Sorell, Walter (1969) *Hanya Holm: The Biography of an Artist*, p. 88. Middletown, CT: Wesleyan University Press

12. Hylborn, Elizabeth H. (1945) Hanya Holm at Colorado College, *Colorado Spring Gazette,* Aug. 18. Republished in *Dance Observer*, XII, 8

13. Sorell, Walter (1969), p. 100.

14. Ibid., p.102

15.   Siegel, Marcia (1979) *The Shapes of Change*, p. 277. Boston: Houghton Mifflin Co.

16.   Ibid., pp. 320-321

17.   Jowitt, Deborah (1988) *Time and the Dancing Image*, p. 354. New York: William Morrow and Co. Inc.

18.   Wigman, Mary (1913) Wrote this sentence in her early diary. She made it one of her basic principles of dance composition, and I later heard it in class

19.   Nikolais, Alwin (1986) Notes from the Wigman Centennial Conference: Speech about Wigman's influence on the Modern Dance in America at the Academy of the Arts, Berlin, September 25-28

20.   Martin, John (1948) The Dance Debut. Hanya Holm in Bow as Choreographer for *Kiss Me, Kate*. *New York Times*, Dec. 30

21.   Lloyd, Margaret (1937) Resonance in the Dance. *Christian Science Monitor*, May 4

22.   Wigman, Mary (1913) Notes from her diary. Wigman Archiv, Berlin, Academy of the Arts

CHAPTER VI: DANCE FOLLOWING WORLD WAR II.

CULTURAL CLIMATE IN GERMANY IMMEDIATELY FOLLOWING WORLD WAR II, 1945-1948

To postwar generations in America and Europe it might appear that the most significant effect of World War II was the state of physical destruction in which Europe was left. Most large cities of England and Germany had been heavily damaged. The central areas of Warsaw, Vienna, Dresden and Rotterdam were razed and because communication and transportation facilities were disrupted, people were completely isolated, unable to locate their families or make contact with the rest of the world. Although pure survival took most of their physical energy, survivors did not view the end of the war as Armageddon--total ruin--but rather, as the end of the Third Reich and of fascist abuse. With the political perversion of Germany halted, they hoped for a radical new beginning and dreamed of a European democracy with free expression of opinions and fresh content in the arts.

The first attempts at cultural revival occurred in Germany with private initiative and at the grass roots levels. While the occupation forces helped to re-establish some order and stability after the unconditional capitulation of Germany in 1945, their main focus was to restore bearable conditions of life for their troops as well as for the population of their zone. The question of spiritual and cultural renewal in the years between 1945 and 1948 was not the most urgent problem for the occupation administrators, who confronted a country lacking nearly all necessities of life. It was left to the artists themselves to show their work. Visual artists organized local shows and some even opened galleries in the midst of ruins to exhibit work they had done in exile during the Nazi regime, under extremely restrictive conditions.

The first "General German Art Exhibition" after World War II opened in Dresden in 1946, presenting artists from all four zones.[1] Their work revealed no unified style; it was evident, however, that artists were painting in different ways than they had before National Socialism had suppressed artistic production twelve years earlier. The cultural climate had changed drastically, and these changes demanded expression in the arts.

In music, the works of Paul Hindemith, Igor Stravinsky and Bela Bartok, banned from the concert stage during the Third Reich, were performed again. Also, composers like Ernst Bloch, who had been considered "not wanted" for racial reasons, presented their music. International summer courses for contemporary music drew attention to Darmstadt, Germany, with premieres of music by Hans-Heinz Stuckenschmidt, Karlheinz Stockhausen, and Hans Werner Henze, starting in 1946.[2]

In the theater, Berlin was exemplary. Initially a "bridge between East and West" because of its four-power administration, Berlin became the focal point of the Cold War. In those first years after the war, prominent authors like Berthold Brecht, Georg Kaiser and Carl Sternheim reappeared and set the model for contemporary production styles. Pieces by foreign as well as German dramatic writers were performed. The plays of two young German playwrights had a particularly strong impact: Günther Weisenborn's *Die Illegalen* (*The Illegals*) and Wolfgang Borchert's *Draussen vor der Tür* (*Outside the Door*). These two pieces found tremendous audience response since they related so directly to the immediate experience of the homecoming soldier. At the same time, theater pieces of American authors were also shown all over West Germany: Thornton Wilder's play *Our Town* was very popular in 1946/1947. *Antigone* by Jean Anouilh was also often performed, and found imitators. The classics started to appear in contemporary versions on substitute stages.[3] Thus, out of the destruction of the war, a quest for cultural renewal was voiced in all the arts. It was only natural that dancers, too, would re-enter the cultural scene.

As soon as the war ended, Gret Palucca and Harald Kreutzberg, the great solo performers of the late twenties, both of whom had once been pupils of Mary Wigman, reappeared on the concert stage. Both dancers had pursued Ausdruckstanz in their individual ways and had found international acclaim in their youth, before the National Socialists assumed power. Both had managed to continue as dancers despite the severe restrictions imposed on artists under the Third Reich. Indeed, Palucca, who had the reputation of being the most humorous and lighthearted of the modern dancers, had needed to adjust her programs only slightly in order to continue performing in Germany during the thirties, under the stifling demands of the Minister of Propaganda. However, after 1939, because of Palucca's relationships with some of the leading artists of German Expressionism, such as Emil Nolde, Wassily Kandinsky, Ludwig Kirchner, and Paul Klee, whose work was banned by the Nazis for being "degenerate art," she, too, had been prohibited from performing. She had lost her position as director of her dance school in Dresden as well. After the war, Gret Palucca reclaimed her Dresden school and also returned to the stage as a solo performer, appearing in recitals until 1950. Then, she decided to turn her main focus to dance education, this time as director of one of the two well-established state schools for dance in Dresden in East Germany. In 1986, on the occasion of her eighty-fifth birthday, the Art Museum of Dresden honored her by organizing an exhibition of art works by "Artists Around Palucca."[4] The exhibition not only recognized her for her work in keeping creative dance alive in Dresden at a time when Modern Dance was receiving no support whatsoever in East Germany, but also demonstrated the links between Palucca and the great artists of German Expressionism. On August 1, 1991, the President of the Federal Republic of Germany, Richard von Weizsäcker, congratulated Gret Palucca on her ninetieth birthday, "in gratitude and high esteem" (according to a note in the *Frankfurter Allgemeine Zeitung*).

Harald Kreutzberg was in his forties when he returned to the stage as a solo performer after the war. Despite the fact that his programs, out of necessity, had become increasingly shallow during the decade of the late thirties and no longer showed the strength of their original spirit, he was well received at first by the circle of admirers from his earlier years and even by the critics. Kreutzberg reappeared with a repertory that he had basically built up during the thirties, and his dances still reflected those years, seemingly oblivious to all that had happened in the meantime. John Martin had already recognized a change in Kreutzberg's performance in 1935, when he commented:

If Kreutzberg were not equipped with a vivid and ingratiating personality, a phenomenal technical facility and an inborn aptitude for movement, it would perhaps be more difficult in a way to explain the unsatisfying quality of his current performance. As it is, however, his excellence as a dancer serves only to accentuate the shallowness of his compositions.[5]

In 1947, reviewing his performance at the First International Music Festival at Vienna, Doris Hering described his work in terms of "refinement of style and nicety of structure."[6] Kreutzberg's style evidently had lost the vitality he had demonstrated in performances during his American tours before 1933; his dances had become increasingly decorative. He did not have a fresh approach to choreography. Nevertheless, he continued to appear as a solo performer on the concert stage until 1955 and, thereafter, he worked mostly as a teacher in his own school until his death in 1968.

The very last of the great soloists of this era was the Austrian dancer and choreographer Rosalia Chladek. Slightly younger than Gret Palucca and Harald Kreutzberg, but also continuing the tradition of European solo concerts, she had trained in Hellerau in the Dalcroze method. Born in 1905 in Brünn, she had studied under Valeria Kratina and Jamila Kroeschlova in the Austrian Hellerau-Laxenburg School. Chladek never worked directly under Dalcroze, who actually did not approve of the institute's new direction. Chladek, however, worked very methodically to integrate kinetic knowledge into the teaching method originally developed by Dalcroze. Her early group work *Contrasts* drew attention during the choreographic competition in Paris. In 1932, Chladek won second prize; Kurt Jooss's *The Green Table* had won first prize. Chladek created dance visions out of a poetic image, as in her choreography *Jeanne of d'Arc*, performed at the Basel Conservatory in 1934. Through the thirties, Chladek gained increased international recognition as choreographer of Greek tragedies performed in open-air ancient theaters in Italy and Greece. In 1939, she went on tour to Indonesia with the solo dancer of the Berlin Opera, Alexander von Swaine. She also performed at the Dance Festival in Berlin in 1940 with Kreutzberg and Dore Hoyer. Niedecken-Gebhard, the so-called father of the modern dancers, suggested Chladek, because of her outstanding international achievements, as director of Modern Dance education in the German Masterstätten für Tanz (German Masters Institute for Dance). But because of inherent political and professional tensions, she preferred to return to Vienna as the director of Modern Dance education for professional dancers and movement educators at the Conservatory of the City of Vienna. Simultaneously she performed her solo dance repertory with sublime refinement, reaching the height of her performing career when she danced *Echo Songs* (*Echo Gesänge*) in 1946.

Because of her isolation during the wartime years and after, Chladek did not receive the recognition she deserved--at least not in Germany, since Vienna was in a foreign country after 1945. This is even more true in regard to her choreography for Greek drama, which was seen in Greece in several memorable performances, but not in the rest of Europe or America. As a result, she will probably be remembered more as a highly analytical pedagogue than as a performer and choreographer. Chladek added a systematic Body Movement study to the Dalcroze method of experiencing music through movement. While director of the dance institute at Hellerau-Laxenburg, she consolidated a very exact system of dance education, based on gymnastics. After the war, as director of the Dance Department of the Academy of Music and Performing Arts in Vienna, she articulated the possibilities of differentiating energy and its effects on the body in space with a rare clarity. Recognizing early the dangers of concentration solely on self-realization in Modern Solo Dance, Chladek managed to find a balance between her life as a performer and as a pedagogue. It was this balance that helped her to survive the difficult period in which she lived.[7]

The highly individualistic form of pure Modern Dance solo performance represented by Palucca, Kreutzberg and Chladek was soon pushed aside in postwar Germany. The career of Dore Hoyer, the strongest and most prolific dancer of this period, best illustrates the fate of solo performers. Born in 1911, Dore Hoyer did not grow up absorbing the educational ideals of the German middle class bourgeoisie, as Wigman or Palucca did. Rather, she came from a family of workmen and she belonged to a transitional generation of modern dancers. Without any trace of the Romanticism still inherent in Wigman's and Kreutzberg's dances, Dore Hoyer could not hope to escape from the political reality of her times into a state of harmony through fantasy as they did. She was the first existentialist in Modern Dance, for she directly confronted the hostile reality of contemporary life.

Dore Hoyer studied dance in her native Dresden, 1927/1928, in a dance school which was based on the system of Hellerau-Laxenburg, and in 1929 to 1930 she studied with Gret Palucca. In 1933, Hoyer gave her first solo concert in Dresden. She became a dancer in Mary Wigman's concert group in 1935/1936. Hoyer reached the height of her performing career during the Second World War as soloist with the German Dance Stage (Deutsche Tanzbühne) in Berlin in 1940/1941. In 1945, she became the director of the previous Wigman School at Dresden, which had been taken away from Wigman for political reasons in 1942. A group from this school presented a dance cycle, *Dances for Käthe Kollwitz (Tänze für Käthe Kollwitz),* at the State Opera at Dresden in 1946 and afterward went on tour with Dore Hoyer in Germany.

It was not accidental that Dore Hoyer chose the work of Käthe Kollwitz as the inspiration for her dance composition. Like Kollwitz, Hoyer detested elitism, and she found in Kollwitz a strong voice for the underprivileged. Hoyer joined with Kollwitz in declaiming violence and misuse of power. Like Käthe Kollwitz's art, Dore Hoyer's dances were cries. They were sparse, intense, uncompromisingly ugly when the theme demanded it. They were also highly abstract, basically without hope, and deeply felt. Perhaps because it was so compelling, her cycle of modern dances was one of the few events which reached over the borders of occupation zones in the immediate postwar period.

However, for financial reasons, Hoyer was forced to dissolve her promising group in 1948, the year of the currency reform in Germany. While the currency reform brought regular funding to the state supported municipal theaters, the unaffiliated groups of Modern Dance found it more difficult to survive without any financial backing. Fortunately, Rennert, the well-known director of the Hamburg Opera at that time, offered Dore Hoyer the leading position with the Hamburg Opera dance ensemble, giving her complete freedom in her stylistic direction, something unheard of in German theater in the 1950s. Dore Hoyer experimented for two years with this ensemble of mostly classically trained dancers. The collaboration was unsuccessful, because she was too extreme in her expectations of herself and of the ensemble. Also, the world of the theater was foreign to her. For a short period she was willing to give it a try, but her choreographic imagination did not work within the framework of German theater, even if it was progressive theater.

In 1957, Mary Wigman convinced Hoyer to dance the part of the chosen virgin in her production of *Le Sacre du Printemps* at the Berlin Opera. Wigman knew Hoyer well as Hoyer had been member of her group in 1935/1936. After the war, impressed by the solo *Der grosse Gesang (The Great Song)*, Wigman recognized Hoyer as the last true solo dancer. In a letter to a friend, Pola Nirenska, Wigman called her "ice-cold, but compelling."[8] Intense and uncompromising, Hoyer surpassed Wigman's highest expectations, portraying the part with cold passion. Her solo also was a last compelling statement of Wigman's absolute dance, a final affirmation of Ausdruckstanz, now integrated into a magnificent theatrical event.

Since Hoyer had no basis of existence as an independent, modern choreographer in Germany at this time, after this great success she left for South America, where she made European Modern Dance popular in Argentina, Uruguay and Brazil. Nevertheless, she was continually torn between her successes in these countries and her homesickness for Germany; she never felt completely comfortable in her self-imposed exile. In a letter written in 1961, Hoyer asked, "Why is Germany so completely mesmerized by the ballet?"[9] Her question could be easily misinterpreted as an animosity she harbored toward ballet. This was not the case. Hoyer just could not conform to the new climate in postwar Germany. The answer to her plaintive question explains much about the history of German Modern Dance in the postwar period.

Two events stimulated significant change in the postwar cultural climate in Germany. These were the Berlin blockade and the currency reform. With the division of Germany into East and West, hopes for a truly fresh start in the arts vanished, as ideological as well as geographical lines were drawn. Disappointment over the division of Germany was mitigated, at least in the West, by the fact that people had money, because the currency reform strengthened the economy and, as we have seen, provided funding for municipal theaters. Moreover, whereas under Russian occupation the population of East Germany continued to pay reparations to the Soviet Union, West German citizens, thanks largely to American support, started to enjoy an improved standard of living. Economic priorities now became uppermost as West German citizens turned their interest to the rebuilding of their cities, including their arts centers.

In this era of Chancellor Konrad Adenauer, a period of political consolidation as well as economic reconstruction, the state-supported theaters had to please the new, well-to-do middle class in a society that had just undergone the screening process of the Nuremberg war crimes trials. As politics shifted noticeably to the right, the schedules of performances reflected the changed mentality: operetta, *Kaiserwaltz, and Cinderella*. The tastes of the late nineteenth century dictated the repertories of the reconstructed theaters and opera houses. Great directors like Erwin Piscator, Fritz Kornter, or Berthold Brecht, who had enjoyed brief comebacks immediately after the war, now worked only as guest directors, because they came to be considered too far left in their political orientation.

Classical ballet seemed to match the new audiences' need for security and diversion; their tastes reverted to those of the nineteenth century. The very same ballet masters who had been accepted by the Nazi regime as good entertainers, continued to produce *Cinderella*. They had made their reputations during the thirties and were often still in the same opera houses. Whereas in other cultural venues the purge from Nazism had been more thorough, in the opera houses the same faces reappeared, and with them the same stylistic stereotypes. The German middle class once again enjoyed renting velvet seats in the opera houses and willingly supported their municipal theaters, but these patrons of culture were not willing to support either the art of the Weimar Republic or contemporary, innovative work. Audience reaction to the Bavarian State Opera's production of the ballet *Abraxas*, performed in Munich in 1948, captured the bourgeois sensibilities of the times. Set to music by Werner Egk and choreographed by Louipart, the ballet, with its overtly erotic choreography and its suggestive costumes, caused a scandal. The performance was prohibited, and heated discussions followed in the press. Significantly, *Abraxas* went on to become a great success, when it was performed in Berlin with new, toned-down choreography by Jeannine Charrat. She engaged soloists of international repute especially for her presentation. Several West German theaters followed the Berlin example, and as a result, for the first time German audiences experienced ballet that was very different in scope from their civic opera house productions.[10]

When the Sadler's Wells Ballet first appeared in Cologne, in 1948, it further exposed the gap between international standards and the local municipal opera house ballet routines. The young Germans who grew up during World War II had never seen *Swan Lake*. The poetry of the choreography, the musical precision and the fine tuned quality of the English classical dancers greatly impressed them.

Of even greater impact on German dance audiences was the New York City Ballet, which came in the early fifties. The neoclassicism of George Balanchine's choreography was absolutely overwhelming, particularly in a country like Germany, which had a very strong tradition of classical music. The critic George Zivier wrote in *Die Neue Zeitung*, Berlin, September 4, 1952:

> The renaissance of ballet is of a young date. One of its most magnificent manifestations is the New York City Ballet. The first evening of the guest appearance at the Berlin Festival could have been called "Le Ballet Blanche." The performance opened with an austere suite, *The Four Temperaments*, to the music by Paul Hindemith, accompanied by Simon Sadoff. These spirited etudes choreographed by George Balanchine were absolutely a high point for the admirer of the pure, classical ballet. Music was never interpreted by dance motion with more musical sensitivity; the patterns of the classical dance composition were never performed more precisely and vivaciously.... These variations made evident that men such as Dalcroze had not worked in vain; eurhythmic principles had

amalgamated with the technique of ballet.

It is ironic that critics coming from a music background influenced the public's opinion of Balanchine by praising his progressive musicality in terms of his debt to Dalcroze while failing to credit the heirs of this tradition--the German modern dancers who built their art strongly on rhythm (until the Nazi regime labeled it "degenerate art" and banned it from the German stage). For ten years, from 1936 until 1946, German Modern Dance had not been in the public eye. After the war, German audiences had no chance to compare Modern Dance with Classical Dance, because the German tradition of Modern Dance had disappeared altogether by the end of the war, and the age of restoration showed no interest in reviving the art of the Ausdruckstanz of the Weimar Republic.

By the late 1940s, audiences in West Germany generally preferred seeing what came from America. American Ballet, together with Jazz and Musical Theater, captivated German audiences. The surviving German modern dancers sustained themselves either by teaching or by going abroad, unable to attract audiences at home because their countrymen found them either too passé or too polemical for their tastes. In the 1950s in West Germany neither the refined solo dances of a Kreutzberg nor the intensely powerful dance cycles of a Hoyer could compete with Contemporary American Dance trends for the hearts of German audiences. The neoclassicism of George Balanchine, however, brought about a renaissance in German Ballet. A new generation of ballet masters arose, gradually replacing the old guard of ballet masters in the municipal opera houses of the thirties. In 1954, Erich Walter, born 1927, became ballet master at the Municipal Opera House at Wuppertal. Collaborating with scenic designer Heinrich Wendel, he experimented in neoclassical style with his ballet ensemble. From 1954 to 1964, both Walter and Wendel aimed for a closer integration of music, scene and dance in Wuppertal. Their imaginative and musically sensitive productions set an encouraging example of Contemporary Ballet in Germany. This extended, in the sixties, to the Opera on the Rhein in Düsseldorf-Duisburg, when Walter and Wendel accepted the leading positions at this institution.

MARY WIGMAN'S MOVE TO BERLIN

While American Dance captured audiences in West Germany, Mary Wigman lived in obscurity in East Germany. This great artist of the era of the Ausdruckstanz had moved to Leipzig in 1942, surviving the war by working as a guest teacher at the Academy of Music and Dramatic Arts in Leipzig. Prohibited from performing since 1942, she was largely forgotten by Germans living in the English, French, and American occupied zones, who were not informed of events in the Russian zone. Although Wigman had opened a school again in 1945, the severe food shortage in Leipzig and Wigman's own weakened physical condition--she suffered from malnutrition--made Leipzig an impossible place to promote her work. At the end of her physical and mental energies, her only hope, as she wrote in her diary, was to make a new start in West Berlin. For three frustrating years she prepared for the move, which became a reality in 1949, thanks to the help of the district mayor of Berlin, Wilmersdorf.

Leipzig is only two hours by train from Berlin, but Mary Wigman arrived there as if from another world. This center of productive artists and theater professionals was no longer the Berlin of the intellectuals that Wigman remembered from the nineteen-twenties. Many of her old friends, such as the great director Erwin Piscator, Fritz Kortner, and Berthold Brecht, had already left for West Germany. These men, who in 1945 had awakened the Berlin theaters after returning from their exiles, were now under suspicion as leftists, and managed to find work only as guest artists in different cities. Wigman herself joined the Academy of the Arts (Akademie der Künste) in West Berlin. Here, from colleagues who also had lived through the wartime period in Germany, she found recognition for her more famous works, those created in the late twenties. The magistrate of Berlin also paid his respects by supporting her school, but for only one year, after which time she was expected to manage by herself. Struggling to keep the school going, in October 1950, Wigman wrote:

> It is inexplicable how we should make progress in this crazy town, which
> is vibrant with activity, but where nobody can truly create, since there is
> always anxiety in the back of one's mind. The "Cold War" between East
> and West is a constant fear inhibiting, separating, hindering.[11]

Wigman's students in Berlin were a very different group from those she had taught before. They had never seen her perform. Also, they did not know about Modern Dance, having grown up during World War II. They were very much taken by the athleticism the American guest companies displayed in their brilliant performances. This generation of young Germans lived in a tremendously changed world which they perceived as a basically hostile environment. They knew that they had lost at least six years of their lives to the war and they were extremely cynical; so many things in their lives had turned out to be an illusion. It was hard for Wigman to reach these young people with her language of imagery. The problem of communication intensified when Elvis Presley's rock and roll reached West Berlin and started a new youth culture there. The rudeness of their behavior and their seeming lack of any discipline were highly objectionable traits to the Adenauer state. Mary Wigman understood this spirit of rebellion; however, she found the students difficult to deal with since their way of looking at things came from a very different mentality. Wigman felt like an outsider, feelings she occasionally expressed in her diary. Wigman's relationship with her assistants was also tense. Marianne Vogelsang, one of the promising younger dancers of the same generation as Dore Hoyer, did not show any interest in collaborating with Wigman in the school, and thus she left. Manya Chmiel, an original Wigman pupil, worked well with the students, but felt that she needed more room for her artistic development. Wigman's last assistant, Hellmut Gottschild, explained, at the Wigman Centennial Conference in Berlin in 1986, that Mary Wigman's language of imagery created a generation problem.[12]

Wigman was plainly exhausted from years of artistic struggle, depression and self-doubt, and she refused to involve herself with the crises of identity of her younger collaborators. She recognized that neither her students nor her assistants had the kind of intense involvement with dance that had led her to devote her life to it at Monte Verita. In a letter written on March 18th, 1954, to Trudi Wulf she evaluated the situation quite realistically:

In order to understand the apparent decline of Modern Dance [in Europe], it is necessary to turn one's eyes toward the short development of this movement. For years [Modern Dance] was the struggle of individual creative personalities. Then a breakthrough occurred which brought dance to the public attention and gave dance an extraordinary impulse. It forced into the open the statements of human expression, new forms of movement material for dance and also a new treatment of elements of music in regard to rhythm and melody. Style and form started to clarify and that made it possible to begin to teach these aspects which were of greatest value for the creatively talented dancer. The time was not ripe yet for a systematization or narrowing down to a specific technical system. Therefore it is understandable that Modern Dance declined during the years of the Hitler regime to a far greater extent than the Classical Ballet which corresponded better to the dancers of this period. The Modern Dance was not yet able to recover from this decline. Its impact, however, should not be underestimated. Theatrical productions, opera and drama, are interspersed today with elements of dance derived not from Classical Ballet, but from the Modern Dance. The Ballet has been enriched tremendously because its earlier form of gesticulation [pantomime] has extended under the influence of the Modern Dance and has acquired new wealth of expression. There is no large ensemble of Modern Dance [in Germany] which is able to compete with the larger state-supported Ballet ensembles or with international dance companies. Private initiative is very limited considering our present general situation.... [13]

Mary Wigman's assessment of the times showed very clearly her pragmatism. Living in West Berlin under tremendous pressures, she saw that the only way Modern Dance could survive in the postwar era was by allying itself with the music theater. She recognized that the general trend went in the direction of large scale, technically spectacular production in the style of the international guest companies, and she was able to adapt to the new situation. Wigman herself now turned to the music drama; she aimed at a contemporary rebirth of the ancient Greek chorus. This was not a new idea. It linked her to her very early beginnings at the Dalcroze Institute at Hellerau in 1913, where she had observed a rehearsal for the opera *Orpheus and Euridyce* by Gluck and had written her impressions in her diary:

These actors became enraptured with words but they did not know anymore the beauty of the sound of a phrase. They had forgotten the melody inherent in language, a wonderful fluctuating of phrases and nuances...and it was as if space joined in demanding forms of expression in correspondence with its own reality.[14]

The young Mary Wigman had intuitively understood spatial dynamics. It was in this field that she created masterworks in the fifties, collaborating with leading German directors.

Not accidentally, Wigman's breakthrough into music drama occurred once again in connection with the opera *Orpheus and Eurydice*. In 1943, she had already proven herself a master of the musical stage with her choreography for Carl Orff's *Carmina Burana*, which she created with the ensemble of the Municipal Opera in Leipzig. After the war, in 1947, the culmination of her years in Leipzig was her production and directing of the opera *Orpheus and Eurydice*, which she choreographed mainly using the students of her school. Although Wigman expressed some doubts in her diaries about her ability to undertake complete responsibility for the entire production, she achieved the greatest realization of her choreographic vision in this version. Only citizens of Leipzig were able to see this production, however, since it was not performed outside the city.[15]

Wigman occasionally wrote about her choreographic process in her diaries. These entries reveal the careful thought and planning she put into her work. Regarding *Orpheus*, she wrote: "The style of the production was determined by the rhythmic and kinetic structure of the scene of the furies. There was no other choice than to continue in this initial direction."[16]

Wigman went through a very thorough process of preparing herself. Working with colored pencils, she designed choreographic sketches that captured her choreographic ideas. They show succeeding generations the detailed choreographic planning preceding rehearsals.[17] Mary Wigman also verbalized her scenario before beginning the choreographic process. In 1957, for example, before she started to do the choreography for Igor Stravinsky's *Sacre du Printemps* with the dance ensemble of the Municipal Opera Berlin, she wrote a a quite detailed outline.

> The basic theme of Stravinsky's *Sacre* is the idea of weight of the earth....
> The painter [Roerich] had to present the rigidity, the crust of the earth still captured by hibernation, the composer, the elementary force of bursting spring, the painful germination of young life. The dancers had to present the weight of the Earth--here was an essential innovation in the field of balletic presentation.... The human sacrifice was the symbolic offering which every human being has to make by his death to provide for the continuity of life.[18]

Despite her careful preparation, rehearsals for her concerts were often grueling. Yet, the enthusiasm of the audiences made up for the anxiety she experienced. She wrote in a letter to Pola Nirenska in 1957:

> Never in my life have I fought so much and struggled as I did with *Sacre*, and then suddenly, while rehearsing, I saw that it really was coming together. The enormous and incredible audience applause was a wonderful response to my doubts and bitter depressions during the preparation time with the Ballet ensemble of the Municipal Opera in Berlin. Dore Hoyer was splendid as the sacrifice. [Hoyer had temporarily returned to Germany to perform this role under Wigman's direction.] [19]

According to Hedwig Müller, Dore Hoyer's interpretation of the chosen virgin gave the work a breathtaking climax and conclusion.[20]

With this choreography for *Le Sacre du Printemps* Mary Wigman was once more the center of attention. Audiences and press both joined in the celebration of this masterwork as an uncompromising statement of Wigman's artistic beliefs. *Sacre* was her last unqualified success.

For Mary Wigman the year of 1957 was significant not only for the success of *Sacre du Printemps*, but also because she had the opportunity to reunite with leading American modern dancers. The occasion was Martha Graham's solo performance of *Judith* at the Berlin Festival in fall 1957. This historic meeting between these two pioneers in the development of Modern Dance was described by Hedwig Müller:

> Martha Graham had finished her dance; a moment of complete silence followed. Then Mary Wigman rose from the orchestra and Martha Graham walked toward her from the stage. They embraced each other and a standing ovation honored the two artists.[21]

Wigman was now surrounded by the leading American artists of the Modern Dance: Doris Humphrey, Agnes de Mille and José Limón. It was an exhilarating time. "Suddenly," she wrote, "it seemed that the bridge which was broken down was rebuilt again. Even correspondence could not achieve what a personal meeting did in a flash!"[22]

In the following year, Mary Wigman, at age 72, visited the United States once more. She went to New York, the Middle West and California and met with Martha Graham and Ruth St. Denis. This last American visit renewed contacts with old friends, giving her the opportunity to reconnect with the happiest periods of her early success in America. She also made new friends; the writer Walter Sorell became her close friend in this period and encouraged her to write. Although Wigman ignored his advice, the exchange of ideas helped her to come to terms with her eventful past. In America, Wigman saw how the seeds of the Wigman approach had grown along different lines in foreign soil. She saw the realization of her concepts in Margarethe Wallmann's very impressive production for the music theater. Wallmann had taught the Wigman approach in Berlin in the late twenties and had also danced in Wigman's company. Being Jewish, she had had to leave Germany and had carried on Wigman's ideas in her work as director of opera in Europe and America.

Wigman's influence also was seen in the Sacred Dance Movement. Erika Thiemey, another early student of Wigman, had worked in America since 1932, bringing dance into various churches. Over a lifetime, she introduced Wigman's concepts to American students in her Washington Dance Theater, which she directed from 1943 to 1979.

In regard to dance education and Modern Dance production, Hanya Holm exerted the most visible and direct influence as a carrier of the Mary Wigman approach to dance.

The pupils of Hanya Holm started to occupy the strategically important positions of the leading colleges in no time, in Wisconsin and Colorado, in Texas and California, to mention just a few. Valerie Bettis, Alwin Nikolais, Glen Tetley, among others, grew up under Hanya's direction based on Wigman's philosophy, to pave the way as well recognized dance artists....[23] A view expressed by Walter Sorell.

In Berlin, in 1960, at the opening of an exhibition of dance photographs of leading artists of the American Modern Dance, Wigman summarized her impressions from this last American visit:

> American dancers have one thing in common. It is not a question of dance themes nor of gestural forms or the rhythmic organization of their dances. It is rather a tone, something which is implied reading between the lines, an atmosphere created. It does not matter what is said, but how it is told.... America can be proud of the many artists at work in dance nowadays.[24]

It is interesting to compare Mary Wigman's very positive evaluation of the American Modern Dance after her last visit, with Dore Hoyer's observations of the New York and New London dance scene after she had danced at the tenth American Dance Festival, in 1957, at Connecticut College. When Hoyer came back, she published an article on her impressions of the American Modern Dance scene, entitled "New York: Stronghold of Modern Dance."

> The Modern Dance in America has many faces. American Modern Dance is far ahead of the European development due to the fact that there are many important dance schools teaching American Modern Dance techniques and choreography, a modern technique created for use on stage and full of vitality and of electrifying directness. The American dancer seems to operate on a higher energy level than the European dancer.... The total systematization of Modern Dance exercises, however, holds also a danger of limiting creative individuality.[25]

Dore Hoyer, a superb technician, recognized the immense possibilities of the American Modern Dance method. As the last German solo performer of expressive dance (Ausdruckstanz), she was unwilling to give up her creative individuality. Like Wigman, she was opposed to any set vocabulary of Modern Dance that would, in her view, necessarily restrict the individual's expressiveness. In the sixties, finding no basis for her existence in the D.B.R. (the German Bundesrepublik), where all cultural support went to the municipal theater ensembles, this individualistic personality, unlike Mary Wigman, refused to adapt to the changed times. In one of the last letters before her suicide, she wrote: "Only in dance could I communicate."[26]

WIGMAN'S LAST YEARS

As soon as Wigman returned from America, she threw herself into the preparation of the opera *Alceste* by Gluck for the National Theater in Mannheim, Germany.

Physically, the rehearsals became increasingly difficult for her. Although it was performed in 1958, just one year after *Le Sacre Du Printemps*, reviewers of *Alceste* felt that the work was dated. In spite of their respect for Wigman's choreographic skill, they felt *Alceste* carried the spirit of a period definitely past. This critique hurt Wigman, but it did not discourage her from producing one more work, in collaboration with the well known German director Sellner. It was her beloved opera *Orpheus and Eurydice*, performed at the German Opera Berlin during the Berlin Festival of 1961. The choreography for this opera was Mary Wigman's summing up her ideas of choral dance. In the program for the festival's performance, Wigman commented: "The unyielding demand of the choral dance on its creator, the choreographer, is: simplicity and once more simplicity in the organization of space, in its rhythmic content, in the dynamic shadings of walks, body attitude and gesture."[27] These words echo the young Mary Wigman's comments on spatial dynamics, at Hellerau. It seems evident that Wigman's strongest influence on the postwar choreographers was her large choral works, which demonstrated that space can be used as a dynamic force in the best Laban tradition.

After this last shared production with opera director Sellner, Mary Wigman finally followed Walter Sorell's encouragement to write a book. Actually, Wigman had kept a diary since 1913 when she first came to Laban, and writing had helped her to clarify her thoughts on many occasions. Wigman entered into a dialogue with Walter Sorell during this last period of her Berlin Studio, between 1961 and 1967. Out of this collaboration grew a synopsis of her artistic works as dancer and choreographer, beginning with her works of the twenties and encompassing forty years of intense artistic production. *Die Sprache des Tanzes (The Language of Dance)*[28] was translated into English by Walter Sorell in 1967. He also edited some of her early diaries, going back to her first year of study with Laban, in the *Mary Wigman Book*.[29]

After 1961, Wigman continued to teach. Two of the pupils trained in this last period of the Wigman Studio, from 1961 to 1967, successfully found a balance between the Wigman heritage and their own needs as contemporary artists. Hellmuth Fricke-Gottschild, Wigman's last assistant, and Susanne Linke both declared their allegiance to Wigman after coming to terms with their own artistic goals. After the closing of the Wigman Studio, Fricke-Gottshild experimented with his own first company, Group Motion Berlin, which he transplanted to Philadelphia in 1968. Presently he is directing The Zero Moving Company. While Fricke-Gottschild is obviously articulating his own group style in a contemporary way, Susanne Linke is redefining solo dance as one facet of Tanz-Theater, combining elements of her two mentors, Wigman and Jooss.

Mary Wigman closed the Wigman Studio in 1967. Shortly afterward, she learned of Harald Kreutzberg's death; at the close of the same year, Dore Hoyer ended her life. These two events moved Wigman very deeply. It was hard for her to survive these two artists who had pursued careers of their own while simultaneously following Wigman's example in so many ways. Their deaths signaled the end of the era of Ausdruckstanz. In her eulogy for Dore Hoyer, Wigman, who was one of Hoyer's few friends, said tellingly, "Dore Hoyer was the last modern dancer who still had something to say."[30]

After 1967, Mary Wigman faded from the dance scene. Her eyesight weakened, and when she died in 1973, she was completely blind. Only a few articles in German newspapers recorded the news of her death.

What then is Mary Wigman's legacy to Modern Dance? The question of Mary Wigman's contribution to dance was raised at the centennial celebration of her birth, organized by the Academie der Kunste (Academy of the Arts), in Berlin in 1986. The answer seemed to differ depending on which generation of dancers responded. "Wigman's strength was her insistence that the student should be sincere in communicating his feelings,"[31] was the answer from well known dance therapist Lilian Espanak, a member of the first generation of students at the Wigman School at Dresden, between 1920 and 1932. Espanak based her therapeutic method on this absolute reliance on individualism-- on being true to one's own self. Communication was the main concern of this first group of pupils, a reflection of the expressionistic twenties.

Dancers representing the second phase of the Wigman School, from 1932 to 1942, were less philosophical in their orientation to dance and more interested in technical details. They were dance pedagogues and had had less direct contact with Wigman, since she had been on tour a great deal during those years. Moreover, by this time, the Wigman School offered a more structured approach to dance. Ballet classes were required, and examinations were organized by the new Ministry of Propaganda. Dancers from this generation tended to work either in the German theater or to become teachers in one of the German music academies. The dance materials taught then as "dance practice" proved without question that Wigman had maintained her high standards as a teacher even during the war years.

It is interesting to compare the reflections of Susanne Linke and Alwin Nikolais. The last German dancer trained in the Wigman School in Berlin, Susanne Linke said: "I experienced spiritual-physical unity only with Wigman."[32] In contrast, Alwin Nikolais, who had been exposed to Wigman's approach in the United States only through Hanya Holm, recollected Holm's technique as not a style, but a way of thinking. Linke's recollections refer to a person, the artist Mary Wigman; Nikolais' recollection refers to an abstraction. The difference in these two evolutions of Wigman's influence reflects the complexity of her work as well as the transformations of her dance on American soil.

The Wigman Centennial Conference in 1986 in West Berlin was the first German attempt to re-open the dialogue, hopefully leading to a revision of Mary Wigman's image from the perspective of the nineties. It is my conviction that Mary Wigman created the crosscurrents in Modern Dance between America and Germany; this has to be recognized for a fair evaluation to be made of Mary Wigman as an artist and as a person.

NOTES FOR CHAPTER VI

1. Roters, Eberhard (1975) Als der Krieg zu Ende war. *Catalogue of the exhibition Art in Germany 1945-1950,* p.10, Berlin, Academy of the Arts

2. Ibid., Herling, Nele. Musik, p. 43

3. Ibid, Scheper, Dirk & Schmidt, Willy. Darstellende Kunst, (Performing Arts) pp.59-60

4. Artists around Palucca, exhibition and publication of the *Staatliche Kunstsammlungen Dresden Kupferstich-Kabinett* honoring Gret Palucca's 85th birthday, August 1987. She has brought representatives of the American Modern Dance to teach summer courses in Dresden.

5. Martin, John (1935) The Dance: Kreutzberg. *New York Times,* March 31

6. Hering, Doris (1947) *Dance Magazine,* December, 9

7. Alexander, Gerda (1980) *Tänzerin, Choreographin, Pädagogin Rosalia Chladek,* 3rd edn.Vienna: Östereichischer Bundesverlag.

8. Sorell, Walter (1986) *Mary Wigman: Ein Vermächtnis,* p. 222. Wilhelmshaven: Florian Noetzel Verlag

9. Loesch, Ilse (1987) A close friend of Dore Hoyer and writer on dance, read this personal letter of Hoyer at the first Dresden Dance Symposium, Oct.5

10. Schlicher, Susan (1987) *Tanz Theater,* p.133. Reinbek: Rowholts. Enzyklopädie

11. Wigman, Mary (1913) Diary entry. Wigman Archive, Berlin, Academy of the Arts, Translation by I. Bergsohn

12. Fricke-Gottschild, Hellmut (1986) At the Mary Wigman Conference in Berlin Academy of the Arts, September 24-27

13. Wigman, Mary (1954) Sie fragen nach der Berechtigung, (You ask for the justification), March 18, directed to Trudie Wolff. Wigman Archive, Berlin, Academy of the Arts. Translation by I.Bergsohn.

14. Wigman, Mary (1913) Diary entry from Hellerau. Wigman Archive, Berlin, Academy of the Arts

15. Ludewig, Jutta (1987) Soloists, and Leipzig school assistant, 1945-48, discussing Wigman's breakthrough to creations in music drama *Orpheus*. The fact that all performers were trained by Wigman herself, made this production the clearest example of Wigman's choreographic intentions.

16. Wigman, Mary (1947) Diary entry, August. Wigman Archiv, Berlin

17. Steinbeck, Dietrich (1987) *Mary Wigmans Choreographisches Skizzenbuch 1930-1961 (Choreographic Sketch book 1930-1961).* Berlin: Edition Hentrich. This publication gives eloquent evidence of Mary Wigman's process of conceptualizing

18. Wigman, Mary (1957) Excerpts from The Basic Idea of Stravinsky's Ballet *Rite of Spring,* Wigman Archive. Berlin, Translation by I.Bergsohn

19. Wigman, Mary (1957) Letter to Pola Nirenska, one of the two Jewish members in Wigman's company who Wigman dismissed under pressures of the Ministry of Propaganda. Published in Walter Sorell's *Mary Wigman: Ein Vermächtnis* (1986). p.241. Wilhelmshaven: Florian Noetzel Verlag. Translation by I. Bergsohn

20. Müller, Hedwig (1986) *Mary Wigman: Leben und Werk der grossen Tänzerin,* p. 299. Berlin: Quadriga.

21. Ibid., p.295. Translation by I. Bergsohn

22. Sorell, Walter. (1986) *Mary Wigman: Ein Vermächtnis* p.241.

23. Ibid., p. 262

24. Wigman, Mary (1960) Excerpt from Wigman's speech at the opening of the exhibition of American Dance Photographs. Translation by I.Bergsohn Berlin:Wigman Archiv

25. Hoyer, Dore (1957) New York: Hochburg des Modernen Tanzes. (New York: stronghold of Modern Dance.) *Singchor und Tanz,* publication of the official Theatre organization, fall. Written after her return from the 10th American Dance Festival in New London, CT. Translation by I.Bergsohn

26. Loesch, Ilse (1986) Personal letter of Dore Hoyer. Read at the first Dance symposium at the Music Academy at Dresden, Oct.4-7

27. Wigman, Mary (1961) Excerpt from Chorischer Tanz (Choral Dance). *Berliner Festwochen Almanach,* April 7. Translation I.Bergsohn.

28.   Wigman, Mary (1963) *Die Sprache des Tanzes*. Stuttgart: Ernst Battenberg
       Verlag.(Translated by Walter Sorell, *The Language of Dance,* Middletown,
       CT: Wesleyan University Press,(1967).

29.   Wigman, Mary. (1975) *The Mary Wigman Book* edited and translated by Walter
       Sorell. Middleton, Conn: Wesleyan University Press. The Mary Wigman
       Book filled the need for English language documentation on this
       essential artist of the European Modern Dance tradition.

30.   Müller, Hedwig (1986) *Mary Wigman*, p.298. Berlin: Quadriga

31.   Espanak, Lilian (1986) Notes from the Centennial Wigman Conference,
       Sept.24-27. Berlin, Academy of the Arts

32.   Linke, Susanna (1986) Statement at the Centennial Wigman Conference, Sept.
       24-27

CHAPTER VII: FROM *THE GREEN TABLE*

TO *JOURNEY IN THE FOG* AND BEYOND.

Mary Wigman and Kurt Jooss represent two different responses to the crisis that faced artists in Germany under National Socialism. Wigman, choosing to remain in Germany, had personal rather than political or moral motives. She did not want to separate from a companion who, since 1929, had supported her in many difficult situations, Hanns Benkert. An engineer in a leading position at Siemens and her confidante since the stressful preparations for *Totenmal*, Benkert had given stability to Wigman and also had influenced her to adapt her art to National Socialist ideologies in the years between 1933 and 1936. Their partnership endured until 1942, when Benkert decided to marry another woman. By this time, in the midst of World War II, it was too late for Wigman to leave.[1]

Jooss, recognizing from the onset the true nature of National Socialism, refused to compromise with it and went into exile instead. Both courses of action led to great personal sacrifices and nearly unsustainable artistic challenges. Their different choices, reflecting their different levels of political sophistication as well as their particular generation, temperament, and personal lives, had significant implications for their artistic work. When we look at Wigman's path--great success in the United States, followed by three years of recognition by the Nazis as "Germany's greatest dancer," then, after 1936, an increasing isolation in Nazi Germany and, finally, vilification as a "degenerate artist"--Jooss's choice to leave Germany and immigrate to England might appear the path to a less troubled artistic future. His life, however, also had its ordeals. Having abruptly left Nazi Germany behind him, Jooss lost the support of the German municipal theater (see Chapter IV). He gave up his directorship of the Folkwang School's Dance Department as well as his leading position at the Essen Opera House, his home in Essen and his income. Jooss, recalling these events, wrote in his biographical notes for August 1933:

In Essen during August, the daily difficulties with the NSDAP are constantly increasing. F.A. Cohen, Heinz Rosen and Ruth Harris had been discharged by the municipality in March 1933. Jooss fights for his Jewish, half-Jewish and quarter-Jewish company members, who officially cannot be denied him since the ensemble, "Ballets Jooss," is now under private management. The disputes with the "Gauleitung" at the headquarters of the Nazi Party are increasing daily. Finally, mid-September, two weeks before the planned Dutch tour, Jooss is warned through the Freemasons: He is to leave Essen and Germany immediately, because the 'Gauleitung' has decided to take him into protective custody (i.e, concentration camp). An immediate, adventurous plan is successful, and two days later the entire ensemble crosses the Dutch border near Maastricht. Eighteen hours later a commission (local Gestapo) arrives at the house Brunnenstrasse 5 to arrest Jooss. The home is confiscated.[2]

Without a home base, his first priority became the continuation of Ballets Jooss. Fortunately, the two new works, *The Prodigal Son* and *Seven Heroes*, which he choreographed while the company was on tour in Western and Eastern Europe, England, Scandinavia and America in 1933, received favorable reviews. English reviewers seemed to accept Jooss's attempt to combine the precision of ballet with the dramatic dynamic and imagination of the modern school, as an article in *Theatre Arts Monthly* of February, 1934, reveals:

> The Jooss system is of the day after yesterday rather than of the day before tomorrow. He is completely contemporaneous, without fanaticism, and no one who understands the life and reactions of the present is uncomfortable in his audience. Slightly nostalgic, resentful, caustic he may be, but he is characterized by that admirable frankness and directness which may be remarked in all youth. There is nothing of that agonized guesswork, that abstract experimentation which has blurred much of the dance work of his generation. He is as sure, as free, and as reasonable as a healthy peasant striding through his fields.... There is one vast difference which sets it aside from the great cult of Wigman, her colleagues and followers--Jooss exists for the theatre and has built his art for the stage only. He does not dance for the dance's sake, nor for body's nor the soul's. His dancers are actors, or his actors are dancers, whichever you prefer. And he has, in his best works, come very near to producing a completely new form.[3]

Jooss was also fortunate in receiving concrete support from Leonard and Dorothy Elmhirst, who turned over a part of their Devonshire estate, Dartington Hall, to him. Facilities in a cloistered fourteenth-century courtyard were converted to accommodate the family, faculty and students. There were spacious outdoor stages and a small, intimate theater designed by Walter Gropius. Sigurd Leeder arrived with the staff and twenty-three students from the Folkwangschule Essen in April 1934 to establish the Jooss-Leeder School of Dance.

JOOSS IN ENGLAND

The Dartington years from 1934 to 1939 seem to have been the most fulfilling time in Jooss's life. After months of improvised housing Jooss had a home again. He and his wife, Aino Siimola, could live again as a family with their daughter, Anna. Moreover, the estate offered excellent facilities for dance, and, since living quarters and work areas all surrounded the old courtyard, Aino could share very closely in the choreographic process. Aino's sharp observations and merciless critiques complemented Kurt Jooss's imaginative choreographic process in producing new pieces for the company: *The Mirror* (1935), *A Spring Tale* (1939) and *Chronica* (1939) were added to the repertory of the company in this period. Ballets Jooss gained a unique international reputation and undertook world tours annually between 1935 and 1938. The fame of the company attracted students from all over the world to the Jooss-Leeder School of Dance. Among the students drawn to the School was Lucas Hoving, best known in America as protagonist of José Limón in his well-known modern dance company of the 1950s and

1960s. Lucas came to Dartington in 1938, after "some nonchalant training in his homeland Holland," as he noted, to study at the Jooss-Leeder School. He became a member of the Ballets Jooss in the early years of World War II. Hoving recalled that: "The atmosphere was unbelievable. Jooss, Leeder and Laban were around on campus accessible to us. It was my first meeting with true substance and it settled my own approach to dance for life."[4]

Another student of Jooss in the same period in England was Ann Hutchinson, the founder of the Dance Notation Bureau in New York. Lucas Hoving, as both performer and choreographer, and Ann Hutchinson, as specialist in Labanotation, contributed significantly to American Modern Dance. In later years, whenever Jooss mentioned Dartington Hall his face lit up in a smile; these were the golden years of his life, after his traumatic flight from Nazi Germany.

In 1936, while Jooss had found a balance between his pedagogic work in the Jooss-Leeder School and his choreographic work with his company at Dartington Hall, the political situation worsened in Germany for Laban (see Chapter IV). Dr. Goebbel's cancellation of Laban's movement choir work *Vom Tauwind und der neuen Freude* (*Springwind and the New Joy*) at the dress rehearsal of the opening event of the Berlin Olympic Games abruptly terminated all of Laban's activities in Germany; Laban was kept in custody for nearly a year, until he escaped to Paris. He was in dire straits when Jooss met him in Paris in November, 1937, and brought him as a guest to Dartington Hall.

Laban only gradually recovered from the shock of having his extensive work in Germany annihilated. Besides Jooss and his wife, Aino, Lisa Ullmann also took care of Laban and she became his closest companion in his work and his life during his English period. At this point in his life Lisa Ullmann, a former student of Laban, who had taught Modern Dance at the Folkwang School, was just the right person to help him restore his energies. Laban distanced himself from his expressionistic past and also from active practical theater dance, but he took enough interest in Jooss's artistic development to write the following letter to Jooss on his way to Geneva, on Christmas, 1938:

My dear Jooss,

It gave me great pleasure before my departure from Dartington to watch some rehearsals of your two new ballets. I found confirmed what we have both known for a long time: namely, that although your work has developed in an individual and original manner, its source is as clear and its enthusiasm as genuine as it was when I had the privilege to introduce you to the Noble Art of Dancing.

And that means much, not only of personal satisfaction to myself, but to the dance in general. I see how through your work, more than through the work of any other of my disciples and collaborators, a great hope nears fulfillment: that the language of movement might become apt to express in easily understandable form those deep and essential things which can only be stated by the dance. For the driving force of the new creative dance is still the desire to express those things which cannot be rendered articulate in any other language....

> Your *Spring Tale* is a dance of life and love, a worthy counterpart to *The Green Table*, which is a dance of death. Your *Chronica* is a moving example of how life, under the rigid enforcement of human will-power, becomes numbed; and how this power-instinct then destroys itself: for life means eternal freedom-eternal youth....

> In true friendship.... [5]

Jooss considered *Chronica*, a metaphor for the Nazis' tyranny, to be one of his major choreographic works, on a par with *The Green Table* and his later dramatic work, *Journey in the Fog*. All three dealt directly with a political reality. As the following review by Ashley Dukes in *Theatre Monthly* suggested, *Chronica* was Jooss's prediction of political catastrophe:

> A free urban community of the great Italian age develops that remarkable and mystic complex, the hero-worship of a "Leader." Just how this comes about is shown discreetly, reasonably, even sympathetically. The hero is not without his very likeable qualities. But inevitably the system introduced to secure peace and order evolves in the direction of tyranny and conquest.... The development of the tale is straightforward and lacks both psychological subtlety and humor, neither of which would be in place. Dr. Goebbels may easily be identified with the character of impish Filippo, and that is the only element of caricature and an unimportant one. The whole drama is danced before curtains, with an immensely resourceful use of lighting. Here Kurt Jooss has said his say wordlessly, simply and strongly. [6]

Unfortunately, Jooss's productive years at Dartington were cut short by the outbreak of war between Germany and England. The Jooss-Leeder School had to close since it was located too near the coast. Moreover, Jooss, whose application for British citizenship was held up by the war, was interned as an enemy alien; after six months, however, he was released. [7] Unable to leave England, he temporarily had to disband the company in 1942. During this summer of 1942, his second daughter, Christina, was born.

After the closing of the Jooss-Leeder School at Dartington Hall, Lisa Ullman became very active in English physical education developing workshops, conferences and lecture demonstrations with Laban. They showed their model of English educational dance in several English training colleges at various locations. At the same time, Laban started to collaborate with Frederic Charles Lawrence, a management consultant in industry. They focussed on the social role of movement in industry. They recorded work problems caused by one sided movements in operation of machines in factories. Their aim was to remedy those damages to the bodily and mental wellbeing of workers. In 1942, they also jointly published the findings of this research in a booklet, *Industrial Rhythm and Lilt in Labour*. In 1947, this material was revised, further clarified and published by Laban, with

Lawrence, under the title *Effort*.[8]

In 1942, Laban and Ullmann settled in Manchester where Ullmann founded, in co-operation with Sylvia Bodmer, the Manchester Dance Circle (1943). Their focus was clearly on recreational and educational dance. In 1949, their Art of Movement Studio in Manchester was officially recognized by the Ministry of Education and exerted a decisive influence on English physical education. It became a center for observation and analysis of movement processes in their widest sense. Laban's publications *Modern Educational Dance* (1948)[9] and *The Mastery of Movement on the Stage* (1950)[10] reflect the very broad approach to movement that characterized Laban's last two decades of educational activity in England. Valerie Preston-Dunlop and Marion North were pupils of Laban and Ullmann in Manchester who have carried on his work. North published *Personality Assessment Through Movement*,[11] and Valerie Preston-Dunlop with John Hodgson wrote *Laban*.[12]

Laban died in 1958 in Weybridge, Surrey, England, before he had the chance to witness the further development of Labanotation, choreology or dance therapy in the sixties and seventies in America and Europe. He is remembered in England as the father of the modern educational dance; Germans, however, hold up a very different image of Laban: they recall him primarily as the initiator of the rebellious Modern Dance of the twenties.

In contrast to Laban's broadening perspective on movement education, Kurt Jooss clearly pursued the development of dance theater on a professional level. He felt a deep loyalty to England, which had given him refuge, and he identified very consciously with the democratic values of his adopted homeland. Even when he was interned for six months as an enemy alien, his spirit was unbroken. Unable to leave England, he had to disband the company in 1942 and that was a hard blow. But he adapted to the necessities of war, temporarily reconstituting a company of twelve members. Since there was a shortage of male dancers, Jooss, who had given up performing in 1938, returned to the stage and performed with his company, which played for five weeks in June 1944. The performances took place at the Haymarket, one of only six London theaters still operating despite the V-bombs. Thereafter, the company toured Belgium, Holland, France, Norway, and Denmark.

Kurt Jooss was granted British citizenship in 1947, and he performed in postwar Europe for the British Occupation Army, reentering Germany in British uniform.[13] Ironically, after Jooss finally had become a British citizen, the financial situation in postwar Britain did not allow the continuation of Ballets Jooss. He had to disband his company once again, in 1947, as there was no more support for his work in England.

Facing disaster, Jooss was rescued, this time by three former soloists of Ballets Jooss who had settled in Chile: Ernst Uthoff, Rudolf Pescht and Lola Botka. They invited him to serve as guest choreographer for the Chilean National Ballet for eight months, between May and December, 1948. Jooss staged four works in South America and even danced once more the role of Death in *The Green Table*. In May 1949, he received an invitation from the City of Essen, Germany, to teach a summer course at the Folkwang School. Jooss agreed, since this would give him a chance to take a realistic look at the conditions of his old dance department. Another invitation reached Jooss for the same summer, and fortunately he was able to accept it, too. The Swiss Association of Professionals in Dance and Gymnastics (Der Schweizer Berufsverband für Tanz und Gymnastik) had initiated the first international summer school in Zürich, and asked Jooss to teach there in July, 1949.

Twenty years had passed since the stormy German Dancers' Congresses, which had been filled with polemic discussions, between Wigman on the one side and Laban and Jooss on the other, regarding the function of dance in the German theater. In the meantime, most of the German theaters had been destroyed, and the leaders of Modern Dance who assembled in the peaceful atmosphere of Switzerland in 1949 came as survivors. In a way, it was a miracle for Rosalia Chladek, Mary Wigman, Harald Kreutzberg and Kurt Jooss to spend two weeks together in these lovely surroundings. A much-needed exchange of ideas ensued, and in spite of minor differences in style, the senior leaders reestablished old contacts and friendships, realizing that as members of the same generation, they had much in common.

These Swiss summer events refocussed on European Modern Dance and brought its leaders closer together in the awareness of a common cause. Jooss was joined by his first soloist, Hans Züllig, who came directly from performing with the Sadler's Wells Ballet, and both appeared very much as Englishmen when they first came to Zürich. In the eyes of the other European modern dancers, Züllig seemed very balletic when he demonstrated Jooss's style. It was obvious that Jooss in his Dartington years had created a new style of dance that integrated classical with modern elements, while Chladek, Wigman and Kreutzberg had remained in the Ausdruckstanz tradition. But aside from these differences, the courses in Zürich were for all of them a confirmation that Modern Dance still existed in a world that had drastically changed.

Kurt Jooss became aware of some of these changes which had taken place in Germany when he started his summer teaching at the Folkwang School in Essen in 1949. It was a very different dance department he found than the one he had left in 1932, and it could not compare with the Jooss-Leeder School in England, which Jooss had been forced to give up at the onset of World War II. The condition in which he found the dance department of the Folkwang School, located now in an old German monastery, was deplorable. Even though the department had managed to exist through the nineteen-thirties and early forties under the direction of one of his previous company members, Trude Pohl, the facilities for dance had become badly run down during the war.

Jooss taught daily classes in technique and also in eukinetics. His appearance was very distinguished, with his silver-gray hair accompanying his sculpturally spacious movements. Not yet fifty, he had a wonderful vitality and demonstrated with great clarity and seeming effortlessness. His movements flowed; they had volume and seemed to enjoy weight. Jooss appeared to be completely at ease despite the fact that he found himself working with students of dissimilar backgrounds.

The participants were largely the regular students of the school, in the Ruhr district. They studied under poor physical conditions and the training was not on a professional level. Some dancers from the Swiss summer course had followed him to Essen; also, some German theater dancers used their vacations to work under Kurt Jooss. All students responded instantly to him as a teacher. Whether they were Folkwang students or dancers in one of the German municipal opera houses, they recognized that after years of cultural deprivation they were now being taught by a master teacher of the highest caliber. Jooss certainly saw how he was needed; he also saw how much had to be done to bring this institute up to international standards. Despite certain misgivings, by the end of this course he had agreed to return to his homeland as director of the dance department of the Folkwang School. The City of Essen had promoted progressive cultural activities during the era of the Weimar Republic and looked back with justified pride on the establishment of the Folkwang Museum and the Folkwang School. People nationwide were drawn to these important cultural centers of the Nordrhein-Westfalen region. Administrators were eager to regain Kurt Jooss, co-founder of the Folkwang School, and the first director of its dance department. Jooss's work was now internationally famous and his name would unquestionably add luster to their own reputations as leaders of the postwar West German cultural revival. As funding for culture began to flow again because of the West German currency reform, these officials, their optimism and confidence renewed, chose to promote a project which could bring Essen into the limelight again. However, they were thinking only in terms of the old municipal dance ensembles, and their failure to understand the concept of an independent, cosmopolitan dance company with international scope doomed the project from the start.

For Jooss, the decision to return to Germany was difficult to make. He was a British citizen, and his daughters had grown up within the British educational system. His family had been forced to move several times before and during the war years. His wife, Aino, was not in good health. In addition, he had reservations about the kind of support he could expect to receive from Essen. In his negotiations with the City of Essen, Jooss recognized some of the administrators from previous years; with them, he felt a mutual understanding. However, he sensed in others whom he had only recently met a certain resentment behind their polite smiles. Was it plain envy of him as a successful, internationally known choreographer, or did they have something to cover up? He asked himself who had collaborated with the Nazi regime, and whom he could trust.

Although he retained very serious doubts about returning to Essen, Jooss also saw a chance to achieve the realization of his vision. The City of Essen had agreed to refinance both a new company and a remodeled dance department. This was perhaps the last opportunity to fulfill his dream of a truly contemporary dance ensemble in liaison with an academy of twentieth-century dance. He had been near to this ideal situation at Dartington, but the war had interrupted his work. Now, in 1949, Jooss was willing to try once more, and this time in Germany. He decided to take a chance, as he had done in most of his difficult life decisions, perhaps because his basically positive and optimistic nature won out.

KURT JOOSS IN ESSEN

As soon as Jooss arrived on the scene as the new director of the dance department of the Folkwang Schule, the studios were upgraded, new dance floors were laid, and showers were installed. The abbey in Essen-Werden kept its historic look from the outside, but the inside was completely remodeled to offer three large dance studios, a theory room for dance notation, and adequate dressing rooms.

Accompanying these physical changes were major reforms in the curriculum. Jooss introduced daily classes in modern and classical technique for every student. This alone represented a decisive shift in direction: Jooss was fully aware that times had changed, and he was determined to elevate standards to a professional level. He also added folkloric dance as a regular course, to prepare the dance students for future theater careers. The curriculum further included eukinetics, choreutics, improvisation, composition, rhythmic analysis, traditional dance forms, music for dancers, history of dance, Kinetography Laban taught by Albrecht Knust, and dance pedagogics. Jooss hired professional specialists such as Laura Marris, who came from England to teach classical technique; Giesela Reber; to develop the courses in folkloric dance; and Hans Züllig, an outstanding soloist with the Ballets Jooss who had grown up with Leeder-Jooss in Dartington, to teach modern technique. He also retained Trude Pohl as a teacher of improvisation and modern dance. Finally, the program was expanded from three years to four.

Dancers from all over the world came to study at the new dance department. Many hoped to be considered later for the Folkwang Tanz-Theater der Stadt Essen, the company which Jooss began to form. There was an exuberant spirit of renewal and of high expectations. For one year, 1949/1950, Jooss himself trained this internationally mixed group. He had to prepare them for his special language of movement, which was new to this generation of dancers. They either came with a classical background prepared to perform in an opera ballet ensemble, or they had grown up in the German Ausdruckstanz (expressive dance) tradition and hated ballet. Jooss made them aware of the dramatic and expressive values inherent in the classical system and combined the rich classical material with the achievements of the new German dance. This involved not just placing classical and modern movement forms side by side, but truly integrating the characteristics of both systems into a new, dramatic, twentieth-century language of dance. Jooss had the help of Hans Züllig in preparing students to perform in his movement ensemble style, for which they were trained technically every morning for at least one year. In the afternoon, Jooss's wife, Aino Siimola, sat next to him as he restaged the original Ballets Jooss works (*Big City*, *Pavane*, *A Ball in Old Vienna*, and *The Green Table*). Her thyroid gland condition did not allow her to dance anymore, but her unfailing memory and accurate observation of every movement detail were an immense help to Jooss. She acted as a filter for his choreographic process and ensured the most thorough preparation of the new company.

The Folkwang Tanz-Theater der Stadt Essen had its debut performance on June 8, 1951, at the Essen Opera House. The leading soloists of the previous Ballets Jooss, Rolf Alexander, Noelle de Mosa, Ulla Soederbaum and Hans Züllig performed together with some new members, dancers from Holland, Switzerland, France and Germany, who had joined Jooss at the Folkwang School during the 1949/1950 season.

The debut performance, like the original program, opened with *Big City*, choreographed by Kurt Jooss to music by Alexandre Tansman, with costumes designed by Hein Heckroth. As in the original performance, the ballet was accompanied by two pianos. Following the format of the original Jooss program, an interlude of piano music by César Franck led to the second piece, *Fantasy*, a ballet premiere choreographed by Hans Züllig to Franz Schubert's *Fantasie* in f Minor.

After an intermezzo of Brahms' waltzes, the world premiere of Jooss's *Colombinade* was performed to an adaptation of Johann Strauss's music by Aleida Montijn. For this humorous piece, the following program directions were given: "Take the register of persons, add a snuff of your own fantasy, mix well and serve it fresh, through two open eyes."[14] After the intermission, the evening ended with a restaging of Kurt Jooss's dance drama *The Green Table*. The press reviews were generally enthusiastic. Gerd Vielhaber wrote for the *Frankfurter Neue Presse*:

> After two years of preparation in the seclusion of the Werdener abbey, Kurt Jooss, the great master, trained a new generation of dancers who will find their place side by side with the great European ballet and dance ensembles. The festive debut of the new "Folkwang Tanz-Theater of the City of Essen" at the opera house in Essen became a triumph. The first reencounter with Kurt Jooss surpassed all expectations."[15]

Dr. Gerigk wrote in the *Essener Tageblatt:* "If this daring attempt succeeds, then this work of Kurt Jooss will cause a transformation of the art of dance, and then a new base will be reached, with Essen as its center."[16] This last statement indicated very clearly that the Office of Cultural Affairs in Essen hoped to regain Essen's leading role by financing the Folkwang Tanz-Theater. The reactions of the press also confirmed Jooss's impression that audiences in Germany responded most strongly to his early works. Without question *The Green Table* received the highest praise. *Big City* was reviewed as a period piece, thanks to its original costumes; its social implications, however (Jooss's portrayal of a German ghetto situation of the hopelessly poor), were barely mentioned.

A few months later, in October, 1951, Jooss followed up this encouraging opening performance at the Essen Opera with a second program. It contained three pieces new to the German audience. The evening opened with the European premiere of *Dithyrambus*, a ballet to music by Handel that Jooss had choreographed in Santiago, Chile, in 1948. The reviewer, Fritz Heerwagen, observed that: "Jooss knew how to find movements, attitudes and groupings which bring antique vases, sculptures and scenes of bucolic idylls to our inner view. If *The Green Table* is Jooss's strongest creation, *Dithyrambus* is the most beautiful."[17] The second piece, *Le Bosquet*, a ballet by Hans Züllig to music by Jean Philippe Rameau, transformed a park scene of Watteau quite elegantly into fluent motion. After an intermezzo, played by two pianos, *Ball in Old Vienna* ended the evening. The audience loved it. According to Dr. Gerigk of the *Essener Tageblatt*, it was "the highpoint of this program."

The Folkwang Tanz-Theater of the City of Essen gave several performances in West Germany and in Berlin. It also toured Holland, Belgium, Luxemburg, Switzerland, Scandinavia, England, Scotland and Ireland.[18] Jooss, meanwhile, worked restlessly to add new pieces to the established repertory. One of the new Jooss ballets seen on tour was *The Night Train*, with music by Alexandre Tansman and costumes by Robert Pudlich. Clive Barnes, seeing it performed in London, thought it was one of the most delightful works of the new Jooss repertory. Set in a railway compartment, the ballet related the dreams of two passengers. In Barnes's words, this humorous work made an "amazingly inconsequential counterbalance to the more serious ballets in the repertory."[19] Jooss wanted to show that he was not just resuming his choreographic work in Essen, but that during his years in exile he had crystallized a new form of ballet, which he now presented with his Folkwang Tanz-Theater der Stadt Essen.

The most significant outcome of Jooss's creative energy in the postwar Essen years was *Journey in the Fog*. Like *The Green Table*, a monumental work of dramatic dance that had grown out of the problematic years following World War II, *Journey in the Fog* made an artistic statement of similar proportion about the more recent past. For this large group choreography, however, he chose a more abstract language of movement to portray man's suffering and insecurity. *Journey in the Fog* is a symphonic work, set to the music of Aleida Montijn, in four movements: exile, barbed wire, shadows, and journey. The four images, like movements of a symphony, are poetic rather than representing any realistic action, and the single dancer is used like a voice in an orchestra. The critic Dr. Gerigk compared the finale "to a counterpoint of bodies who are moved as independent voices of a musical score unified by the conception of Kurt Jooss."[20] The fact that the German critics compared the structure of this work to a musical score shows that as late as 1952 they were not yet used to seeing this degree of abstraction in dance. Although the English critic Clive Barnes praised this immense work as a "distinguished" ballet and lauded the last movement's "choreographic craftsmanship,"[21] and although Jooss himself considered *Journey* to be one of his most important works, on a par with *The Green Table*, the audience in Essen, while responding respectfully, did not fully grasp the work's significance.

Journey in the Fog was performed again in 1952 at the second German Dancers' Congress at Recklinghausen before the assembled leaders of German dance. At the Congress, Jooss pleaded for a synthesis combining the historically developed forms of dance (classical ballet) and the new achievements of Modern Dance, those that concentrated on true expression and were relevant to contemporary times. The old controversy flared up again; both Tatjana Gsovsky and Mary Wigman argued for a clear separation of ballet and Modern Dance. However, *Journey in the Fog* proved that this polemic was really outdated; Jooss had already forged a language that blended ballet and Modern Dance to express contemporary issues in dramatic ways. At least some of his professional colleagues recognized the significance of Jooss's new work. As Kurt Peters wrote in the official publication of the German dance organization, "*Journey in the Fog* presented magnificent male dancers who exemplified the superb ensemble structures of Jooss in symbolic images of our time."[22]

THE DISSOLUTION OF THE FOLKWANG TANZ-THEATER

Unfortunately, *Journey in the Fog* was barely seen outside Germany. Despite his promising beginnings and rave press reviews both at home and abroad, in May 1953, Jooss was suddenly asked to disband his company. The City of Essen refused to continue its financial support, and the Folkwang Tanz-Theater was forced to cancel its touring commitments. The news of this strange change in German cultural policy spread quickly to other countries in Europe. The Dutch press interpreted this unexpected turn of events as political in motivation:

> It would be tragic and absolutely irresponsible if the most famous German dance group should now be obliged to end its successful activity. In Bonn circles there are rumors that the more or less forced ending of the Jooss Ballet is due to political motives. The pacifist trends, it is said, of *The Green Table*, Jooss's world-famous creation, do not agree with certain circles in the Federal Republic. But Essen's mayor Toussaint and Jooss himself assure that only financial reasons and no political implications influenced the decision of the Essen administration. However, the Jooss affair reveals a noteworthy deficiency in the organization of the Bundesrepublik. Bonn does not have a Ministry of Education, Art and Sciences. The cultural concerns of West Germany are the responsibility of the state governments. However, these states do not have the necessary financial means at their disposal to ensure the most important cultural activities. At least the Federal Government should guarantee the continuity of such an enterprise as the Jooss Ballet.[23]

Was the Dutch press correct in its explanation of the causes behind this sudden change in Essen's cultural policy? The City of Essen had actually guaranteed financial support for the company for only one year. It seems obvious to anybody dealing with theater, however, that a dance ensemble cannot be self-supporting after one year. Even Diaghilev, with all his initial success, struggled tremendously during the second period of the Ballet Russe to gain financial independence for the company. The Folkwang Tanz-Theater der Stadt Essen was the first attempt of a dance company to achieve economic solvency in postwar Germany. Not even Tatjana Gsovsky was able to build an independent dance ensemble before the middle of the fifties, and that was in Berlin, where she had been the queen of ballet for many years.

The actual reason for discontinuing support of Jooss's work was neither political nor financial but rather reflected the parochial perspective of Essen's city fathers. A deep discrepancy obviously existed between Jooss's artistic aims, which were of international proportion, and the more narrow aims of the City of Essen, which were mostly concerned with its own reputation, as a comment in the *Essener Tageblatt* showed very clearly: "The payments of the citizens of Essen for the 'Folkwang Tanz-Theater' were discontinued after it became apparent that the fruits of this work essentially benefitted the German and European cultural centers, but barely the City of Essen!"[24]

Cultural concerns, to be sure, may have been tied in to local politics. Jooss had not felt on firm ground ever since his return to Essen. He had discovered on more than one occasion how society had changed. His old friends of the twenties greeted him cordially, but he also had to negotiate with men whose political activity during the Third Reich was unclear. He himself had returned with an absolutely clean political record, but he felt an animosity from people who preferred not to remember their political past. He was met with respect, but did this really indicate a willingness to support his artistic endeavors, especially when his major works had obvious political implications? Jooss had not taken the time to analyze these relationships, however; he was much too involved with his artistic work.

Whatever the reason was for Essen's decision, Jooss was deeply disappointed and discouraged. The loss of financial support in the midst of the second season of performances stunned Jooss. He informed his company of the news in a terse note, saying only that after 300 performances and great success in Germany and abroad he had to cancel the performance in Paris and the last performances in Amsterdam and The Hague due to the disbandment of the company. Several guaranteed tours to the United States, South America and England were also canceled. Jooss had worked relentlessly to reestablish an international dance ensemble with the Folkwang Tanz-Theater der Stadt Essen. The success of the company had exceeded the expectations of any administrator, and the withdrawal of the financial support seemed almost unbelievable. Ironically, Jooss's experiences in postwar Germany turned out to be similar to Mary Wigman's. She too had received support for only a short time from the Berlin magistrate and had then been left to her own devices. She, however, had not been wooed as ardently as Essen had wooed Jooss.

He now felt betrayed. He had exchanged his international, independent company for one dependent upon local administrators' patronage. He had relocated his family and his soloists, who were devoted to his work, hoping to reestablish himself in his homeland as an artist and choreographer. He was forced to accept the fact that in postwar Germany, cultural concerns had less importance than material restoration. The voice of dancers had little weight in the age of the economic miracle. Jooss made one final effort to keep his work alive when he accepted a position as chief choreographer with the Opera Düsseldorf in 1954. He was promised that he could reestablish his dance theater there in his second season with the Opera. He moved to Düsseldorf, which meant commuting daily by a local train to Essen-Werden to fulfill his teaching obligations at the Folkwang School. The situation at the Opera was not without difficulties since Jooss had to take over a ballet ensemble accustomed to its own standard repertory. After one frustrating year at the Opera, a change of directors brought a new policy for the Opera. Jooss resigned in the fall of 1956.

Jooss now reached the lowest point in his own "Journey in the Fog." He came to the realization that his plan of building an international company once again was premature. This effort had cost him a tremendous amount of energy, and the exhaustion from having driven himself so relentlessly the last seven years finally caught up with him. While climbing into a tram, he was hit by a car and temporarily immobilized. His wife's illness, by this time, had worsened, and he had serious financial worries.

While recuperating from the accident Jooss spent some time thinking over his own situation, and he decided to refocus on his pedagogic work. He had re-established the prestige of the Folkwang School Dance Department as the leading state-supported institution offering dance in West Germany in the fifties. Now, thinking about future needs, one of his early memoranda, written in 1927 when he founded the Folkwang Dance Department, came back to his mind. He had been intensely involved with Laban's dance and movement concepts at that time and had started to work on plans for a German Dance Academy.

Originally, his proposal had conceived an "Institute for Pure Dance." This vision for a "Studio for Dance and Movement Art" recaptured his imagination. Richer from the experience of choreographing and teaching for nearly thirty years, Kurt Jooss revised his earlier proposal, focussing on the apparent needs of the stage dance in postwar Germany. Since the Dance Department of the Folkwang School was the most diversified of public dance institutions in Germany of the mid-fifties, Jooss formulated his new proposal as "Plan for a Dance Academy as a Superstructure to the Professional Classes of the Dance Department of the Folkwang School in Essen."[25]

RAISING STANDARDS OF STAGE DANCE IN WEST GERMANY

Jooss's ambitious plan combined a program to prepare ballet masters, choreographers and teachers of professional studios, and movement educators in schools. It also included an institute for kinetography, an institute for comparative dance studies, and a seminar in dance criticism, with a special adjacent library offering translations of key works of French, Italian, and English dance writers. If this amazingly comprehensive plan had ever been realized, it would have fulfilled dreams which Laban himself had never specified in such detail. This complex model is still unattained in Germany and in America, and it remains a goal for future dance administrators to implement. Nevertheless, it served to guide Jooss as pedagogue from this time on in his efforts to gradually lay the foundation for a future academy in Essen.

Jooss was not alone in his concern about raising the standards of German stage dance. In the mid-fifties, some German theater professionals had started to express concern about the deplorable state of affairs in dance, and, in 1955, Jooss was invited by this group of theater professionals to chair the founding ceremonies of a Society for the Promotion of Artistic Dance in Krefeld. On this occasion, Heinz Laurenzen brought up the idea of an International Summer Academy. After two years of organization and preparation by the society, an International Summer Academy was first offered in Krefeld. It gave German dancers and students a wider perspective by offering courses taught by Victor and Tatjana Gsovsky side-by-side with the Austrian modern dancer Rosalia Chladek. The International Summer Academy became an annual event in dance, moving to Cologne after two initial years in Krefeld, where it became a very influential institution for dance in Germany in the sixties.

By this time, Laurenzen, the director of the six-week Summer Academy, the Institute for Stage Dance, and the Ballet Academy Cologne, started his own completely independent cultural program in Cologne and focussed particularly on offering American

Modern Dance. Leading American instructors taught fundamentals of American jazz and Graham technique in set exercise sequences to large classes of enthusiastic German dance lovers. The Summer Academy familiarized European dancers and students with American artists Mary Hinkson, who taught Graham technique, Walter Nix, who taught American jazz, and Alvin Ailey, who introduced his own style, based on the work of Lester Horton.

The International Summer Academy of Dance in Cologne has been in existence for nearly thirty years. Hundreds of European dancers have trained there in classical, folklore, tap and contemporary Modern Dance during their summer break, gradually improving their technical level. A week of guest performances of American choreographers with their companies, such as Paul Taylor in Modern Dance and Todd Bolender in ballet, has become the annual high point of the summer sessions. The Tenth Summer Academy started to offer classes on three different levels, which considerably helped to raise the technical level of the participants. Ballet masters came to Cologne looking for dancers for the next season, and the American guest teachers started to consider Cologne as one of the promising dance centers, as Donald McKayle recognized.[26] At the twelfth annual session 1968, a new generation of young German choreographers-- John Neumeier, Gerhard Bohner, and Pina Bausch among them--made a mark with highly individual, socially critical works. These led to the German Tanztheater of the seventies and eighties. The International Summer Academy in Cologne retrained German theater dancers to a technically better standard of performance of contemporary ballet and forms of American jazz, and certainly contributed to a more diversified training for the stage.

Kurt Jooss had supported the beginnings of the Krefeld Summer Academy, though the institute in Colgne developed along its own lines. After recovering from his accident in 1956, he turned his undivided attention to his senior students at the Folkwang School. Jooss had always enjoyed teaching; it was the proving ground for his choreographic experimentation, and the rising standards of technical and performance skills of members of his senior class encouraged him gradually to prepare them to become his master students. To provide his students and faculty with a more personal, firsthand encounter with American dance teaching, he invited three American teachers to the school: Pearl Lang (Graham technique); Alfredo Corvino (classical ballet); and Jerry Bywaters (American jazz). They successfully taught three weeks at the Folkwang School in 1959. Jooss encouraged his students and faculty "to learn and share what efforts are being made toward our common goal of contemporary dance." [27]

In the same year, Jooss, as an independent choreographer, joined with the director Dr. Erich Schumacher and the designer Jean-Pierre Ponnelle of the Opera Essen in the Schwetzinger Festspiele (Schwetzinger Festival) production of Henry Purcell's *The Fairy Queen*. In fall 1959, the premiere and first German version, prepared by Kurt Jooss, was staged in the intimate, French rococo-styled theater in Schwetzingen, a small residence near Stuttgart, Germany. For this fanciful extravaganza, Jooss combined soloists of his previous Folkwang Tanz-Theater with Folkwang dance students in the chorus to create a beautifully integrated dance ensemble. Like Fokine, Jooss developed the appropriate dance language for each work. In his famous *The Green Table*, for instance, Jooss had used weight impact as an expressive tool; in the *Fairy Queen*, he emphasized a different, not less typical, aspect of his movement qualities. He elaborated on lightness. Rhythmic structures were parallelled in dance phrases, and, mixing classical legwork with the fluidity of the modern dance, he achieved an amalgam of styles which uniquely reflected the Baroque atmosphere. A.V. Cotton, familiar with Kurt Jooss's work since the Dartington years, praised the choreography for its "blending of a restrained balletic classicism with Jooss's personal dramatic dance idiom--a recent development of his work and here used with full appropriateness."[28] The premiere of *Fairy Queen* turned out to be a sensational event which drew international audiences to Schwetzingen. Jooss was again in the limelight, together with director Erich Schumacher and designer Jean-Pierre Ponnelle. The City of Essen, sponsoring this extraordinary event, finally received appropriate credit and gained the reputation it had craved.

Kurt Jooss was celebrated in rave reviews in the English and German press, which also referred to his skillful directing of Shakespeare's *A Midsummer Night's Dream* for the Folkwang School in 1931. This change of attitude toward Jooss manifested itself also quite concretely; in 1961, recognition was given in the form of funds. Nordrhein/Westfalen gave surplus money to its leading art schools: Detmold in music and the Folkwang School in dance.

The funds were limited, but they enabled Kurt Jooss to establish master classes for dance at the Folkwang School, and the first step of his academy plan was realized. Two-year stipends enabled a small group of advanced students to continue to work under Jooss, who also provided exposure to internationally known guest choreographers. Thus, Jooss reentered the international dance scene, once again, in the sixties. His own personal "Journey in the Fog" during the fifties lay behind him, and his efforts for an academy now bore fruit. The 1960 master classes at the Folkwang School consisted of former Folkwang students and four leading dancers. One of the four was Pina Bausch, who graduated from the Folkwang School as a member of the first postwar generation, in 1959. Bausch had returned from a year of intense studies at the Dance Department of the Juilliard School in New York City, and one season dancing under Tudor at the Metropolitan Opera House in New York. Dancing under Jooss in this experimental set-up, Bausch reached maturity as a performer.

Since the dancers needed performing opportunities and the space of the Folkwang Studio was too limited, touring became a necessity, and an agent was hired. The master class performed as "Folkwang-Ballett." Kurt Jooss did not want to dominate the repertory. His intention was to combine classical ballet, central European Modern Dance and American Modern Dance as dynamically contrasting forces within the same program. Antony Tudor came to set *Jardin aux Lilas* on this ensemble and Lucas Hoving composed his *Songs of Encounter* for them. He also restaged one of his well-known works, *Icarus*, for them. Hoving combined sources of European and American Modern Dance in a fine balance, and his style complemented the Jooss repertory very well. A pupil of Sigurd Leeder, Jean Cebron, who had danced under Jooss in Chile, contributed three short dancing poems under the title *Recueil*, set to an interesting modern score for clarinet, trumpet, trombone, cello and percussion and danced by Pina Bausch and Michael Diekamp. Still, *The Green Table* had the strongest impact; it acted as a trademark and set the company apart from other dance ensembles performing contemporary dance.

The Folkwang Ballet continued in spite of some difficulties, and Jooss created a new work, *Phases,* for them. The English dance critic John Percival described it as "a pleasant, smoothly flowing piece of invention, both musically and in dance: not burning itself on the memory as a great distinctive work, but enjoyable and making good use of its leading soloists." According to Percival, however,

> there were two remarkable things about *Phases.* One was the fact that it is the first completely plotless work we have seen from Jooss, and that it continues and develops the inclination he has shown over the years towards a more classical approach (in mood, not technique). The other is that, in its freshness, lyrical feeling, and even slight blandness, it looks like the work of a young aspirant, not a man in his sixties.[29]

Percival was right: the more classical approach was more typical of Jooss's works of the postwar period. Percival's second point was true too; Jooss was young in spirit. This review was written in 1967.

According to German regulations, Jooss had already reached retirement age; he was, however, not at all ready to give up his artistic work. Nevertheless, in 1968, the year that the Folkwang School finally received Academy status, Kurt Jooss was forced to leave the department he had created. Three years later, in February 1971, Jooss lost his wife, Aino, his closest professional associate. With no further reason to remain in Essen, he moved to Kreuth in Bavaria, preferring the rustic mountain air of Kreuth to the industrial climate of Essen.

Jooss never stopped working. To the end of his days he was involved with dance. He travelled as an independent choreographer, restaging *The Green Table* in Eastern and Western Europe. With the collaboration of his daughter, Anna Markard, he worked on the revision of the Kinetography Labanotated scores of the four works that built the first touring program of Ballets Jooss, in 1932: *Big City* (1932), *Pavane on the Death of an Infanta* (1929), *Ball in Old Vienna* (1932), and, concluding the evening as the fourth work, *The Green Table* (1932).

In 1976, thanks to the thorough revision of the original scores, the Joffrey Ballet performed this entire Jooss program in New York in Jooss's presence in honor of his seventy-fifth birthday. At last he had received the kind of recognition from American ballet that he had already enjoyed from American Modern Dance audiences.

In that same year, he taught a choreographic workshop in Santa Barbara, California; it was his last visit to the United States. By then 75 years old, he confessed that his thoughts were waking him up early in the morning, "since I have to think through Laban's ideas to their last consequence." He made the remark to me on one of his last days of the workshop. He had the feeling that his life's work was still unfinished. In the following three years, he frequently travelled to Greece, which became his last great love. On May 22, 1979, Kurt Jooss, still vigorous, died tragically after a car accident in Heilbronn.

Kurt Jooss was ahead of his time in many ways. If his work did not enjoy full recognition in postwar Germany, it is perhaps because he did not at all fit into the period of German reconstruction. He was not an expressionist, and he also did not represent "German dance." Nor did he want to be remembered as the founder of a "Jooss approach." Kurt Jooss passionately worked to overcome the separation between classical and Modern Dance, because for him, there was only one dance, the dance that reflects the spirit of the twentieth century. The international recognition he achieved outside of his own country of birth suggests that he achieved his goal. While he influenced dance in both Germany and the United States, ultimately his life work belongs to the historical period we have come to call "modern," rather than to a particular country, and in this sense, he transcended nationality to become an artist of our times and a citizen of the world.

NOTES FOR CHAPTER VII

1. Müller, Hedwig (1986) *Mary Wigman: Leben und Werk der Grossen Tänzerin*, *(Life & Work of the Great Dancer)*, p.257. Berlin: Quadriga 2. Markard,

2. Markard, Anna & Herman (1985) *Jooss*, p. 53. Köln: Ballett-Bühnen-Verlag

3. Five Facets of the Dance. (1934) *Theatre Arts Monthly,* vol.18, Number 2, 139-140

4. Hoving, Lucas (1985) Interview, by I. Bergsohn, Tucson, University of Arizona, Nov. 15

5. Laban, Rudolf (1938-1939) Excerpt from an open letter written in Dec., printed in Ballets Jooss' program (Fourth Transcontinental Tour)

6. Dukes, Ashley (1939) Ballet 1939 *Theatre Arts Monthly,* Sept. vol. 23, pp. 630-631

7. Markard, Anna & Hermann (1985) *Jooss*, p. 5

8. Laban, Rudolf with Lawrence. F.C. (1947) *Effort*. London: MacDonald & Evans

9. Laban, Rudolf (1948) *Modern Educational Dance*. London: MacDonald & Evans

10. Laban, Rudolf (1950) *The Mastery of Stage Movement*. London: MacDonald & Evans

11. North, Marion (1972) *Personality Assessment Through Movement*. London: MacDonald & Evans

12. Hodgson, John & Preston Dunlop, Valerie (1990) *Rudolf Laban*. Plymouth: Northcote House

13. Markard, Anna & Hermann (1985) *Jooss*, p. 59

14. Program note for Colombinade (1951) Festive opening performance of the Folkwang-Tanz Theater, June 11

15. Vielhaber, Gerd (1951) Meeting with Jooss Again. *Frankfurter Neue Presse*, June 11

16. Dr Gerigk (1951) Festive Opening of the Folkwang Tanztheater. *Essener Tageblatt,* June 11

17.   Herwagen, Fritz (1951) Dithyrambus *Frankfurter Allgemeine Zeitung,* Oct. 5

18.   Markard, Anna & Hermann *Jooss* p. 67

19.   Barnes, Clive (1953) The Importance of Ballets Jooss. *Dance and Dancers,* June 10

20.   Dr Gerigk (1952) Jooss Premiere: Essen Opera House, *Journey in the Fog,* *Essener Tageblatt,* June 23

21.   Barnes, Clive (1953) The Importance of Ballet Jooss, *Dance and Dancers,* June, 10

22.   Peters, Kurt (1952) The Purpose of Dance. *Official Newsletter of German Professional Dance Organization.* Aug. 29

23.   Markard, Anna & Hermann (1985) *Jooss,* p. 69

24.   Public Notice, (1954) *Essener Tageblatt.* Jan. 26

25.   Markard, Anna & Hermann (1985) *Jooss,* p. 151

26.   Peters, Kurt (1982) Report on the 25 years of the Summer Academy at Krefeld and Köln, Germany

27.   Jooss, Kurt (1959) Remarks at the opening of the fall semester at the international Folkwang school

28.   Coton, A. V. (1960) Rave Notices for Purcell in Germany. *Daily Telegraph,* Feb.23

29.   Percival, John (1967) Ballets Jooss at the Congress Theatre in Eastbourne, *Dance and Dancers,* January

BIBLIOGRAPHY

BOOKS AND ARTICLES

Alexander, Gerda, and Groll, Hans (1980) *Tänzerin, Choreographin, Pädagogin Rosalia Chladek,* 3rd edn. Vienna: Österreichischer Bundesverlag (1rst. edn. 1965, 2nd edn.1975)

Appia, Adolphe (1899) Die Inscenierung als Schöpfung der Musik. In *Theater im 20. Jahrhundert*, edited by Manfred Braunbeck. pp.39-46. Hamburg: Rowohlts Enzyclopädie

Armitage, Merle (1978) *Martha Graham: The Early Years.* New York: DaCapo Press (Reprint of original edn,1937)

Arnheim, Rudolf (1974) *Art and Visual Perception*, New Version, exp. and rev.edn. Berkeley: University of California Press

Bach, Rudolf (1933) *Das Mary Wigman-Werk.* Dresden: Carl Reissner Verlag

Bardsley, Kay (1979) Isadora Duncan's First School: The First Generation Founders of the Tradition. *CORD Dance Reseach Annual X*, pp.219-250. New York: CORD

Barnes, Clive (1953) The Importance of Ballets Jooss. *Dance and Dancers,* June, 10

--------------(1966) Wigman at 80: Still an Influence. *New York Times*, sec.2, Nov.13

Bartenieff, Irmgard with Lewis, Dori, (1981) *Body Movement, Coping with the Environment.* New York: Gordon and Breach

Bie, Oscar (1923) *Der Tanz.* Berlin: Julius Bard Verlag

Blass, Ernst (1921) *Das Wesen der Neuen Tanzkunst.* Weimar: Lichtenstein Verlag

Brandenburg, Hans(1921) *Der Moderne Tanz*, 3rd edn. Munich: Georg Müller

------------(1929) Laban als Stilreformer (Laban as Reformator of Style). *Singchor und Tanz* Heft 24, 297.

Cage, John (1967) *Silence*. Cambridge, MA.: Massachusetts Institute of Technology   Press

Chujoy, Anatole, and Manchester, P.W.(1967) *The Dance Encyclopedia.* New York: Simon and Schuster

Cohen, Selma Jeanne (1958) Laban dies at age 78.*Dance Magazine*, Aug, 28 and 71.

-------(1972) *Doris Humphrey: An Artist First*. Middletown, Ct: Wesleyan University Press

Cohen, Selma Jeanne (1974) *Dance as a Theatre Art: Source Readings in Dance History from 1581 to the Present*. New York: Dodd, Mead and Co.

Coton, A.V. (1946) *The New Ballet: Kurt Jooss and his Work*. London: Dennis Dobson

------------(1975) *Writings on Dance 1938-68*. London: Dance Books

Craig, Edward Gordon (1906) *Isadora Duncan: Sechs Bewegungsstudien*. Leipzig:

Denby, Edwin (1968) *Looking at the Dance*. New York: Horizon Press.

Doubler, Margaret N.H'(1957) *Dance A Creative Art Experience*, first edn. 1940,   second edn. 1957. Madison: University of Wisconsin Press

Dukes, Ashley (1939) Ballet 1939. *Theatre Arts Monthly,* Sept, vol.23, 630-631.

Duncan, Irma (1965) *Duncan Dancer: An Autobiography*. Middletown, Ct.: Wesleyan University Press.

Duncan, Isadora (1927) *My Life*. New York: Horace Liveright

Duncan, Isadora (1977) *The Art of the Dance*. edited by Cheldon Cheney. New York: Theatre Art Books (revised edn. of original, 1928)

Enkelmann,S (1937) *Tänzer unserer Zeit*. Munich: R.Piper and Co.

Flade, Tina (1925-38) Press Voices from Germany and America. Unpublished print, Columbus, by Tina Flade, Ohio

Goldberg, RoseLee (1979) *Performance: Live Art 1909 to the Present*. New York: Harry N.Abrams

Graham, Martha (1972) *The Notebooks of Martha Graham*. New York: Harcourt Brace Jovanovich

---------------(1991) *Blood Memory*. New York: Doubleday

Green, Martin (1986) *Mountain of Truth*. Hanover, N.H. and London: University Press of New England

Gropius, Walter, Gropius, Ise, and Bayer, Herbert, editors.(1959) *Bauhaus 1919 to 1928*. Boston: Charles T.Branfort Co.

Haftmann, Werner (1986) *Banned and Persecuted; Dictatorship of Art under Hitler*. Cologne: DuMont Buchverlag

Hildebrant, Hans (1952) *Oskar Schlemmer*. Munich: Prestel Verlag

Hodgson, John & Preston-Dunlop, Valerie (1990) *Rudolf Laban: An Introduction to his Work and Influence*. Plymouth: Northcote House

Holm, Hanya (Nov.1935) Mary Wigman, *Dance Observer*, vol. 2, 8

-------(1937) Trend grew upon me. *Magazine of the Art*, No.3,137

-------(1956) Wigman at 70: Who is Mary Wigman? *Dance Magazine* Nov, 22-25.

-------(1966) The Mary Wigman I Know. In *The Dance has Many Faces*, edited by Walter Sorell (revised from the 1st. edn., 1951). New   York: Columbia University Press

Horst, Louis (1961) *Modern Dance Forms*. New York: Dance Horizon Books

Hoyer, Dore (Fall 1957) New York: Hochburg des Modernen Tanzes (New York, Stronghold of Modern Dance). *Singchor und Tanz*, publication of the official Theater organization, fall

Hutchinson, Ann (1956) *Labanotation*, with preface by Rudolf Laban.
New York: New Directions

Joffrey, Robert (1979) Remembrances of Kurt Jooss. *Ballet News*, Sept.,29-30

Jooss, Kurt (1927) Tanzerziehung in der Folkwang Schule (Dance education at the Folkwang School). *Essener Zeitung*. Translated by Anna Markard, Wiesbaden, Jooss Archiv

-----------(1929) Rudolf von Laban und das Ballett. *Singchor und Tanz*, Heft 24, 296-297. Translated by Anna Markard

-----------(1935) Die Sprache des Tanztheaters (The Language of Dance Theater) .*Ballett 1986*, edited by Regitz, Hartmut, p.17 Translated by Anna Markard

-----------(1958) Gedanken über Stilfragen, (Thoughts Concerning Questions of Style), lecture presented at the Folkwang Schule Essen. *Folkwang Schule für Gestaltung* (School for Design), vol.5

-----------(1959) Remarks at the opening of the fall semester at the Folkwang school.

Jooss (1981) Venezia Danza Europa '81. Catalogue of the exhibition with introduction by Mario Pasi, pp.7-14, and preface and biography by Anna Markard, pp.15-63. Venice: Marsilio Editori

Jowitt, Deborah (1977) *Dance Beat*. New York: Marcel Decker

----------------(1988) *Time and the Dancing Image*. New York: William Morrow

Kandinsky, Wassily (1977) *Concerning the Spiritual in Art,*
    translated by M. T. H. Sadler. New York: Dover Publications

King, Eleanor (1978) *Transformations*. Brooklyn: Dance Horizons

Kirstein, Lincoln (1970) *Movement and Metaphor*. New York: Praeger Publishers

Knust, Albrecht (1929) Laban als Erzieher (Laban as Educator).
    Singchor und Tanz, Heft 24, 295

Koegler, Horst (1963) *Yvonne Georgi*. Hannover: Friedrich Verlag

----------------(1974) In the Shadow of the Swastika: Dance in Germany 1929-1936. *Dance*
    Perspectives, 57, (Spring).

----------------(1983) Zehn Jahre nach Crankos Tod. *Ballet 1983,* pp. 48-52. Zürich: Orell Füssli
    & Friedrich

----------------(1984) Eine Vitale Vielseitigkeit: Das Ballett in Deutschland. *Tanz in Deutschland*
    Ballett seit 1945. edited by Hartmut Regitz, pp. 7-31. Berlin: Quadriga Verlag

--------and Günther, Helmut, (1984) *Reclams Ballett Lexikon*. Stuttgart: Philipp Reclam

Kostelanetz, Richard (1968) *The Theatre of Mixed Means: An Introduction to Happenings,*
    Kinetic Environment and Other Mixed Means Performances. New York: Dial Press

Kreutzberg, Harald (1939) *Über mich Selbst (About myself)*. Detmold: Hamann Verlag

Kriegsman, Sali Ann (1981) *Modern Dance in America: The Bennington Years*. Boston:
    G.K. Hall

Laban, Rudolf (1920) Kultische Bildung im Feste (Spiritual education in festival) *Die Tat,*
    (Monthly for the Future of German Culture), Heft 3, 161-168

--------------(1920) *Die Welt des Tänzers (A Dancer's World)*. Stuttgart: Walter Seifert
    Verlag

--------------(1922) Festwille und Festkultur(Desire for festival and culture of festival). *Die Tat,*
    XIII.Jahrgang, Heft 11, 846-848

--------------(1926) *Choreographie*, Heft I. Jena: Eugen Diederichs

--------------(1926) *Gymnastik und Tanz (Gymnastics and Dance)*. Oldenburg: Gerhard Stalling

------------(1926) *Des Kindes Gymnastik und Tanz (The Child's Gymnastics and Dance)*. Oldenburg: Gerhard Stalling Verlag

------------(1927) Tanztheater und Bewegungschor (Dance Theatre and Movement choir).In *Tanz und Reigen*, edited by I. Gentges, pp.72-79. Berlin: Bühnenvolksbund-Verlag

------------(1928) Tanzkomposition und Schrifttanz. *Schrifttanz*, Heft II, 19-20

_____ (1935) *Ein Leben für den Tanz*. Dresden: Carl Reisner Verlag. (For translation see Laban 1975 below as *A Life for Dance*)

--------(1938) Excerpt from an open letter written in Dec., printed in Ballets Jooss'program (Fourth Transcontinental Tour).

--------(1948) *Modern Educational Dance*. London, MacDonald and Evans

--------(1950) *The Mastery of Movement*. London: MacDonald and Evans

--------(1954) The Work of the Art and Movement Studio. *Journal of Physical Education,* vol 46, no.137, 22-30

--------(1954) Foreword. In *Labanotation*, by Ann Hutchinson. New York: New Directions

--------(1975) *A Life for Dance*, translated and annotated by Lisa Ullmann. London: MacDonald & Evans

--------and Lawrence, Frederick Charles (1947) *Effort*. London: MacDonald & Evans

Lämmel, Rudolf (1928)(*Der Moderne Tanz The Modern Dance*). Berlin: P.J. Ostergard Verlag

Laqueur, Walter (1974) *Weimar: A Cultural History 1918-1933*. New York: G.P. Putnam's Sons

Lauterer, Arch (1937) Design for Dance. *Magazine of the Arts*, no.3, 137 and 148

Lewitan, Joseph (1929) Laban der Tanz-Tribun. *Der Tanz*, Heft 14, 6-7

Magriel, Paul (1977) *Nijinsky, Pavlova, Duncan*. New York: Dacapo Paperback

Maletic, Vera (1987) *Body Space Expression: The Development of Rudolf Laban's Movement and Dance Concepts*. Berlin, New York: Mouton de Gruyter

Manning, Susan (1989) Ideology and Performance Between Weimar and the Third Reich: The Case of *Totenmal*. *Theatre Journal*, May, 222

Markard, Anna & Hermann (1985) *Kurt Jooss*. Cologne: Ballett Bühnen Verlag

Martin, John (1930) The Dance: Mary Wigman's Art. *New York Times*, Aug.3

------------(1930) Triumph in Dance by Mary Wigman. *New York Times*, Dec. 29

------------(1931) The Dance: Vital Issues. *New York Times*, March 8

------------(1931) Cordial Reception for Mary Wigman. *New York Times*, Dec.11

------------(1932) Festival of Dance opened by Wigman. *New York Times,* Dec.26

------------(1933) The Dance: Art of Jooss. *New York Times*, Nov.5

------------(1935) The Dance: Kreutzberg. *New York Times*, March 31

------------(1937) New York Debut for Hanya Holm. *New York Times*, Dec. 29

------------(1939) Tragic Exodus. *New York Times*, Feb.20

------------(1965) *Introduction to the Dance* (Reprint of the original edn. 1939). Brooklyn, N.Y.: Dance Horizons

------------(1940) Dance since Isadora. *Theatre Arts*, 24, Sept.

Morgan, Barbara (1941) *Martha Graham: Sixteen Dances in Photographs*. New York: Duell, Sloan and Pearce

Müller, Hedwig (1986) *Mary Wigman: Leben und Werk der grossen Tänzerin*. Berlin: Quadriga Verlag

Niedecken-Gebhard, Hanns (1927) Tanz und Bühne (Dance and Stage). *Die Tat,* November

Niehaus, Max (1981) *Isadora Duncan: Triumph und Tragik einer legendären Tänzerin*. München: Wilhelm Heyne Verlag

North, Marion (1972) *Personality Assessment Through Movement*. London: MacDonald and Evans

Orff, Carl (1976) *The Schulwerk*. Tutzing: Hans Schneider Verlag

Patterson, Michael (1981) *The Revolution in German Theatre 1900-1933*. Boston: Routledge and   Kegan, Paul

Percival, John (1971) *Experimental Dance*. New York: Universe Books (1980) *Modern Ballet*, rev.ed. London: The Herbert Press (1st edn,1970)

Peters, Kurt (1950) An Rudolph von Laban (To Rudolph von Laban). *Tanz Prisma*, Dec.,3-20

------------(1952) The Purpose of Dance. *Official Newsletter of German Dance Organization*, Aug. 29

Preston-Dunlop, Valerie (1984) Point of Departure: The Dancer's Space. London: Lime Tree Studios

Preston-Dunlop (1988) Laban and the Nazis. London: Dance Theatre Journal, vol.6, 2,4-7

Prevots, Naima (1985) Zürich Dada and Dance: Formative Ferment. *Dance Research Journal*, 17/1 (Spring/Summer), 3-9

Regitz, Hartmut (1984) *Tanz in Deutschland: Ballett seit 1945*. Berlin: Quadriga Verlag

Regner, O.F. (1954) *Das Ballett Buch*. Hamburg: Fischer Bücherei

Reidemeister, Leopold (1983) *Brücke*. Catalogue of the Brücke Museum, p.2. Berlin: Hartmann

Rose, Barbara (1975) *American Art Since 1900*. New York: Holt, Rinehart and Winston (1st edn.: Frederick A. Praeger, 1967)

Roslavleva, Natalia (1975) Prechistenka 20: The Isadora Duncan School in Moscow. *Dance Perspectives*, 64, vol.16, 3-48

Roters, Eberhard (1975) "Als der Krieg zu Ende war." *Catalogue of the Exhibition: Art in Germany 1945-1950*,the Visual Arts, pp.9-11, Berlin: Academy of the Arts

Scheper, Dirk, & Schmidt, Willy. (1975) Ibid. The Performing Arts. pp. 59-60.

Schlicher, Susanne (1987) *Tanz Theater*. Hamburg: Rowohlts Enzyklopädie/Kulturen und Ideen

Schlundt, Christena L. (1989/90) Tamiris: a Chronicle of her Dance Career 1927-1955. *Studies in Dance History,* 1:1 (Fall/Winter)

Schönberg, Bessie (1992) Letter to the author,March 18

Schuftan, Werner (1928) *Handbuch des Tanzes*. Mannheim: Verlag Deutscher Chorsänger Verband und Tänzerbund E.V.

Shawn, Ted (1954) *Every Little Movement*. Pittsfield, Ma.: Eagle Printing Press

Shelton, Suzanne (1984) *American Dance Festival Brochure*. Durham, N.C., American Dance Festival, Duke University.

Shurr, Gertrude and Yocom, Rachael Dunaven (1980). *Modern Dance Techniques and Teaching*, 2nd edn., New York: Dance Horizons,(1st edn.,New York: Ronald Press) 1949)

Siegel, Marcia (1979) *The Shapes of Change*. Boston: Houghton Mifflin Co.

---------------(1973) Mary Wigman 1886-1973: A Tribute. *Dance Magazine*, Nov., 80

Snell, Gertrude (1930) Grundlagen einer Allgemeinen Tanzlehre: III. Eukinetik. *Schrifttanz*, Heft II, 48-50

Sokolow, Anna (1981) Biographical statement from 1937.In *Modern Dance in America: The Bennington Years*, edited by Kriegsman, Sali Ann. Boston: G.K. Hall & Co., p. 264

Sorell, Walter (1966) with Mary Wigman in Ticino. *Dance Magazine* Nov.,40-41

-------------- (1969) *Hanya Holm: The Biography of An Artist*. Middletown, Ct: Wesleyan University Press

---------------(1981) *Dance in its Time*. Garden City, N. Y.: Anchor Press, Doubleday

---------------(1986) *Looking Back in Wonder*. New York: Columbia University

---------------(1986)*Mary Wigman: Ein Vermächtnis*. Wilhelmshaven: Florian Noetzel Verlag

Steinbeck, Dietrich (1987) *Mary Wigman's Choreographisches Skizzenbuch 1930-1961* (*Mary Wigman's Choreographic Sketchbook 1930-1961*). Berlin: Edition Hentrich

Topaz, Muriel (1988) Specifics of Style in the Works of Balanchine and Tudor. *Choreography and Dance: An International Journal.*(London: Harwood Academic Publishers), I, 3-36

Ullmann, Lisa (1979) Rudolf von Laban in England 1938-1958. *Tanzarchivreihe*,19/20,26-28

Weidt, Jean (1984) *Auf der grossen Strasse:Jean Weidt's Erinnerungen*. Berlin: Henschel Verlag

Welzien, Leonore. (1990) From Rhythm to Movement, from Movement to Dance (interview with Rosalia Chladek). *Tanzdrama*, Heft 11, 18-23

Wigman, Mary (1913) Notes from Mary Wigman's diary. Wigman Archiv, Berlin: Academy of the Arts

------------(1921) Rudolf von Labans Lehre vom Tanz (Rudolf von Laban's Theory of Dance). *Die Neue Schaubühne*, 5/6, Heft, 3. Jahrgang (Sept) 99-106

------------(1929) Rudolf von Laban. In *Singchor und Tanz*, Heft 24, p. 295 (in honor of Laban's fiftieth birthday)

------------(1954) Sie fragen nach der Berechtigung (You ask for the justification), March 18. Berlin: Wigman Archiv (Unpublished article directed to Trudi Wulff).

------------(1956) My Teacher Laban. *Dance Magazine*, Nov., 27-28, 71-78

------------(1960) Excerpts from Wigman's speech at the opening of the exhibition of American Dance Photographs. Berlin: Wigman Archiv, Academy of the Arts. Tranlation byI.Bergsohn

------------(1961) Excerpt from Chorischer Tanz (Choral Dance). *Berliner Festwochen Almanach*,Ap.7. Translation by I. Bergsohn

------------(1963) *Die Sprache des Tanzes*. Stuttgart: Ernst Battenberg Verlag. (Translated by Walter Sorell, as *The Language of Dance*. Middletown, Ct: Wesleyan University (1967)

------------(1975) *The Mary Wigman Book*, edited and translated by Walter Sorell. Middletown, Ct: Wesleyan University Press

INTERVIEWS:

All interviews were done by Isa Bergsohn, except as otherwise indicated.

Bodmer, Sylvia (Dec. 5, 1987), Manchester, England

Cohen, Selma Jeanne (July 16, 1989), New York City

Hill, Martha (July 18 and 20, 1989), Brooklyn, N.Y.

Holm, Hanya (July 17 and 19, 1989), New York City

Hoving, Lucas (Nov. 15, 1985), Tucson, Arizona

Jooss, Kurt (1973). Interviewed by John Hodgson, Kreuth, Bavaria

------------(Sept. 20, 1976) Santa Barbara, CA

------------(Sept. 1976), Interviewed by Tobias, Tobi. The New York Public Library, Oral Project Dance Collection

Kloepper, Louise (March 18, 1990), Madison, Wisconsin

Lewitzky, Bella (April 20, 1990), Tucson, Arizona

Ludewig, Jutta (July 20, 1988), Mainz, Germany

Shurr, Gertrude (May 27, 1990), Tucson, Arizona

Wilson, John M. (June 6, 1990), Tucson, Arizona

(1986) NOTES FROM THE WIGMAN CENTENNIAL CONFERENCE, Berlin: Academy of the Arts, Sept. 24-27

Espanak, Liljan spoke about her studies with Wigman during the twenties.

Fricke-Gottschild, Hellmut, last assistant of Wigman in the Berlin school, commented on Wigman's teaching during the nineteen-sixtees.

Linke, Susanne, leading German contemporary modern dancer and choreographer expressed her gratitude to Wigman.

Nikolais, Alwin discussed Wigman's Influence on American Modern Dance.

REVIEWS

author not given (1928) *The World*, May 16

Chotzinoff, Sarah (1930) Other Music. *New York World*, Dec. 29

Coton, A.V.(1960) Rave Notices for Purcell in Germany. *Daily Telegraph*, Feb. 23

Dr Gerigk (1951) Festive Opening of the Folkwang Tanz Theater of the City of Essen. *Essener Tageblatt*, June 11

----------(1952) Jooss Premiere: *Journey in the Fog*. Essen Opera House. *Essener Tageblatt*, June 23

Goode, Elizabeth (1939).*Danzas Mexicanas. Dance Observer*, 203 (José Limón)

Hering, Doris (1947) Harald Kreutzberg. *Dance Magazine*, December, 9

Herwagen, Fritz (1951) *Dithyrambus*. Folkwang Tanz Theater. *Frankfurter Allgemeine Zeitung*, Oct. 5

Hoyer, Dore (1957) New York: Hochburg des Tanzes (New York: Stronghold of Dance). *Official Newsletter of German Professional Dance Organization*, (Fall)

Hylborn, Elizabeth (1945) Hanya Holm at Colorado College. *Dance Observer*,no.12, 8 (Oct.)

Peters, Kurt(1952) The Purpose of Dance. *Official Newsletter of German Professional Dance Organization*, Aug.29

------------(1982) Report on the 25 years of the summer Academy at Krefeld & Cologne. *Official Newsletter of German Professional Dance Organization,* fall

Krevitzky, Nik (1946) Jooss Ballet at New York City Center. *Dance Observer*, Dec. 3-22

Koegler, Horst (1956) Mary Wigman und der moderne Tanz. *Frankfurter Allgemeine Zeitung*,

--------Nov.13 (1972) Tanz durch die Zeiten. *Frankfurter Allgemeine Zeitung*, Nov.13

Lloyd, Margaret (1937) Resonance in the Dance. *Christian Science Monitor*, May 4

----------------(1939) review of the School of the Dance at Mills College. *Christian Science Monitor*, June 10

Martin, John (1929) The Macabre in Germany's Dance. *New York Times*, Feb. 16

-------------(1930) A Futile Congress. *New York Times,* July 20

-------------(1933) Jooss Ballet To make Debut at Forrest Theatre. *New York Times*, Oct. 29

-------------(1948) The Dance: Debut Hanya Holm in Bow as Choreographer of *Kiss Me, Kate*. *New York Times*, Dec. 30

Percival John (1967) Ballets Jooss at the Congress Theatre in Eastbourne. *Dance and Dancers*, January

Selden, Elizabeth (1930) Masters of the New Mode Gather at Munich. *New York Evening Post*, March 31

Terry, Walter (1937) Jooss Ballet Combines Modern Dance with Classic Forms. *Boston Herald*, October 17

Vielhaber, Gerd (1951) Meeting with Kurt Jooss again. *Frankfurter Neue Presse*, June 11

Zivier, George (1952) The Renaissance of Ballet. *Die Neue Zeitung*, Sept. 4

Index